INVESTING: THE LAST LIBERAL ART

INVESTING

THE LAST LIBERAL ART

SECOND EDITION

ROBERT G. HAGSTROM

Columbia University Press
Publishers Since 1893
New York   Chichester, West Sussex
cup.columbia.edu
Copyright © 2013 Robert G. Hagstrom
All rights reserved

Library of Congress Cataloging-in-Publication Data
Hagstrom, Robert G., 1956–
Investing : the last liberal art / Robert G. Hagstrom. — 2nd ed.
p. cm.
Includes bibliographical references and index.
ISBN 978-0-231-16010-0 (cloth : alk. paper)
ISBN 978-0-231-53101-6 (ebook)
1. Investments.   I. Title.
HG4521.H2263   2012
332.6—dc23   2012036489

∞

Columbia University Press books are printed on permanent
and durable acid-free paper.
This book is printed on paper with recycled content.
Printed in the United States of America

c 10 9 8 7 6 5 4 3 2 1

Cover design: Noah Arlow

References to Internet Web sites (URLs) were accurate at the time of writing. Neither
the author nor Columbia University Press is responsible for URLs that may have
expired or changed since the manuscript was prepared.

CONTENTS

PREFACE

In 2000, I wrote a book then titled *Latticework: The New Investing*. It was a liberal arts interpretation of investing, inspired by Charlie Munger's lectures on the art of achieving what he called "worldly wisdom." For those who don't know Charlie, he is vice-chairman of Berkshire Hathaway and investment partner to Warren Buffett, who is, arguably, the world's greatest investor.

Latticework—the title—was deliberately chosen to make clear its linkage to Charlie's approach. His concept of a "latticework of mental models" is well known to investors and instantly identifiable. Or so I thought. I have since learned that authors are best at writing books but marketing professionals are best at titling and publicizing them. In the year following the publication of *Latticework*, the publisher decided to relaunch the book as a paperback with a new title—*Investing: The Last Liberal Art*. Result? A definite spike in interest in the book. Then, when Columbia University Press asked if I would be interested in revisiting the original work with a second edition, I immediately accepted the opportunity. One, because I deeply believe in the values and lessons of the book but more importantly, because of the amount of new knowledge (new to me, at least) that I have gained over the past decade. For one small example, there are about one hundred new entries in the Bibliography.

The overall structure of the book is the same. We take a look at the major mental models in physics, biology, sociology, psychology, philosophy, and literature. To that we have added an entirely new chapter on mathematics. The book then concludes with a chapter on decision making. For those who have read the first edition, you will revisit many of the classical models, but you will also receive substantially new knowledge and understanding based on new material in each chapter—proof positive that learning is a continuous process.

Keep one thing firmly in mind: this is not a how-to book on investing. You won't find a new set of step-by-step instructions on how to pick stocks or manage your portfolio. However, after reading this book, what you will have, if you are willing to spend some time with challenging ideas, is a new way to *think* about investing and a clearer understanding of how markets and economies work. It is an understanding derived not from the economics and finance textbooks, but from the basic truths embedded in a number of seemingly unrelated disciplines, the same disciplines you would find in a classical liberal arts education.

To develop this new understanding, you and I will walk together through those areas of knowledge, investigating the basic and fundamental concepts in each field. Sometimes we will begin with a historical overview to see how the concepts originated and then move forward; always we shall examine how those concepts relate to investing and the markets. One chapter at a time, one piece at a time, with some of the greatest minds of all time, we shall assemble a new and original way to think about investing.

I must confess that writing this book was difficult. It required delving deeply into several disciplines and then distilling the essence of each into one short chapter. The discussions are, of necessity and without undue apology, both brief and general. If you happen to be an expert in any one of these disciplines, you may quibble with my presentation or may conclude I have omitted certain concepts. However, I hope you appreciate that to do otherwise would have resulted in a book with chapters one hundred pages long and a final manuscript equal in proportion to an encyclopedia. While writing this book, I came to believe it was far more important to deliver an abbreviated sermon to a larger number of people than to restrict its overall message to the few who would be willing to tackle a dissertation. For this reason, I hope you will recognize it was necessary to limit the descriptions in each discipline to the very basics.

Even so, many readers may find that reading this book is something of a challenge, no less than the writing was for me. It was challenging on two levels. First, some of the chapters may deal with disciplines that are un-familiar to you, and reading them may remind you of an intensive college-level seminar. Nonetheless, it is my hope that you will find the exposure to new ideas stimulating and rewarding. Second, because each chapter presents a completely different field of study, the total benefit of the book may not be fully clear until you reach the end. It is a cumulative process, with each chapter adding a new layer of ideas. I have tried to point out common themes and mental links, but my comments are no substitute for your own personal revelation that will come from careful study and thoughtful reflection.

Reading this book requires, then, both an intellectual curiosity and a significant measure of patience. In a world that increasingly seeks to solve our needs in the shortest amount of time, this book may be an anomaly. However, I have always believed there are no shortcuts to greater under-standing. You simply have to work through the basics.

This broad-based approach to understanding is the heart of a liberal arts approach to investing. It is no longer enough to just acquire and master the basics in accounting, economics, and finance. To generate good investment returns, I believe, requires much more. It is driven by a keen mental appetite to discover and use new insights regardless of what Dewey decimal number they bear or how unrelated they may at first appear.

Mistakes in investing most often occur because of investor confusion. In my opinion, the basic investment lessons we have learned thus far have not given us a complete view of how markets work or how investors operate within markets. No wonder we're confused. No wonder we make mistakes. When we don't understand something, there is always a fifty-fifty chance we will make the wrong decision. If this book improves, even slightly, your understanding of investing and how markets work, then the odds of success will tilt in your favor.

Robert G. Hagstrom
Villanova, Pennsylvania
September 2012

INVESTING: THE LAST LIBERAL ART

1

A Latticework of Mental Models

In April 1994, at the Marshall School of Business of the University of Southern California (USC), students in Dr. Guilford Babcock's Student Investment Seminar got a rare treat: a powerful dose of real-world knowledge from a man whose thoughts on money are widely considered priceless.

Charles Munger—Charlie, as he is known throughout the investment world—is vice chairman of Berkshire Hathaway, the holding company run by Warren Buffett, the world's most famous investor. Trained originally as an attorney, Charlie is Buffett's business partner, friend, and straight man. He commands attention whenever he speaks.

Charlie Munger is an intellectual jewel somewhat hidden behind his more celebrated partner. The anonymity is not Buffett's fault. Charlie simply prefers the lower profile. Except for his occasional appearances such as the one at USC and his prominent role at Berkshire Hathaway's annual meetings, Charlie remains largely out of public view. Even at those annual meetings, he deliberately keeps his remarks brief, allowing Buffett to answer most of the questions from shareholders. But occasionally Charlie does have something to add, and when he speaks, the shareholders straighten and shift forward to the edge of their seats, straining to get a better view, to catch every word.

In Dr. Babcock's classroom that day in April, the atmosphere was much the same. The students knew whom they were listening to, and they knew they were about to receive the benefit of considerable investment expertise. What they got instead was something infinitely more valuable.

At the outset, Charlie mischievously admitted that he was about to play something of a trick on his audience. Rather than discussing the stock market, he intended to talk about "stock picking as a subdivision of the art of worldly wisdom."[1] For the next hour and a half, he challenged the students to broaden their vision of the market, of finance, and of economics in general and to see them not as separate disciplines but as part of a larger body of knowledge, one that also incorporates physics, biology, social studies, psychology, philosophy, literature, and mathematics.

In this broader view, he suggested, each discipline entwines with, and in the process strengthens, every other. From each discipline the thoughtful person draws significant mental models, the key ideas that combine to produce cohesive understanding. Those who cultivate this broad view are well on their way to achieving worldly wisdom, that solid mental foundation without which success in the market—or anywhere else—is merely a short-lived fluke.

To drive his point home, Charlie used a memorable metaphor to describe this interlocking structure of ideas: a latticework of models. "You've got to have models in your head," he explained, "and you've got to array your experiences—both vicarious and direct—on this latticework of models." So immediate is this visual image that "latticework" has become something of a shorthand term in the investment world, a quick and easily recognized reference to Charlie's approach.

It is a theme he returns to often. At the Berkshire Hathaway annual meetings, for instance, he frequently adds to Buffett's answers by quoting from a book he has recently read. Often the quote at first appears to have no direct link to investing, but with Charlie's explanation it quickly becomes relevant. It is not that Buffett's answers are incomplete. Far from it. It is just that when Charlie is able to connect Buffett's ideas to similar ideas in other disciplines, it tends to elevate the levels of understanding among the group.

Charlie's attention to other disciplines is purposeful. He operates in the firm belief that uniting the mental models from separate disciplines to create a latticework of understanding is a powerful way to achieve superior investment results. Investment decisions are more likely to be correct when ideas from other disciplines lead to the same conclusions. That is the topmost payoff—broader understanding makes us better investors. It will be immediately obvious, however, that the ramifications are much wider. Those who strive to understand connections are well on the way to worldly wisdom. This makes us not only better investors but better leaders, better citizens, better parents, spouses, and friends.

How does one achieve worldly wisdom? To state the matter concisely, it is an ongoing process of, first, acquiring significant concepts—the models—from many areas of knowledge and then, second, learning to recognize patterns of similarity among them. The first is a matter of educating yourself; the second is a matter of learning to think and see differently.

Acquiring the knowledge of many disciplines may seem a daunting task. Fortunately, you don't have to become an expert in every field. You merely have to learn the fundamental principles—what Charlie calls the big ideas—and learn them so well that they are always with you. The following chapters of this book are intended to be a starting point for this self-education. Each one examines a specific discipline—physics, biology, social studies, psychology, philosophy, literature, and mathematics—from the perspective of its contribution to a latticework of models. Of course, many other sources are available to the intellectual explorer.

A protest is commonly heard at this point. "Isn't that what a college education is supposed to do for us, teach us critical concepts that have been developed over the centuries?" Of course. Most educators will tell you, in passionate terms, that a broad curriculum grounded in the liberal arts is the best way, perhaps the only way, to produce well-educated people. Few would argue with that position in theory. But in reality we have become a society that prefers specialization over breadth.

This is wholly understandable. Because students and parents spend a small fortune on a college education, they expect this investment to pay off promptly in the form of good job offers after graduation. They know that most corporate recruiters want workers with specialized knowledge who can make an immediate and specific contribution to the organization. It is little wonder that most of today's students, faced with this pressure, resist a broad, liberal arts education in favor of a specialty major. Understandable, as I say. Still, I believe we are all the poorer for it.

At one point in our history, we were given a superb model of what constitutes a good education. Perhaps we should have paid better attention.

In the summer of 1749, subscribers to the *Pennsylvania Gazette* received, along with their newspaper, an additional pamphlet written by the newspaper's publisher, Benjamin Franklin. He described this pamphlet, entitled *Proposals Relating to the Education of Youth in Pensilvania*, as a "Paper of Hints" to address the regret that the "youth of the Province had no academy."[2] The young men in Connecticut and Massachusetts were already attending Yale and Harvard, Virginians had the College of William and Mary, and students in New Jersey were served by the College of New Jersey (later called Princeton). But Philadelphia, the largest and richest city in the Colonies, known as the Athens of America, had no institution for higher learning. In his pamphlet, Franklin explained his proposal to remedy that with the establishment of the Public Academy of Philadelphia.

Franklin's concept was unique for its day. Harvard, Yale, Princeton, and William and Mary were schools for educating the clergy; their curricula stressed the classical studies rather than the practical lessons that prepared young men for business and public service. It was Franklin's hope that the Philadelphia Academy would stress both the traditional classical areas (which he termed "ornamental") as well as the practical. "As to their studies," he wrote, "it would be well if they could be taught everything that is useful and everything that is ornamental. But art is long and their time is short. It is therefore proposed that they learn those things that are likely to be most useful and most ornamental, regard being had to the several professions for which they are intended."

Today Franklin's Public Academy of Philadelphia is the University of Pennsylvania. The former dean of its College of Arts and Sciences, Dr. Richard Beeman, describes the scope of Franklin's achievements.[3] "Benjamin Franklin proposed the first modern-day secular curriculum," he explains, "and the timing was perfect." In the eighteenth century the world's knowledge base was exploding with new discoveries in math and sciences, and the classical curriculum of Greek, Latin, and the Bible was no longer sufficient to explain this new knowledge. Franklin proposed including these new areas in the academy, and then he went further still: he also recommended the students acquire the necessary skill sets to become successful at business and public service. Once students mastered these basic skills, he said, which at that time included writing, drawing, speaking, and arithmetic, then they could devote attention to acquiring knowledge.

"Almost all kinds of useful knowledge would be learned through reading of history," wrote Franklin. But he meant much more than the definition we customarily attach to a history discipline; for Franklin, "history" encompassed all that is meaningful and worthwhile. By encouraging young men to read history, Franklin meant for them to learn philosophy, logic, mathematics, religion, government, law, chemistry, biology, health, agriculture, physics, and foreign languages. To those who wondered whether such a burdensome task was really necessary, Franklin replied that it was not a burden to learn but a gift. If you read the universal histories, he said, "it would give you a connected idea of human affairs."

Benjamin Franklin was the originator of a "liberal arts education," Beeman points out. "He was in the business of cultivating habits of mind. The Philadelphia Academy was a broadly based platform for lifelong learning. Of course Franklin is the perfect role model. He kept his mind open and his intellectual ambition fully fueled. As an educator he is my hero."

Beeman continues: "Benjamin Franklin's success as an educator was based upon three standing principles. First the student must acquire the basic skill sets: reading, writing, arithmetic, physical education, and public speaking. Then the student was introduced to the bodies of knowledge, and finally the student was taught to cultivate habits of mind by discovering the connections that exist between the bodies of knowledge."

In the 250 years since Franklin's proposal, American educators have continued to debate the best method to train young minds, and college administrators have continued to adjust their curricula in the hope of attracting the best students. Critics of our current education system remain, and many of their criticisms seem valid; yet for all its faults, our education system today has done a reasonably good job of providing skills and producing knowledge—the first two of Franklin's key principles. What is often lacking is his third principle: the "habits of mind" that seek to link together different bodies of knowledge.

We can change this. Even if our days of formal schooling are behind us, we can search on our own for the linkages between ideas in various arenas, the connections that illuminate real understanding.

It is of course easy to see that cultivating Franklin's "habits of mind," to use Professor Beeman's wonderful phrase, is the key to achieving Charlie Munger's "worldly wisdom." But seeing this is one thing; acting on it is another. For many of us, this goes against the mental grain. After having invested many years in learning one specialty, we are now being asked to teach ourselves others. We are told not to be bound by narrow confines of the discipline we were trained in, but to leap over the intellectual fences and look at what's on the other side.

For investors, the rewards for making the effort are enormous. When you allow yourself to look beyond the immediate fences, you are able to observe similarities in other fields and recognize patterns of ideas. Then, as one concept is reinforced by another and another and then another, you know you are on the right track. The key is finding the linkages that connect one idea to another. Fortunately for us, the human mind already works this way.

In 1895, a young graduate student named Edward Thorndike began to study animal behavior under the psychologist and philosopher William James at Harvard University. We shall meet William James later in this book, in another capacity; for now our interest in Thorndike is his groundbreaking research into how learning takes place, in humans as well as animals. Thorndike was the first to develop what we now recognize as the stimulus-response framework in which learning occurs when associations—connections—are formed between stimuli and response.

Thorndike continued his studies at Columbia University, where he worked closely with Robert S. Woodworth. Together they investigated the process by which learning is transferred. They concluded, in a paper published in 1901, that learning in one area does not facilitate learning in other areas; rather, they argued, learning is transferred only when both the original and the new situation have similar elements. That is, if we understand A, and recognize something in B that resembles A, then we are well on our way to understanding B. In this view, learning new concepts has less to do with a change in a person's learning ability than with the existence of commonalties. We do not learn new subjects because we have somehow become better learners but because we have become better at recognizing patterns.

Edward Thorndike's theory of learning lies at the core of a contemporary theory in cognitive science called *connectionism*. (The cognitive sciences encompass how the brain works—how we think, learn, reason, remember, and make decisions.) Connectionism, building from Thorndike's studies of stimulus-response patterns, holds that learning is a process of trial and error in which favorable responses to new situations (stimuli) actually alter the neural connections between brain cells. That is, the process of learning affects the synaptic connections between neurons, which are continually adjusting as they recognize familiar patterns and accommodate new information. The brain has the ability to link together related connections into a chain and to transfer what was learned to similar situations; intelligence, therefore, can be viewed as a function of how many connections a person has learned.

Connectionism has received a great deal of attention from business leaders as well as scientists because it is at the heart of a powerful new system of information technology known as *artificial neural networks*. These neural networks, as they are more commonly called, attempt to replicate the workings of the brain more closely than has been possible with traditional computers.

In the brain, neurons function within groups called networks, each with thousands of interconnected neurons. We can therefore think of the brain as a collection of neural networks. Artificial neural networks, in turn, are computers that mimic the basic structure of the brain: they consist of hundreds of processing units (analogous to neurons) that are cross connected into a complex network. (Surprisingly, neurons are several orders of magnitude slower than silicon chips, but the brain makes up for this lack of speed by having a massive number of connections that afford enormous efficiencies.)

The great power of the neural network, and the quality that sets it apart from a traditional computer, is that the weighting of the connections between its units can be adjusted, just as the brain's synapses adjust, becoming weaker or stronger or even rewired altogether as needed to perform different tasks. So, just like the brain, a neural network can learn. Just like the brain, it has the ability to recognize complex patterns, classify new information into patterns, and draw associations between the new data.

We are only beginning to understand how this technology can be applied in the business world. A few examples: A manufacturer of baby foods uses the technology to manage trading cattle futures. Soft drink bottlers use it as an "electronic nose" to catch and analyze unpleasant odors. Credit card companies use it to detect forged signatures and to spot fraud by identifying deviations in spending habits. Airlines use it to forecast flight demand. Postal services use neural networks to decipher sloppy handwriting, and computer companies use them to develop software that will recognize handwritten notes sent via email and engineering schematics sketched on a cocktail napkin.

The process of building and using a latticework of mental models is an innovative approach to thinking, and one that can be intimidating to many, to the point of mental paralysis. Fortunately there is a road map to the process that is easy to understand.

The Santa Fe Institute, Santa Fe, New Mexico, is a multidisciplinary research and education facility where physicists, biologists, mathematicians, computer scientists, psychologists, and economists come together to study complex adaptive systems. These scientists are attempting to understand and predict immune systems, central nervous systems, ecologies, economies, and the stock market, and they are all keenly interested in new ways of thinking.

John H. Holland, a professor in two fields at the University of Michigan—psychology, and engineering and computer science—is a frequent visitor to the Santa Fe Institute, where he has lectured extensively on innovative thinking. According to Holland, innovative thinking requires us to master two important steps. First, we must understand the basic disciplines from which we are going to draw knowledge; second, we need to be aware of the use and benefit of metaphors.

You will recognize the first step as being exactly the same as the first part of Charlie Munger's process for acquiring worldly wisdom. The ability to link mental models together and then benefit from the connections assumes that you have a basic understanding of each model in the latticework. There is no benefit to stringing mental models together if you have no idea how each model works and what phenomena it describes. Remember, though, it is not necessary to become an expert in each model but merely to understand the fundamentals.

The second step—finding metaphors—may at first seem surprising, especially if it makes you think of your ninth-grade English class. At the simplest level, a metaphor is a way to convey meaning using out-of-ordinary, nonliteral language. When we say that "work was a living hell," we don't really mean to say that we spent the day beating back fire and shoveling ashes, but rather we want to communicate, in no uncertain terms, that it was a hard day at the office. Used this way, a metaphor is a concise, memorable, and often colorful way to express emotions. In a deeper sense, metaphors represent not only language but also thought and action. Writing in *Metaphors We Live By*, the linguists George Lakoff and Mark Johnson suggest that "our ordinary conceptual system, in terms of which we can think and act, is fundamentally metaphorical in nature."[4]

But, Holland argues, metaphors are much more than merely a colorful form of speech, even more than representations of thoughts. They can also help us translate ideas into models. And that, he says, represents the basis of innovative thinking. In the same way that a metaphor helps communicate one concept by comparing it to another concept that is widely understood, using a simple model to describe one idea can help us grasp the complexities of a similar idea. In both cases we are using one concept (the source) to better understand another (the target). Used this way, metaphors not only express existing ideas, they stimulate new ones.

In the book *Connections*, based on a memorable PBS series, James Burke describes several cases in which inventors were led to a discovery by first observing the similarities that existed between a previous invention (source) and that which the inventor wished to build (target). The automobile is a prime example. The carburetor is linked to a perfume sprayer, which in turn is linked to an eighteenth-century Italian who was trying to understand how to harness the hydraulic power of water. Alessandro Volta's electric pistol, initially created to test the purity of air, eventually sparked the fuel sprayed by the carburetor 125 years later. An automobile's gears are the direct descendant of the waterwheel, and the engine's pistons and cylinders can be traced to Thomas Newcomen's pumping engine, originally designed to drain coal mines. Each major discovery is connected to an earlier idea, a model that stimulated original thinking.

In our case, the main subject we wish to understand better (the target model) is the stock market or the economy. Over the years we have accumulated countless source models within the finance discipline to explain these phenomena, but too often they fail us. In many ways, the operation of markets and economies is still a mystery. Perhaps it is time we expanded the number of disciplines we call upon in our search for understanding. The more disciplines we have to explore, the more likely are we to find commonalties of mechanisms that clarify the mysteries. Innovative thinking, which is our goal, most often occurs when two or more mental models act in combination.

A latticework of mental models is itself a metaphor. And on the surface, quite a simple one at that. Everyone knows what latticework is, and most people have some degree of firsthand experience with it. There is probably not a do-it-yourselfer who hasn't made good use of a four-by-eight sheet of latticework at some point. We use it to decorate fences, to create shade over patios, and to support climbing plants. It is but a very small stretch to envision a metaphorical lattice as the support structure for organizing a set of mental concepts.

Yet, like many ideas that at first seem simple, the more closely we examine the metaphor of latticework, the more complex it becomes and the more difficult it is to retain as a pure mental-model concept. One thing we understand about the human mind is the variability with which it receives and processes information. Any educator knows that the best way to teach a new idea to one student may have no effect whatsoever with another; the best educators, therefore, carry with them a virtual key ring with many different keys for unlocking individual minds.

In much the same way, I have found myself using various analogies to present the concept of a latticework of mental models. For those with a high-technology background, I often compare the process of constructing a mental latticework to designing a neural network, and they instantly recognize the possibilities for immense power. Talking with mathematicians, I may ask them to think about the concepts first envisioned by George Boole and later formalized by Garrett Birkhoff of Harvard University in his book entitled *Lattice Theory*; this gives us the double reinforcement of a comparable theoretical framework that happens to be called by the very same name. Psychologists easily relate latticework to connectionism; educators link it with the brain's capacity to seek and find patterns. For people whose intellectual comfort zone is firmly planted in the humanities, I talk about the value of metaphors as devices for expanding the scope of our understanding. Many others, nonscientists like myself, often respond best to my description of a real piece of latticework with tiny lights at the junction points.

I hit upon this analogy one afternoon while staring out the window at the fence in our backyard. The entire fence is topped with a decorative strip of latticework that is visually broken into sections that echo the sections of the fence itself as defined by the posts. While looking at this fence and thinking about mental models, I gradually began to see each section of latticework as one area of knowledge; the section nearest the garage became psychology, the next one biology, and so on. Within each section, it was easy to think of the points where two lattice strips connect as nodes. Then, in that marvelous way that our brains skip from one analogy to the next, I suddenly thought of outdoor Christmas decorations, and I began to see, in my mind's eye, miniature lightbulbs at each node.

Suppose I was struggling to understand some marketplace trend or make an investment decision, and I arrayed my uncertainty on that latticework. Looking at the question from my perspective of biology, I might see several lights pop on. When I move to the next section, perhaps psychology, maybe a few other bulbs light up. If I also see lights in a third section, and then a fourth, I would know I could proceed with reasonable confidence, for my original insecure thinking would now have been confirmed and ratified. Conversely, if I saw no lights going on while I pondered the problem, I would take that as a clear indication not to proceed.

That's the power of a latticework of mental models, and it extends far beyond the narrow question of picking stocks. It leads to understanding the full range of market forces—new businesses and trends, emerging markets, the flow of money, international shifts, the economy in general, and the actions of people in markets.

Two years after Charlie Munger startled the finance students at USC by challenging them to consider investing as a subdivision of worldly wisdom, he reprised his notion of a latticework of models at Stanford Law School, this time in some more detail.[5]

He first reiterated his basic theme: true learning and lasting success come to those who make the effort to first build a latticework of mental models and then learn to think in an associative, multidisciplinary manner. It may take some work, he warned, especially if your education has forced you to specialize. But once those models are firmly set in your mind, you are intellectually equipped to deal with many different kinds of situations. "You can reach out and grasp the model that better solves the overall problem. All you have to do is know it and develop the right mental habits." No doubt Benjamin Franklin would approve.

I believe extraordinary rewards are possible for those who are willing to undertake the discovery of combinations between mental models. When that happens, what Charlie calls "especially big forces" take over. This is more than one plus one; it's the explosive power of critical mass, what Charlie—the master of colorful language—calls "the lollapalooza effect."

This is the heart of the investing philosophy that is presented in this book: developing the ability to think of finance and investing as one piece of a unified whole, one segment of a body of knowledge. Done right, it produces nothing short of a lollapalooza effect. I believe it is our best hope for long-term investment success.

Let's give Charlie the final word on the subject. In response to questions from Stanford students concerned about the process of uncovering the models, he remarked:

"Worldly wisdom is mostly very, very simple. There are a relatively small number of disciplines and a relatively small number of truly big ideas. And it's a lot of fun to figure out. Even better, the fun never stops. Furthermore, there's a lot of money in it, as I can testify from my own personal experience.

"What I am urging on you is not that hard to do. And the rewards are awesome. . . . It'll help you in business. It'll help you in law. It'll help you in life. And it'll help you in love. . . . It makes you better able to serve others, it makes you better able to serve yourself, and it makes life more fun."

2

Physics

Physics is the science that investigates matter, energy, and the interaction between them—the study, in other words, of how our universe works. It encompasses all the forces that control motion, sound, light, heat, electricity, and magnetism and their occurrence in all forms, from the smallest sub-atomic particles to the entire solar system. It is the intellectual foundation of many well-recognized principles such as gravitation and such mind-boggling modern concepts as quantum mechanics and relativity.

This is all very serious stuff and frequently intimidating to nonscientists. Does it have a place in our latticework of mental models for investors? I believe it does.

Of course many people assume that physics is too hard for ordinary mortals to grasp or too abstract to have any real application to modern finance. If you are among them, think for a moment about the last time you were in an antiques store. If the shop owner has too much inventory, prices suddenly become negotiable. On the other hand, if you fall in love with a special one-of-a-kind item, you know that it will command a high price because it is rare, but you may be willing to pay the price because your desire to own the item is equally high. What happens in the shop is governed by the rule of supply and demand, which in turn is a pure, classic example of the law of equilibrium at work. And equilibrium is one of the fundamental concepts in the field of physics.

How these concepts were uncovered, and the degree to which they may now be evolving into somewhat different forms with profound implications for finance and economics, is the story of this chapter.

The heart of the story begins with Sir Isaac Newton, the man whom many historians consider the greatest scientific mind of all time. He was born on Christmas Day in 1642 at the family farm in Lincolnshire, England. Nothing about the family circumstances at the time would have indicated that the premature, sickly infant would develop into a genius who would later be knighted. His father, who could neither read nor write, died several months before Isaac was born. Financially destitute, his mother was forced to leave the baby in the care of his grandmother for nine years. The youngster busied himself crafting intricately designed windmills, water clocks, and mouse-driven corn mills. It was a practice that served him well later, when he constructed his own scientific apparatuses to conduct experiments. Then, at age nineteen, with no formal background in mathematics or science, Newtown stepped into Trinity College at Cambridge and into a dazzling world filled with new ideas.

In 1661, the year Newton began his studies at Cambridge, nearly everyone—academics and laypeople alike—believed that God governed the world through inexplicable, supernatural powers. But the movement we now call the scientific revolution was well under way. Outside their formal classrooms, the students at Cambridge were exploring bold and contradictory ideas from the seventeenth century's greatest scientists: Johannes Kepler, Galileo Galilei, and Rene Descartes. Their ideas galvanized the students. What Newton learned from these three eventually led him to a new vision of the workings of the universe and, in particular, the law of equilibrium.

Johannes Kepler began his scientific career as an assistant to Tycho Brahe, a Danish nobleman and scientist, who had designed and built a large quadrant to study the movement of the planets. At that time, astronomers were pulled between two competing theories of the universe. One, originally suggested by Aristotle and amended by Ptolemy some four hundred years later, held that the sun, stars, and planets revolved around the earth. The other, published in 1543 by the Polish astronomer Nicolaus Copernicus and widely considered heretical well into the seventeenth century, held that the sun was at rest, and all the planets, including the earth, were in motion around it.

Before Brahe, scientists in both camps had to depend on the naked eye for celestial measurements; the telescope had not yet been invented. Brahe's quadrant, which looked something like a gun sight, was able to record the positions of planets as two angles, one measured up from the horizon and the second measured around true north.

Over a span of twenty-five years, Brahe recorded in meticulous detail the positions of planets. Just before his death in 1601, he turned over his observations to his young assistant. A talented mathematician, Kepler reanalyzed Brahe's detailed findings and began to draw meaningful conclusions that he summarized as the three major laws of planetary motion. By the time Newton was at Cambridge, Kepler's laws had begun to overrule the existing geocentric theories of astronomy and had firmly established the sun as the center of the universe.

The lesson Newton took from Kepler is one that has been repeated many times throughout history: Our ability to answer even the most fundamental aspects of human existence depends largely upon measuring instruments available at the time and the ability of scientists to apply rigorous mathematical reasoning to the data.

The second influence on Newton's thinking was the work of Galileo Galilei, who died the year Newton was born. Galileo, the Italian philosopher, mathematician, inventor, and physicist, is considered to be the first modern-day experimental scientist. Among his many inventions are the thermometer, the pendulum clock, the proportional compass used by draftsmen, and—most important to our story—the telescope. Galileo was thus the first to actually observe the heavenly bodies described by all the earlier astronomers: Kepler, Copernicus, Ptolemy, and Aristotle. With the technology of the magnifying optical instrument, Galileo could prove once and for all that the earth was not the center of the universe.

Galileo promoted a mathematical view of science. He believed that numerical relationships could be discovered throughout nature but hastened to add that their existence was not contradictory to the teachings of the church. It was important, he felt, to distinguish between "God's word" and "God's work." According to Galileo, primacy was in God's work, and it was the goal of scientists to discover the relationships in nature on the basis of logic. Today, he is best remembered among scientists for his experimental techniques.

The third important influence on Newton was Rene Descartes, the French mathematician and scientist who is often called the father of modern philosophy. He was one of the first to oppose the Aristotelian view of the world and instead embrace an empirical and mechanistic approach. Descartes died in 1650, eight years after Newton was born, and his ideas were gaining acceptance in certain circles by the time Newton entered Cambridge.

Descartes promoted a mechanical view of the world. He argued that the only way to understand how something works is to build a mechanical model of it, even if that model is constructed only in our imagination. According to Descartes, the human body, a falling rock, a growing tree, or a stormy night all suggested that mechanical laws were at work. This mechanical view provided a powerful research program for seventeenth-century scientists. It suggested that no matter how complex or difficult the observation, it was possible to discover the underlying mechanical laws to explain the phenomenon.

In his first days at Cambridge, Newton was unaware of the new discoveries and theories of these three scientists. But with relentless study and by applying his own intense powers of concentration, Newton quickly grasped their basic ideas. What he did with those ideas is the crux of our story.

While still a student, Newton began to synthesize Kepler's celestial laws of planetary motion with Galileo's terrestrial laws of falling bodies, all embraced within Descartes's cosmological view that the universe must operate by fixed mechanical laws. This gave Newton an outline to begin formulating the universal laws of physics.

Then in 1665, Newton's life took an unexpected turn. As the plague descended upon London, Cambridge was shut down and Newton was forced to retreat to his family's farm. There, in solitude and quiet, Newton's genius sprang forth. During what has been described as the *annus mirabilis* ("wonder year"), Newton brought forth new ideas with breathtaking speed. His first major discovery was the invention of fluxions or what we now call calculus. Next he developed the theory of optics. Previously it was believed that color was a mixture of light and darkness. But in a series of experiments using a prism in a darkened room, Newton discovered that light was made up of a combination of the colors of the spectrum. The highlight of that year, however, was Newton's discovery of the universal law of gravitation.

According to the legend, Newton watched an apple fall from a tree and, in a flash of insight, conceived of the idea of gravitation. Whereas

Kepler had defined the three laws of planetary motion and Galileo had confirmed that a falling body accelerates at a uniform rate, Newton, in a stroke of genius, combined Kepler's laws with Galileo's observations. Newton reasoned that the force acting upon the apple was the same power holding the moon in orbit around the earth, and the planets around the sun. It was an incredible leap of intuition.

Surprisingly, Newton did not publish his discovery of gravitation for more than twenty years. Unable at first to present his findings with mathematical precision, he waited until the publication of his masterpiece, *Principia Mathematica*, to describe his three laws of motion. Using these three laws, Newton was able to demonstrate how gravitational forces act between two bodies. He showed that the planets remain in a fixed orbit because the velocity of their forward motion is balanced by the force of gravity pulling them toward the sun. Thus, two equal forces create a state of equilibrium.[1]

Equilibrium is defined as a state of balance between opposing forces, powers, or influences. An equilibrium model typically identifies a system that is at rest; this is called *static equilibrium*. When competing forces are equally matched, a system reaches *dynamic equilibrium*. A scale that is equally weighted on both sides is an example of static equilibrium. Fill a bathtub full of water and then turn off the faucet and you will observe static equilibrium. But if you unplug the drain and then turn on the faucet so the level of the bathtub does not change, you are witnessing dynamic equilibrium. Another example is the human body. It remains in dynamic equilibrium so long as the heat loss from cooling remains in balance with the consumption of sugars.

With the publication of *Principia*, scientists quickly embraced the belief that the entire natural world was governed by universal laws rather than by a godhead whose will no human could ever know. It is impossible to overstate the significance of the shift. It represents nothing less than a complete reversal of the very foundation on which human existence was thought to rest. It meant that scientists no longer relied on divine revelation for understanding. If they could discern natural laws of the universe, they would be able to predict the future based on the present data. The scientific process used to investigate those natural laws is the legacy of Sir Isaac Newton.

The Newtonian view of the world portrays science as the study of an ordered universe that is as predictable as a clock. Indeed, the metaphor frequently used for the Newtonian vision is a "clockwork universe." Just as we can understand how a clock functions by separating its mechanism into individual parts, we can understand the universe by analyzing its separate elements. At its core, this is the definition of physics: reducing phenomena into a few fundamental particles and defining the forces that act on those particles. For more than three hundred years, breaking apart nature into its constituent parts has become the primary activity of science.

Physics has always held an enviable position within the sciences. With its mathematical precision and immutable laws, it seduces us with a sense of certainty and gives us the comfort of absolute answers. We should not be surprised to learn, therefore, that other disciplines generally looked first to physics in a search for answers, for order underneath nature's messiness. In the nineteenth century, for instance, certain scholars wondered whether it was possible to apply the Newtonian vision to the affairs of men. Adolphe Quetelet, a Belgian mathematician known for applying probability theory to social phenomena, introduced the idea of "social physics." Auguste Comte, whom we shall meet again in Chapter 4, developed a science for explaining social organizations and guiding social planning, a science he called *sociology*. Economists, too, have turned their attention to the Newtonian paradigm and the laws of physics.

After Newton, scholars in many fields focused their attention on systems that demonstrate equilibrium (whether static or dynamic), believing that it is nature's ultimate goal. If any deviations in the forces occurred, it was assumed that the deviations were small and temporary—and the system would always revert back to equilibrium. The critical point to our story is how the concept of equilibrium expanded from celestial mechanics into much broader applications, particularly economics.

For more than two hundred years, economists have relied on equilibrium theory to explain the behavior of economies. Alfred Marshall, the British economist, was the chief proponent of the concept of dynamic equilibrium in economics. His celebrated text, *Principles of Economics*, originally published in 1890, is considered one of the most important contributions to economics literature.[2] In Book 5 of *Principles of Economics*, which addresses the relationship of demand, supply, and price, Marshall devotes three separate chapters to economic equilibrium: in individuals, in companies, and in the marketplace.

In regard to individuals, Marshall explains:

> The simplest case of balance or equilibrium between desire and effort is found when a person satisfies one of his wants by his own direct work. When a boy picks blue-berries for his own eating, the action of

picking is probably itself pleasurable for a while; and for sometime longer the pleasure of eating is more than enough to repay the trouble of picking. But after he has eaten a good deal, the desire for eating diminishes; while the task of picking begins to cause weakness, which may indeed be a feeling of monotony rather than fatigue.

Equilibrium is reached when at last his eagerness to play and his disinclination for the work of picking counterbalance the desire for eating.[3]

In explaining how equilibrium affects companies, Marshall writes: "A Business firm grows and attains strength, and afterwards perhaps stagnates and decays; and at the turning point there is a balance or equilibrium of forces of life and decay."[4]

Even in the marketplace, the forces of equilibrium work to maintain a balance between demand and supply and help set prices for goods. According to Marshall, "When the demand price is equal to the supply price, the amount produced has no tendency either to be increased or to be diminished; it is in equilibrium."[5]

In Marshall's opinion, when the economy reaches equilibrium, it achieves stability. In fact, Marshall believed that equilibrium is the natural state of the economy; if the prices, demand, or supply become displaced, the economy will work to return to its natural equilibrium state. Here is his eloquent argument:

When demand and supply are in stable equilibrium, if any accident should move the scale of production from its equilibrium position, there will be instantly brought into play forces tending to push it back to that position; just as a stone hanging by a string is displaced from its equilibrium position, the force of gravity will at once tend to bring it back to its equilibrium position. The movements of the scale of production about its position of equilibrium will be of a somewhat similar kind.[6]

Marshall's *Principles of Economics* was the standard economics textbook for much of the twentieth century until Paul Samuelson introduced his *Economics* in 1948. Although colleges soon favored Samuelson's updated text over Marshall's classic work, the message of equilibrium remained the same. According to Samuelson, millions of prices and millions of outputs are connected to an interdependent weblike system. Within this system, households with preferences for products and services interact with firms that provide those products and services. These firms, each guided by a desire to maximize profits, transform information from households into products sold to households. The logical structure of this exchange, says Samuelson, is a general equilibrium system.

Paul Samuelson, who won the Nobel Prize in Economics in 1970, was a man of great intellect. The stock market fascinated him, and he took a suspicious view of any professional who claimed an ability to predict price changes and thus beat the market. "The respect for evidence," he once wrote, "compels me to incline toward the hypothesis that most portfolio decision makers should go out of business—take up plumbing, teach Greek, or help produce the annual GNP by serving as corporate executives."[7]

An important part of our story is tracing how Samuelson, with his respect for evidence and scientific methods, developed his own theories of how the market establishes prices. And, in yet another demonstration of the cumulative nature of human knowledge, we learn that Samuelson's attitude about the market was shaped by the works of Louis Bachelier, Maurice Kendall, and Alfred Cowles.

In 1932, Alfred Cowles established the Cowles Commission for Research and Economics. Having subscribed to several investment services, none of which predicted the 1929 stock market crash, Cowles set about to determine whether market forecasters could actually predict the future direction of the market. In one of the most detailed studies ever conducted, the commission analyzed 6,904 forecasts from 1929 through 1944; according to Cowles, "the results failed to disclose evidence of ability to predict successfully the future course of the stock market."[8]

Maurice Kendall, a professor of statistics at the London School of Economics, looked past the market forecasters the Cowles Commission studied and instead analyzed individual stock prices. In a 1953 paper entitled "The Analysis of Economic Time Series," Kendall studied the behavior of stock prices dating back over fifty years and was unable to find any patterns for structure in prices that would lead someone to make an accurate forecast. According to Peter Bernstein, whose *Capital Ideas* explores the origins of modern financial theory, Samuelson's interest in the stock market was triggered in large part by the news that Kendall's paper was greeted enthusiastically at the Royal Statistical Society.

In thinking about Kendall's work, Samuelson connected the idea of stock price movements with the classical economic theory of price and value. For nearly two hundred years, since the 1776 publication of Adam

Smith's *The Wealth of Nations*, economists had agreed there is a fundamental value, the "true value," that underlies the marketplace, and prices
tend to bounce above and below this value. Of course, what has haunted
economists and investors alike ever since is the debate over what is the
true value. Alfred Marshall tells us competition ultimately determines
equilibrium price. If price is oscillating, it is because there is a temporary
imbalance between supply and demand, but this is ultimately corrected by
the marketplace.

For his part, Samuelson believed stock prices bounced around because
of the perceived uncertainty over a stock's future value. Whether IBM is
worth a hundred dollars per share or fifty dollars per share is a debate in
the marketplace over the future growth of its earnings, the competitive
landscape, and attitudes about inflation and interest rates. In his 1965
landmark paper, "Proof That Properly Anticipated Prices Fluctuate Randomly," Samuelson introduced the concept of "shadow prices"—a stock's
intrinsic, but perhaps not obvious, value. Of course, the problem is how to
bring shadow prices to the forefront of the market. What Samuelson did
next created a seismic shift in how people began to frame the behavior of
the stock market.

Relying on a little-known doctoral dissertation written in 1900 by the
French mathematician Louis Bachelier, Samuelson began to weave together
a theory of market prices. Bachelier had argued that price changes in the
market were impossible to predict. His reasoning was straightforward.
"Contradictory opinions concerning market changes diverge so much," he
wrote, "that at the same time instant buyers believe in a price increase and
sellers believe in price decrease." Believing that, on average, neither buyers
nor sellers possessed any great insight, Bachelier made a startling conclusion. "It seems that the market, the aggregate of speculators, at a given instant can believe in neither a market rise nor a market fall, since, for each
quoted price, there are as many buyers as sellers." Thus, according to Bachelier, "the mathematical expectation of the speculator is zero."[9]

Bachelier's logic gave Samuelson a pathway for moving his shadow
prices from behind the market to the forefront. In one giant leap, Samuelson suggested that the best measure of shadow prices was Bachelier's market
prices. It may not always be perfectly accurate, he said, but there was no
better way to gauge intrinsic value than by Bachelier's aggregated collection
of buyers and sellers.

To strengthen the shadow price theory, Samuelson next introduced the
"rational expectations hypothesis." Samuelson writes, "We would expect

people in the marketplace, in pursuit of avid and intelligent self-interest, to take an account of those elements of future events that in a probability sense may be discerned to be casting their shadows before them."[10] Samuelson, in other words, believed that people make rational decisions consistent with their individual preferences. Hence, stock prices at any point in time are a reflection of these rational decisions; thus, shadow prices and market prices are one and the same.

Another way to think about this is that Samuelson took the concept of equilibrium in the economy and moved it to the stock market, connecting the idea of stock price movement with the classical idea that price and value exist in equilibrium. His notion that investors act on the basis of rational expectations is what upholds the concept of equilibrium in the stock market.

The individual credited with taking Samuelson's theoretical view of the market to the next level is Eugene Fama. His University of Chicago doctoral dissertation entitled "The Behavior of Stock Price" immediately caught the attention of the investment community. The dissertation was published in its entirety in the *Journal of Business* and later was excerpted in *The Financial Analysts Journal* and *Institutional Investor*. It is the foundation of what has come to be called "modern portfolio theory."

Fama's message was clear. Stock prices are unpredictable because the market is too efficient. In an efficient market, a great many smart people (Fama called them "rational profit maximizers") have simultaneous access to all the relevant information, and they aggressively apply that information in a way that causes prices to adjust instantaneously—thus restoring equilibrium—before anyone can profit. Predictions about the future therefore have no place in an efficient market, because share prices fully reflect all available information.

It's important to remember that Fama's efficient market theory is applicable only in the much broader view of market equilibrium promoted by Marshall, Samuelson, and one other individual: a finance professor and economic thinker, William Sharpe.

Sharpe was awarded the Nobel Prize in Economics for developing "a market equilibrium theory of asset prices under conditions of risk." His theory was originally outlined in a 1964 paper entitled "Capital Asset Prices: A Theory of Market Equilibrium under Conditions of Risk." Sharpe explained, "In equilibrium, there is a simple linear relationship between the expected return and standard deviation of return (defined as risk)."[11]

According to Sharpe, the only way to achieve a greater return is to incur additional risk. To increase expected returns, investors need only march further out the capital market line. Conversely, if investors wished to assume less risk, they would step down the capital line and by doing so receive less return. In either case, equilibrium is maintained.

The concept of equilibrium is so deeply embedded in our theory of economics and the stock market, it is difficult to imagine any other idea of how these systems could possibly work. As we have seen, equilibrium is not only the backbone for classical economics, but it also serves as the foundation for modern portfolio theory. To question the validity of the equilibrium model is to enter into combat with a legion of scholars who have made it their career to defend this ideal. Although the analogy may be a stretch, debating existing dogma is not unlike the challenge Copernicus faced when he questioned the religious view of a geocentric universe. Yet despite the risk, a number of scientists have begun to question the equilibrium theory that dominates our view of the economy and the stock market.

One place where the question is being raised is the Santa Fe Institute, where scientists from several disciplines are studying complex adaptive systems—those systems with many interacting parts that are continually changing their behavior in response to changes in the environment. A simple system, in contrast, has very few interacting parts. Examples of complex adaptive systems include the central nervous system, ecologies, ant colonies, political systems, social structures, and economies. To this list of complex adaptive systems we must add one more: stock markets.

Every complex adaptive system is actually a network of many individual agents all acting in parallel and interacting with one another. The critical variable that makes a system both complex and adaptive is the idea that agents (neurons, ants, or investors) in the system accumulate experience by interacting with other agents and then change themselves to adapt to a changing environment. No thoughtful person, looking at the present stock market, can fail to conclude that it shows all the traits of a complex adaptive system. And this takes us to the crux of the matter. If a complex adaptive system is, by definition, *continuously adapting*, it is impossible for any such system, including the stock market, ever to reach a state of perfect equilibrium.

What does that mean for the market? It throws the classic theories of economic equilibrium into serious question.[12] The standard equilibrium theory is rational, mechanistic, and efficient. It assumes that identical individual investors share rational expectations about stock prices and then efficiently discount that information into the market. It further assumes there are no profitable strategies available that are not already priced into the market.

The counterview from Santa Fe suggests the opposite: a market that is not rational, is organic rather than mechanistic, and is imperfectly efficient. It assumes the individual agents are, in fact, irrational and hence will misprice securities, creating the possibility for profitable strategies. In later chapters we will consider the underlying psychology that causes people to behave irrationally where money is concerned.

The catalyst for this alternative view of markets was the 1987 stock market crash. According to classical equilibrium market theory, sudden price changes occur because rational investors adjust to new market information. However, several post-1987 studies failed to identify any information that might have caused a correlating decline in price. In a strict interpretation of market equilibrium, there would be no booms or crashes, no high trading volume or high turnover ratios. But as we know all too well, trading volume and turnover ratios have continued to climb, and heightened volatility has become the norm rather than the exception. Is it possible that automatic acceptance of market equilibrium, and the efficient market hypothesis that is its corollary, can no longer be defended?

In all fairness, I must point out that classical economists and proponents of modern portfolio theory recognize that their systems are not capable of perfect equilibrium. Near the end of his life, even Alfred Marshall went public with his misgivings. Paul Samuelson acknowledged that people do not begin with perfect rationality but believed that over time the rational and thoughtful investor will win out over the irrational and visceral. Likewise, Fama believes that an efficient market requires neither total rationality nor perfect information; however, because it *is* efficient, he says, it is all but impossible for any one individual to beat the market.

For my part, I suspect that most economists, if pressed, would confess that the idea of a market composed of only rational investors who process perfect information is an idealized system, displaying all the limitations inherent in any idealized system. Louis Bachelier's equal number of buyers and sellers who exhibit Samuelson's rationality and process Fama's perfect information is obviously at odds with what occurs in the real world of investing. Investment professionals who continue to promote an idealized system over what is exhibited in the real system may be leading us down the wrong path.

Yet we still hold on to our belief that the law of equilibrium is absolute. We cling to it because the entire Newtonian system, of which equilibrium is one part, has been our model for how to think about the world for three hundred years. Letting go of such deeply embedded ideas is not easy. However, in the spirit of Newton, Galileo, and Copernicus, we must be willing to see the world as it is, and that means making room for new ideas.

Let me say very clearly here that I am not asking you to surrender your trust in equilibrium or to conclude that the law of supply and demand is hereby revoked. The world is not nearly so simple that I could make such black-and-white dictums—and that, in fact, is the point. In an environment of complexity, simple laws are insufficient to explain the entire system.

Equilibrium may indeed be the natural state of the world, and restoring it when it is disturbed may be nature's goal, but it is not the constant condition that Newtonian physics would suggest. At any given moment, *both* equilibrium and disequilibrium may be found in the market. It's a bit like those trick photographs that show two different scenes; one well-known example seems at first to depict a wineglass, until you shift your perspective and see that it also portrays a silhouette of a woman in an old-fashioned dress. Both images are correct; both exist simultaneously. Which one we focus on is a matter of personal perspective. In much the same way, the balance between supply and demand, between price and value, will always be in evidence in the daily operation of the market, but it no longer gives us the full answer.

Just as our viewpoint of the world changed when it was demonstrated the earth was no longer the center of the universe, so will your viewpoint of the market change, I believe, when we accept that it is not governed strictly by the mechanical laws of Newton. The obvious question then becomes, if the Newtonian perspective is inadequate by itself, what other mental models should we add? The answer, described in the following chapter, may surprise you.

3

Biology

The market crash of 1987 caught most scholars, economists, and investment professionals by surprise. Nowhere in the classical, equilibrium-based view of the market so long considered inviolate was there anything that would predict or even describe the events of 1987. Then, some thirty years later, we learned this hard lesson all over again. The stunning events of 2007–2009 and their devastating dominoes only served to reinforce this unsettling sense of being blindsided by something wholly unpredictable. This double failure of the existing theory left open the potential for competing theories. Chief among them was the belief that the market and the economy are best understood from a *biological* perspective.

Turning to biology for insight into finance and investing may at first seem a startling move, but just as we did in our study of physics, we focus here on just one core idea from the field of biology: evolution. Whereas in nature the process of evolution is one of natural selection, seeing the market within an evolutionary framework allows us to observe the law of economic selection.

The concept of evolution is not the sole intellectual franchise of any one mind. As far back as the sixth century B.C.E., the possibility of species developing in different forms had been expressed by Greek and Chinese philosophers. Yet today, the evolutionary principle is firmly associated with one individual, a man whose ideas triggered a scientific revolution every bit as profound as that emanating from the work of Sir Isaac Newton a century and a half earlier.

Charles Robert Darwin was born in Shrewsbury, England, in 1809, into a family of scientists. His paternal grandfather was the physician and scientist Erasmus Darwin, and on his mother's side, his grandfather was the famous potter Josiah Wedgwood.[1]

His father, Robert, also a respected physician and very forceful personality, insisted that Charles study medicine and enrolled him in the University of Edinburgh. Darwin was uninterested. He found the classroom studies boring and became violently ill at the sight of surgery performed without anesthesia. The natural world was far more fascinating to him, and the young Darwin spent many hours reading geology and collecting insects and specimens.

Realizing his son would never become a physician, Robert Darwin sent Charles to Cambridge University to study divinity. Once again a less than stellar student, he nonetheless earned a bachelor's degree in theology. More significant than the formal course of study were the associations he formed with several of the Cambridge faculty. The Reverend John Stevens Henslow, professor of botany, permitted the enthusiastic amateur to sit in on his lectures and to accompany him on his daily walks to study plant life. Darwin spent so many hours in the professor's company that he was known around the university as "the man who walks with Henslow." After graduation, Darwin joined a geological trip to Wales, an experience that moved him to consider a career as a geologist. But when he returned home from Wales, Darwin found waiting for him a letter that would change his life forever.

Professor Henslow wrote to say that he had recommended Darwin for the position of naturalist on a naval expedition. HMS *Beagle*, under the command of Captain Robert FitzRoy, was soon to leave on a voyage of scientific exploration with two purposes: to continue the process of charting the coast of South America, and to add to the investigation of longitude by taking a series of chronological readings. It would require sailing completely around the world, a trip of at least two years (as it turned out, the trip took five years). The position of naturalist carried no salary—in fact, the naturalist would have to pay his own expenses—but Darwin was thrilled at the prospect.

He almost did not make the journey. Faced with his father's strong objections, Charles at first declined the offer. Fortunately, Charles's uncle,

Josiah Wedgwood II, whom Dr. Darwin respected, intervened and convinced his brother-in-law that it was a splendid opportunity for the young man. And thus, when the *Beagle* set sail from Plymouth, England, on December 27, 1831, Charles Darwin was aboard, charged with the responsibility of collecting, recording, and analyzing all of the flora and fauna and every other aspect of natural history that would be encountered. He was twenty-two years old.

Always more comfortable on land than sea, Darwin was frequently seasick, and during the voyage he often kept to himself, reading from the ship's library and his own personal collection of scientific texts. But whenever the ship landed, he plunged eagerly into exploring the local environment. What we know to be his most significant observations occurred fairly early in the trip, on the Galapagos Islands, near the equator on the Pacific side of South America, about six hundred miles west of Ecuador. This island group would prove to be the perfect laboratory for studying the mutability of species.

Darwin, the amateur geologist, knew that the Galapagos were classified as oceanic islands, meaning they had risen from the sea by volcanic action with no life forms aboard. Nature creates these islands and then waits to see what shows up. An oceanic island eventually becomes inhabited but only by forms that can reach it by wings (birds) or wind (spores and seeds). In the Galapagos, Darwin surmised that the tortoise and marine iguana, swimmers capable of staying under water for long periods of time, could have made the long journey from South America, possibly attached to floating debris pulled along by the current. He also figured that other animals he observed had been brought to the islands by earlier sailors and adventurers. But much of what he saw in the island group puzzled and intrigued him.

Darwin was particularly fascinated by the presence of thirteen types of finches. He first assumed these Galapagos finches, today called Darwin's finches, were a subspecies of the South American finches he had studied earlier and had most likely been blown to sea in a storm. But as he studied distribution patterns, Darwin observed that most islands in the archipelago carried only two or three types of finches; only the larger central islands showed greater diversification. What intrigued him even more was that all the Galapagos finches differed in size and behavior. Some were heavy-billed seedeaters; others were slender billed and favored insects. Sailing through the archipelago, Darwin discovered that the finches on Hood Island were different from those on Tower Island and that both were different from those on Indefatigable Island. He began to wonder what would happen if a few finches on Hood Island were blown by high winds to another island. Darwin concluded that if the newcomers were pre-adapted to the new habitat, they would survive and multiply alongside the resident finches; if not, their number would ultimately diminish. It was one thread of what would ultimately become his famous thesis.

When Darwin returned home in 1836, he was enthusiastically welcomed into England's scientific community. He was immediately made a fellow of the Geological Society and three years later was elected to the Royal Society. He quickly settled into work. Publicly, Darwin was busily preparing the publication of his many geological and biological discoveries. But privately, he was also constructing a new theory.

Reviewing his notes from the voyage, Darwin was deeply perplexed. Why did the birds and tortoises on some islands in the Galapagos resemble the species found in South America while those on other islands did not? This observation was even more disturbing when Darwin learned that the finches he brought back from the Galapagos belonged to different species and were not simply different varieties of the same species, as he had previously believed. Darwin also discovered that the mockingbirds he had collected were three distinct species and the tortoises represented two species. He began referring to these troubling questions as "the species problem," and outlined his observations in a notebook he later entitled "Notebook on the Transmutation of the Species."

Darwin now began an intense investigation into the species variation. He devoured all the written work on the subject and exchanged voluminous correspondence with botanists, naturalists, and zookeepers—anyone who had information or opinions about species mutation. What he learned convinced him that he was on the right track with his working hypothesis that species do in fact change, whether from place to place or from time period to time period. The idea was not only radical at the time, it was blasphemous. Darwin struggled to keep his work secret.

As he continued to study and think, Darwin was increasingly certain that evolution was taking place, but he did not yet understand how. It wasn't until 1838 that he was able to put the pieces together. In the fall of that year, Darwin began to read *Essay on the Principle of Population* by the British economist Thomas Malthus. After exploring the relationship between the food supply and human population, Malthus concluded that population was increasing geometrically while the means of subsistence (food production) progressed arithmetically. Thus population growth would always outrun the growth of food supplies and populations would grow until checked by war, famine, or disease.

Darwin saw an immediate parallel between Malthus's work and the unanswered questions about animal and plant populations. Malthus's theory decreed that a limited food supply would force an increasing population into a permanent struggle for survival. From his years of observation, Darwin recognized the Malthusian process in the animal world. "Being well prepared to appreciate the struggle for existence which everywhere goes on from long-continued observation of the habits of animals and plants," he wrote in his notebook, "it at once struck me that under these circumstances, favorable variations would tend to be preserved and unfavorable ones to be destroyed. The result of this would be the formation of new species. Here, then, I had at last got a theory—a process by which to work."[2]

The originality of Darwin's theory lay in the idea that the struggle for survival was occurring not only between species but between individuals within the same species. If having a longer beak, for example, increased a bird's chances of survival, then more birds with long beaks would be more likely to pass this advantage on. Eventually, the longer beak would become dominant within the species.[3] By this process of natural selection, Darwin theorized, favorable variations are preserved and transmitted to succeeding generations. After several generations, small gradual changes in the species begin to add up to larger changes—thus, evolution occurs.

In 1842, Darwin had completed a brief outline of his new theory, but resisted publication. Perhaps sensing the furious controversy the theory would generate, he insisted on developing further documentation. Then on June 18, 1858, Darwin received a paper from the naturalist Alfred Russel Wallace that summarized perfectly the theory Darwin had been working on for twenty years. For advice, Darwin called on two close colleagues, the geologist Robert Lyell and the botanist Joseph Hooker, and they decided to present the work of both men in a combined paper. The following year, Darwin published *On the Origin of Species by Means of Natural Selection, or the Preservation of Favoured Races in the Struggle for Life*. The book sold out on the first day, and by 1872, *The Origin of Species*, as it was popularly called, was in its sixth edition.

Darwin had written the book of the century—perhaps, said the noted evolutionary biologist Richard Dawkins, the book of the millennium. "*The Origin* changed humanity, and of all life, forever," Dawkins wrote.[4] It also changed our view of other areas of knowledge, including economics, and that is the focus in this chapter.

In the years following Darwin's masterpiece, European intellectuals were fascinated with the theory of natural selection; it swirled through conversations, lectures, and writings in many fields of study. Inevitably, the concept of evolutionary change attracted the attention of economists as well.[5]

The first luminary was Alfred Marshall, the leading economist in Britain (and therefore, some might argue, the world) from the last decade of the nineteenth century until his death in 1924. Marshall's magnum opus is *Principles of Economics*, first published in 1890 and revised and expanded seven times afterward. As a comprehensive review of the development of economic thought, it has few equals, and in fact the eighth edition is still used as an important text in many college curricula.

Marshall makes another appearance in our chapter a little later on. For the moment, I point you to the title page of the first edition of his book. Below the title, below the author's name and university affiliation, and below a line that poignantly proclaims this as Volume 1, is this Latin phrase:[6]

Natura non facit saltum.

Marshall's audience needed no translation, but today most of us do. "Nature does not make leaps." Darwin himself used the exact same motto in *The Origin of Species*. So with this homage, Marshall is hinting that he aligns himself with the intellectual revolution triggered by Darwin's work and perhaps also that he sees virtue in viewing economics through a Darwinian prism. His real intention is a tantalizing puzzle for us today, for Marshall was never fully explicit about his position.

Less than two decades after Marshall's text first appeared, a new figure in economic study made an impressive debut. In 1908, at the young age of twenty-five, Austrian-born Joseph Schumpeter, educated in both economics and law, published his first book, titled *The Nature and Essence of Economic Theory*. In it, he sought to differentiate the conventional static view of the economy with his more dynamic theory.

In that first book, Schumpeter advanced the argument that economics is essentially an evolutionary process. He expanded that theme in his next book, *The Theory of Economic Development* (1911), and continued to develop it throughout his life.[7] In fact, Christopher Freeman, a twentieth-century British economist who studied Schumpeter extensively, comments: "The central point of his whole life work is that capitalism can only be understood as an evolutionary process of continuous innovation and creative destruction."[8]

Schumpeter's dynamic economic process was composed of three principal elements: innovation, entrepreneurship, and credit. At the heart of his theory is the idea that the search for equilibrium is an adaptive process. In that process, innovators are the change agents. All changes in the economic system start with innovation.

Innovation, said Schumpeter, is the profitable application of new ideas, including products, production processes, supply sources, new markets, or new ways in which a company could be organized. Whereas standard economic theory believed progress was a series of small incremental steps, Schumpeter's theory stressed innovative leaps, which in turn caused massive disruptions and discontinuity—an idea captured in Schumpeter's famous phrase "the perennial gale of creative destruction."

But all these innovative possibilities meant nothing without the entrepreneur who becomes the visionary leader of innovation. It takes someone exceptional, said Schumpeter, to overcome the natural obstacles and resistance to innovation. Without the entrepreneur's desire and willingness to press forward, many great ideas could never be launched. Lastly, Schumpeter explained, great innovations led by great entrepreneurs can thrive only in certain environments. Such things as property rights, stable currencies, and free trade are all important environmental factors, but credit is paramount. Without access to credit, the ability to promote innovation would be hamstrung.

In 1907, while Schumpeter was still gathering his thoughts for *The Nature and Essence of Economic Theory*, he visited the celebrated economist Alfred Marshall in Cambridge.[9] At that time, Marshall was sixty-five years old and in declining health. Schumpeter knew that Marshall was intrigued with Darwin's theory of evolution and was eager to discuss it.

For some time Marshall had privately chided his colleagues for not recognizing that economic phenomena more closely resembled biological processes than the standard mechanized theory. But he was ambiguous about publicly advancing a radically new theory. When Schumpeter told Marshall he intended to promote a biological interpretation of economics, Marshall turned cautious. As he was leaving, Schumpeter commented that their conversation had cast him "as indiscreet lover bent on an adventurous marriage and you a benevolent old uncle trying to persuade me to desist." Marshall replied in good humor, "And this is as it should be. For if there is anything to it, the uncle will preach in vain."[10]

Thirteen years after their meeting, the eighth and final edition of *Principles of Economics* (1920) was published. Here, for perhaps the first time, Marshall clearly and eloquently presented his ideas on evolutionary economics. In the preface, he wrote:

> The Mecca of the economist lies in economic biology rather than in economic dynamics. But the biological conceptions are more complex than those of mechanics; a volume on Foundations must therefore give a relatively large place to mechanical analogies; and frequent use is made of the term "equilibrium," which suggests something of a statical analogy. This fact, combined with the predominant attention paid in the present volume to the normal conditions of life in the modern age, has suggested the notion that its central idea is "statical," rather than "dynamical." But in fact it is concerned throughout with the forces that cause movement: and its key-note is that of dynamics, rather than statics.[11]

I have always wondered why the biological view of economics, conceived over one hundred years ago, has not yet reached the top rung of academic support. It may be, as Marshall wrote, "biological conceptions are more complex than mechanics." It may also be that a biological interpretation of economics is just now entering the "revolutionary" phase of scientific development.

Fifty years ago, Thomas Kuhn wrote a landmark book titled *The Structure of Scientific Revolutions* ([1962] 1970). In it, he challenged the conventional view that scientific progress moves in a pedestrian fashion as a series of accepted facts and theories. Kuhn believed there are times when advancement occurs only by revolution.

Under "normal science," he explains, puzzles are solved within the context of the dominant paradigm. As long as there is a general consensus about the paradigm, normal science continues. But what happens when anomalies appear?

According to Kuhn, when an observed phenomenon is not adequately explained by the dominant paradigm, a new competing paradigm is born. Scientists left with an ineffectual model go to work on developing a new theoretical outline. Although you might think the transition from old paradigm to new is peacefully led by the collective who are in the pursuit of truth, Kuhn tells us just the opposite happens—hence the term "revolution."

Proponents of the dominant paradigm, when confronted with a new and alternative paradigm, are left with two choices. They can jettison their long-held beliefs and divorce themselves from a lifelong intellectual and professional investment, or they can stand and fight. In the second case, we have what is known as a "paradigm collision," and the tactics for dealing with it are straightforward. First, you seek to discredit the new paradigm in any manner possible; then you begin to repair the dominant paradigm so it better explains the environment. For example, when the geocentric view of the solar system was challenged by Copernicus's evidence that the earth was not the center of the universe, adherents to Ptolemy's *Almagest* simply added orbital rings to his elliptical spheres to explain away the anomalies. When that didn't work, they threw Copernicus in prison until he recanted his theory.

In the midst of a paradigm collision, the scientific community bifurcates.

The older entrenched group seeks to defend the primary paradigm while others seek to institute a new paradigm. Kuhn tells us that once this polarization occurs, "political recourse fails." Although intense intellectual combat is the norm when two competing paradigms collide, there is another, more subtle way, which can ultimately settle the matter—time.

Kuhn notes that the scientific revolutionaries are often "either very young or very new to the field whose paradigm they change." They have very little intellectual capital committed to the older primary paradigm and are more "likely to see that those rules no longer define a playable game and [work] to conceive another set that can replace them."[12] If the new paradigm is indeed robust, over time it will attract more scientists. If the older paradigm cannot compete, lacking any new recruits it will slowly fade away. It is, we might say, undergoing a kind of evolution.

Perhaps we should forgive the economists of the last one hundred years for not fully embracing the idea of evolutionary economics. After all, evolution itself is not easily recognizable. Darwin's evolution was steady, slow, and continuous. Biologists call this gradualism. The beaks of Darwin's finches or the stripes of a tiger were not altered in a few short years but gradually, over hundreds if not thousands of years. Likewise, a business owner who operates in the same industry year after year may not experience any change. If economic transformation is not easily noticeable, how can we then blame the economist who overlooks it? Seen from this perspective, Marshall would be a gradualist.

But in other cases, change can occur swiftly and dramatically. Biologists call this "punctuated equilibrium." For a long period of time there is very little change, then suddenly a few huge changes can occur—perhaps the result of DNA mutations or a dramatic alteration of the environment. This is Schumpeter's evolution. In his world, change occurs very rapidly then settles down again for a period of steady, slow, but continuous alteration.

But no matter its pace, we must remember there is always change. And this is why we must leave Newton's world and embrace Darwin's. In Newton's world, there is no change. You can run his physics experiments thousands of times for thousands of years and always get the same result. But not so with Darwin and not so with economics. Companies, industries, and economies may mark time with no discernible changes, but inevitably they do change. Whether gradually or suddenly, the familiar paradigm crumbles.

Brian Arthur, formerly at Stanford University and a visiting professor at the Santa Fe Institute, was one of the first modern economists willing to take a fresh look at how economics really works. Trained in classical economics, Arthur immersed himself in the teachings of Marshall and Samuelson and in particular the equilibrium of markets—the stability of supply and demand. But the world described by the classical economists was not the same world Arthur saw. No matter how hard he tried to embrace the teachings of stability, he could see only instability. The world was constantly changing, thought Arthur. It was full of upheavals and surprises. It was continually evolving.

In November 1979, Arthur began to record his observations in his personal notebook. One page, which he entitled "Economics Old and New," he divided into two columns in which he began to list the characteristics of both concepts. Under "Old Economics," Arthur listed investors as identical, rational, and equal in ability. The system was devoid of any real dynamics. Everything was in equilibrium. Economics was based on classical physics under the belief that the system was structurally simple. Under "New Economics," Arthur wrote that people were separate and different in ability. They were emotional. The system was complicated and everchanging.

In Arthur's mind, economics was not simple but inherently complex, more akin to biology than physics.

A soft-spoken Irishman, Arthur confesses he was not the first to think about economics in this way, but he was most assuredly the first to confront it.

It was the Nobel Prize–winning economist Ken Arrow who first introduced Brian Arthur to the close-knit group of scientists working at the Santa Fe Institute. Arrow invited Arthur to attend a conference of physicists, biologists, and economists at the institute in the fall of 1987 to present his latest research. The conference was organized in the hope that the ideas then percolating within natural sciences, namely "the science of complexity," would help stimulate new ways to think about economics.[13] Common to the study of complexity is the notion that complex adaptive systems operate with multiple elements, each adapting or reacting to the patterns the system itself creates. Complex adaptive systems are in a constant process of evolving over time. These types of systems are familiar to biologists and ecologists, but the group at Santa Fe thought that perhaps the concept should be expanded, that maybe now the time had come to include the study of economic systems and stock markets within the overarching idea of complexity.

Unshackling themselves from the classical teachings, the Santa Fe group was able to point out four distinct features they observed about the economy.

1. *Dispersed interaction:* What happens in the economy is determined by the interactions of a great number of individual agents all acting in parallel. The action of any one individual agent depends on the anticipated actions of a limited number of agents as well as on the system they cocreate.

2. *No global controller:* Although there are laws and institutions, there is no one global entity that controls the economy. Rather, the system is controlled by the competition and coordination between agents of the system.

3. *Continual adaptation:* The behavior, actions, and strategies of the agents, as well as their products and services, are revised continually on the basis of accumulated experience. In other words, the system adapts. It creates new products, new markets, new institutions, and new behavior. It is an ongoing system.

4. *Out-of-equilibrium dynamics:* Unlike the equilibrium models that dominate the thinking in classical economics, the Santa Fe group believed the economy, because of constant change, operates far from equilibrium.

An essential element of complex adaptive systems is a feedback loop. That is, agents in the system first form expectations or models and then act on the basis of predictions generated by these models. But over time these models change depending on how accurately they predict the environment. If the model is useful, it is retained; if not, the agents alter the model to increase its predictability. Obviously, accuracy of predictability is a paramount concern to participants in the stock market, and we may be able to achieve broader understanding if we can learn to view the market as one type of complex adaptive system.

The whole notion of complex systems is a new way of seeing the world, and it is not easily grasped. How exactly do agents in complex adaptive systems interact? How do they go about collectively creating, and then changing, a model for predicting the future? For those of us who are not scientists, finding a way to visualize the process is helpful. Brian Arthur gives us an answer with an example he dubbed "the El Farol Problem."

El Farol, a bar in Santa Fe, New Mexico, used to feature Irish music on Thursday nights. Arthur, the Irishman, loved to go there. On most occasions, the bar patrons were well behaved, and it was enjoyable to sit and listen to the music. But on some nights, the bar was packed with so many people crammed together drinking and singing that the scene became unruly. Now Arthur was confronted with a problem: How could he decide which nights to go to El Farol and which nights to stay home? The chore of having to decide led him to formulate a mathematical theory he named the El Farol Problem. It has, he says, all the characteristics of a complex adaptive system.

Suppose, says Arthur, there are one hundred people in Santa Fe who are interested in going to El Farol to listen to Irish music, but none of them wants to go if the bar is going to be crowded. Now also suppose the bar published its weekly attendance for the past ten weeks. With this information, the music lovers will build models to predict how many people will show up next Thursday. Some may figure that it will be approximately the same number of people as last week. Others will take an average of the last few weeks. A few will attempt to correlate attendance data to the weather or to other activities for the same audience. There will be endless ways to build models to predict how many people will go to the bar.

Now let's say that every lover of Irish music decides that the comfort level in the small bar is sixty people. All one hundred people will decide, using whatever predictor has been the most accurate over the last few weeks, when the limit is going to be reached. Because each person has a different predictor, on any given Thursday some people will turn up at El Farol and others will stay home because their model has predicted more than sixty people will be attending. The following day, El Farol publishes its attendance and the hundred music lovers will update their models and get ready for next week's prediction.

The El Farol process can be termed an ecology of predictors, says Arthur. At any point, there is a group of models that are deemed "alive"— that is, they are useful predictors of how many people will attend the bar. Conversely, predictors that turn out to be inaccurate will slowly die off. Each week, new predictors, new models, new beliefs will compete for use by other music lovers.

We can quickly see how the El Farol process echoes the Darwinian idea of survival through natural selection and how logically it extends to economies and markets. In the markets, each agent's predictive models compete for survival against the models of all other agents, and the feedback that is generated causes some models to be changed and others to disappear. It is a world, says Arthur, that is complex, adaptive, and evolutionary.

Brian Arthur is not the only Santa Fe scientist exploring the link between biology and economics. J. Doyne Farmer, originally trained as a physicist, knew that classical economics was based on the same equilibrium laws he had studied in college, but he also knew that what he observed in the markets did not always correspond with those laws.

Farmer was already convinced that the market was not efficient. That much was clear to him. Lawrence Summers, who was to become U.S. Treasury Secretary, was one of the original attendees at the 1987 conference on economics and complex systems. Summers researched the one hundred largest daily market moves and was able to connect newsworthy events to only 40 percent of them. In other words, more than half of the largest market movers were occurring without some corresponding informational input. This, Farmer knew, was highly inconsistent with the efficient market theory. It was clear that some internal dynamics were causing the excess volatility in the market. But what were those dynamics? Farmer, who

Table 3.1

Biological Ecology	Financial Ecology
Species	Trading strategy
Individual organism	Trader
Genotype (genetic constitution)	Functional representation of strategy
Phenotype (observable appearance)	Actions of the strategy (buying, selling)
Population	Capital
External environment	Price and other informational inputs
Selection	Capital allocation
Mutation and recombination	Creation of new strategies

possesses a natural sense of the curiosity that constantly pushes him into new arenas, thought that the answer might be found, not in the laws that explain celestial mechanics, but rather in the laws that describe the behavior of ecological systems.

In a Santa Fe Institute paper titled "Market Force, Ecology, and Evolution," Farmer has taken the important first step in outlining the behavior of the stock market in biological terms. His analogy between a biological ecology of interacting species and a financial ecology of interacting strategies is summarized in the table shown here.[14]

Farmer is the first to admit the analogy is not perfect, but it does present a stimulating way in which to think about the market. Furthermore, it links the process to clearly defined science of how living systems behave and evolve.

If we go back through the history of the stock market and seek to identify the trading strategies that dominated the landscape, I believe there have been five major strategies, (which in Farmer's analogy would be species).

1. In the 1930s and 1940s, the discount-to-hard-book value strategy, first proposed by Benjamin Graham and David Dodd in their classic 1934 textbook *Security Analysis*, was dominant.

2. After World War II the second major strategy that dominated finance was the dividend model. As the memories of the 1929 market crash faded and prosperity returned, investors were increasingly attracted to stocks that paid high dividends, and lower-paying bonds lost favor. So popular was the dividend strategy that by the 1950s, the yield on dividend-paying stocks dropped below the yield of bonds—a historical first.

3. By the 1960s, a third strategy appeared. Investors exchanged stocks paying high dividends for companies that were expected to grow their earnings at a high rate.

4. By the 1980s, a fourth strategy took over. Warren Buffett stressed the need to focus on companies with high "owner-earnings" or cash flows.

5. Today we can see that cash return on invested capital is emerging as the fifth new strategy.

Most of us easily recognize these well-known strategies, and we can readily accept the idea that each one gained favor by overtaking a previously dominant strategy and was then itself eventually overtaken by a new strategy. In a word, evolution took place in the stock market via economic selection.

How does economic selection occur? Remember that in Farmer's analogy, a biological population is capital and natural selection occurs by capital allocation. This means capital varies in relation to the popularity of the strategy. If a strategy is successful, it attracts more capital and becomes the dominant strategy. When a new strategy that works is discovered, capital is reallocated—or, in biological terms, there is a change in population. As Farmer notes, "The long-term evolution of the market can be studied in terms of flows of money. Financial evolution is influenced by money in much the same way that biological evolution is influenced by food."[15]

Why are financial strategies so diverse? The answer, Farmer believes, starts with the idea that basic strategies induce patterns of behavior. Agents rush in to exploit these obvious patterns, causing an ultimate side effect. As more agents begin using the same strategy, its profitability drops. The inefficiency becomes apparent, and the original strategy is washed out. But then new agents enter the picture with new ideas. They form new strategies of which any number may become profitable. Capital shifts and the new strategy explodes, which starts the evolutionary process again. It is the classic El Farol Problem described by Brian Arthur.

Will the market ever become efficient? If you accept the idea that evolution plays a role in financial markets the answer would have to be no. Each strategy that eliminates an inefficiency will soon be replaced in turn by a new strategy. The market will always maintain some level of diversity, and this we know is a principal cause of evolution.

What we are learning is that studying economic and financial systems is very similar to studying biological systems. The central concept for both is the notion of change, what biologists call evolution. The models we use to explain the evolution of financial strategies are mathematically similar to the equations biologists use to study populations of predator-prey systems, competing systems, or symbiotic systems.

The concept of evolution should not be foreign to financial analysts. Outside the markets, we can easily observe the multitude of systems that undergo change, from fashions to language to popular culture in all its manifestations. If understanding financial markets in terms of evolution seems intimidating to some, I suspect that may be because of the words biologists use to describe the process: Variation. Adaptation. Mutation. Genetic recombination. These are terms not found in the lexicon of an MBA program.

Perhaps it is easier if we switch to the vocabulary of the corporate world, where the concepts of managing change, encouraging innovation, and adapting to marketplace demands are well established and well understood. Simply put, the whole concept of adaptation is based on the idea that there is a problem, and the species—or the industry, or the company— eventually solves it by adapting to the environment.

The idea of biological economics should also be easier to embrace now that the theory has graduated from the Santa Fe Institute to mainstream universities and consulting firms that study business and management strategies. Richard Foster and Sarah Kaplan, from McKinsey & Company, wrote a very important book titled *Creative Destruction: Why Companies That Are Built to Last Underperform the Market—and How to Successfully Transform Them.* Clay Christensen, professor of business administration at Harvard University, has had a major impact on the curriculum with his best-selling books, *The Innovator's Dilemma: When New Technologies Cause Great Firms to Fail* and *The Innovator's Solution: Creating and Sustaining Successful Growth* (co-authored with Michael Raynor).

Andrew Lo, a finance professor at the Massachusetts Institute of Technology and director of the MIT Laboratory for Financial Engineering, has sought to strike a balance between two competing paradigms by suggesting the economic system actually possesses, simultaneously, the effects of both a Newtonian efficient market hypothesis and a Darwinian biological interpretation.

Remember that in the chapter on physics we postulated that although "equilibrium may indeed be the natural state of the world, and restoring it when it is disturbed may be nature's goal, it is not the constant condition that Newtonian physics would suggest. At any given moment, both equilibrium and disequilibrium may be found in the market." Andrew Lo's *The Adaptive Markets Hypothesis: Market Efficiency from an Evolutionary Perspective* is heading in the same direction. Lo admits he struggled with the conflict between the two schools of thought for many years until it dawned on him that there was no conflict at all.

Lo reminds us of the well-known fable in which six blind priests come upon an elephant. The first priest feels the elephant's leg and declares it to be a tree. The next priest feels the elephant's side and claims it is a huge wall. Each priest touches a different part of the elephant and comes up with a different explanation. Andrew Lo sees the two different interpretations of the market in the same manner. "I realized that the behavioral finance folks and the efficient-market folks were both right," he says. "They were both observing the same phenomenon, but from different angles."

In Lo's opinion, the market is neither exclusively efficient nor always behavioral—it is both. "Behavior is really the outcome of interactions between our logical faculties and our emotional responses," he explains. "When logic and emotions are in proper balance, markets operate in a relatively efficient manner."[16] (We will look more closely at the tug-of-war between logic and emotion and its impact on investors in a later chapter.) Lo's hypothesis seeks to bridge the gap between market efficiency and behavioral inefficiency by applying the principles of evolution, competition, adaptation, and natural selection to the financial interactions.

Many forward-thinking people, including several we have met in this chapter, believe that the theory of evolution may become the most powerful force in finance. "There are many opportunities for biological principles to be applied to financial interactions," J. Doyne Farmer explains, "after all, financial institutions are uniquely human inventions that provide an adaptive advantage to our species. This is truly a new frontier whose exploration has just begun."[17]

It is tempting, therefore, to rush full steam ahead toward a biological interpretation of the economy and the stock market. We can identify more analogies with biological systems than with physical systems. But we must guard our enthusiasm. This approach is still unfolding, and there are several missing pieces. One of them, according to Farmer, concerns the question of speed: innovation in financial markets is rapid, compared to the slow, random-variation process in biological systems. Because of this, Farmer believes the timeline for market efficiency may still be decades away.

There are some who are dismayed that evolutionary biology cannot make firm predictions. But Darwin never claimed that ability. The Darwinian revolution is very much about how change replaced stasis and, in doing so, gave us a more accurate picture of the behavior of all living things. In her book *The Nature of Economies*, Jane Jacobs captures the essence perfectly: "A living system makes itself up as it goes along."[18] For that reason alone, I believe that biological systems (stock markets included), unlike physical systems, will never possess a stable mean.

The German philosopher Immanuel Kant once said there would "never be a Newton of the grass blades." He was wrong. The intellectual revolution caused by Darwin's theory of natural selection is every bit as powerful as Newton's gravitational force.

Indeed, the movement from the mechanical view of the world to the biological view of the world has been called the "second scientific revolution." After three hundred years, the Newtonian world, the mechanized world operating in perfect equilibrium, is now the old science. The old science is about a universe of individual parts, rigid laws, and simple forces. The systems are linear: Change is proportional to the inputs. Small changes end in small results, and large changes make for large results. In the old science, the systems are predictable.

The new science is connected and entangled. In the new science, the system is nonlinear and unpredictable, with sudden and abrupt changes. Small changes can have large effects while large events may result in small changes. In nonlinear systems, the individual parts interact and exhibit feedback effects that may alter behavior. Complex adaptive systems must be studied as a whole, not in individual parts, because the behavior of the system is greater than the sum of the parts.

The old science was concerned with understanding the laws of being. The new science is concerned with the laws of becoming. How ironic it is that biologists, once thought to be the stepchildren of science, are now leading us away from the old science into the new.

It seems fair to give Charles Darwin the last word. He was a gifted writer whose scientific observations have become literary masterpieces. One of his best-known passages is the last paragraph in *The Origin of Species*, and it serves as a fitting end to this chapter.

> It is interesting to contemplate an entangled bank, clothed with many plants of many kinds, with birds singing on the bushes, with various

insects flitting about, and with worms crawling through the damp earth, and to reflect that these elaborately constructed forms, so different from each other, and dependent on each other in so complex a manner, have all been produced by laws acting around us. These laws, taken in the largest sense, being Growth with Reproduction; Inheritance which is almost implied by reproduction; Variability from the indirect and direct action of the external conditions of life, and from use and disuse; a Ratio of Increase so high as to lead to a Struggle for Life, and as a consequence to Natural Selection, entailing Divergence of Character and Extinction of less improved forms. Thus, from the war of nature, from famine and death, the most exalted object which we are capable of conceiving, namely, the production of higher animals, directly follows. There is grandeur in this view of life, with its several powers, having been originally breathed into a few forms or into one; and that, whilst this planet has gone cycling on according to the fixed law of gravity, from so simple a beginning endless forms most beautiful and most wonderful have been, and are being, evolved. (Charles Darwin, *The Origin of Species*)

4

Sociology

"I can calculate the movement of the heavenly bodies," said Sir Isaac Newton, "but not the madness of men"—a humbling confession for a man universally considered the greatest mind of his generation.[1] What on earth could have prompted such a remark? Turns out, intellectual giants are human too.

In February of 1720, Newton invested a modest sum of his substantial wealth in shares of the South Sea Company. This British joint-stock company, founded in 1711, was granted a monopoly to trade in Spain's South American colonies as a part of a treaty from the War of the Spanish Succession.

In three months, Newton's shares had tripled in value, and he decided to sell. Had the story ended here, all would have been well. But Newton could not stay away from the South Sea Company. He watched anxiously as friends who still held their shares continued to get rich. By July, Newton could no longer resist the temptation. He reinvested in the company, paying £700 for each share he had sold earlier for £300. However, this time he did not invest a modest amount—it was a substantial chunk of his entire net worth.

By November, it was all over. The "South Sea Bubble" had popped. Like a raging fever, speculation in shares of the company had quickly come and gone. Newton scrambled to sell his investment, eventually exiting just north of £100 per share. Had he not held the post of Master of the Royal Mint, with its guaranteed salary, Newton's remaining life would have been a financial struggle.

It's unfortunate that Charles Mackay's *Extraordinary Popular Delusions and the Madness of the Crowds* was not available for Newton. But that masterpiece on crowd psychology was not to be written for another 120 years. Still, Newton could have studied Joseph de la Vega, a successful Jewish merchant and philanthropist who had written the first book on the stock market titled *Confusion of Confusions* ([1688] 1996). In it, Vega presents the art of speculation as a dialogue between different market participants. It was a brilliant narrative tool, which helped the reader better understand speculation and trading.

Vega's *Confusion of Confusions* is easily summarized. In the Second Dialogue, Vega lists four basic principles of trading—as relevant today as they were 325 years ago:

> The first principle: Never advise anyone to buy or sell shares. Where perspicacity is weakened, the most benevolent piece of advice can turn out badly.
>
> The second principle: Take every gain without showing remorse about missed profits. It is wise to enjoy what is possible without hoping for the continuance of a favorable conjuncture and the persistence of good luck.
>
> The third principle: Profits on the exchange are the treasures of goblins. At one time they may be carbuncle stones, then coals, then diamonds, then flint-stones, then morning dew, then tears.
>
> The fourth principle: Whoever wishes to win in this game must have patience and money, since values are so little constant and the rumors so little founded on truth. He who knows how to endure blows without being terrified by the misfortune resembles the lion who answers the thunder with a roar and is unlike the hind who, stunned by the thunder, tries to flee.

Together, Joseph de la Vega, Isaac Newton, and Charles McKay are telling us something very important: The relationship between the individual investor and the stock market, which in itself is nothing more than a collection of individuals, is a profound puzzle. For over four hundred years, it has perplexed the rich and the poor as well as the genius and the dimwitted, and it is the story of our current chapter on social systems.

Sociology is the study of how people function in society, with the ultimate hope of understanding group behavior. When we stop to consider that all the participants in a market constitute a group, it is obvious that until we understand group behavior, we can never fully understand why markets and economies behave as they do.

Throughout history, poets, novelists, philosophers, political leaders, and theologians have all submitted ideas about how societies work, but the distinction for social scientists is their recognition of the scientific process. This process, in essence, involves developing a theory (a hypothesis), then testing that theory through controlled, repeatable experiments. This is the same approach used by chemists, physicists, biologists, and all other scientists in their search for answers.

Social scientists, as they work to uncover and explain how human beings form collectives, organize themselves, and interact, have adopted the scientific process, developing theories that lead to the construction of models that can be compared with data collected and then testing and verifying those theories. However, because their investigation by definition involves the subjective and unpredictable behavior of human beings, in the social sciences the process is less precise than in the natural sciences, and in many circles the social sciences have not yet reached the same level of scientific acceptance.

Indeed, some have suggested that the lack of maturity in social sciences is directly attributable to the absence of hard, quantitative results commonly associated with the natural sciences. This is now changing, as immense computer power makes possible the collection of vast amounts of data, but nonetheless, there are those who question the validity of attaching the term "science" to the study of social systems. We might say that the social sciences are still waiting for their Isaac Newton.

The development of the social sciences has followed two distinct paths: a drive for a unified theory and a move toward narrower specializations. The first approach was urged by the French philosopher Auguste Comte, who in the mid-nineteenth century called for a new science to take its place alongside astronomy, physics, chemistry, and biology. This new science, which he named "sociology," would explain social organization and help guide social planning. Comte saw the study of society as a unified pursuit; society is an indivisible thing, he argued, and so too must be the study of it. But despite Comte's efforts at synthesis, the nineteenth century did not end with a single unified theory of social science but rather with the promotion of several distinct specialties, including economics, political science, and anthropology.

Economics was the first discipline to attain the status of a separate study within social science. Some trace the history of modern economics back to 1776, the year that the Scottish economist Adam Smith published his most famous work, *Wealth of Nations*. Considered the founder of economics, Smith was also one of the first to describe its effect on society. He is best known to today's economists for his advocacy of a laissez-faire capitalist system—that is, one free of government interference, including industry regulation and protective tariffs. Smith argued that an economic system works best when it is based solely on its own natural mechanism, what he called the "invisible hand."

Smith believed that division of labor is the cause of increased productivity and, ultimately, wealth for the owners of capital. He was not, however, unaware of the social consequences produced by division of labor: the decline of general skills and craftsmanship, the likely incorporation of women and children into the workforce, and the tendency to divide society into economic classes with opposing interests. He acknowledged that, over time, the owners of capital would seek to limit the wages of labor. Thus was set into motion a countervailing view of economics propounded by Karl Marx and other socialists: that capitalism was but a passing stage of development that would soon be replaced by a more humane economic system based on cooperation, planning, and the common ownership of the means of production.

Given the debate over the interplay of economics and society, it is not surprising that at the same time there was an increasing investigation into the behavior of governments. By the nineteenth century, the role of the state held the same fascination for a group of social scientists, soon called political scientists, as did the impact of capital for economists. These new political scientists were soon investigating the political consequences of Adam Smith's laissez-faire economics. How should the government respond to the new democratic rights of working people while at the same time protecting the private property rights of the owners of capital? Deciding who gets what, when, where, and how became the essence of the new field called political science.

Soon another science took its place alongside economics and politics as a separate discipline within the social sciences: anthropology. From the beginning, anthropology was divided into two classes: physical and cultural. Physical anthropology was chiefly concerned with the evolution of man as a species and with genetic systems such as different races in the world. Cultural anthropology, on the other hand, investigated the social aspects of the many different human institutions, as found in both primitive and contemporary societies. It was here that the science of sociology came into its own. At first it was difficult to separate the identities of cultural anthropologists from the new sociologists, but the distinction was made clearer when sociologists began to limit their inquiry to contemporary societies, leaving the investigation of primitive societies to the anthropologists.

By the twentieth century, sociology had been further separated into social psychology and social biology. Social psychologists studied the ways in which the individual human mind, as well as the collective mind, relates to the social order. They sought to explain how culture affects psychology and, conversely, how collective psychology influences culture. We shall see more about this in the next chapter.

Social biologists, for their part, owe much to Charles Darwin. The increasing academic acceptance and scientific maturity of Darwin's theory of evolution caused several scientists to make considerable advances promoting a biological view of society. There was no greater champion of this approach than the Yale sociologist William Graham Sumner, who founded an intellectual movement known as Social Darwinism, in which he sought to connect Adam Smith's principle of laissez-faire economics to Charles Darwin's concept of natural selection.

In Sumner's mind, there was a strong connection between the struggle of existence within nature and the struggle for existence within society. He believed the market, just like nature, is in a constant struggle for scarce resources, and that the process of natural selection in humans would inevitably lead to social, political, and moral progress.

After World War II, Social Darwinism all but disappeared from academic debate. Only recently has the biological concept resurfaced. Several scientists, most notably Edward O. Wilson, have reintroduced the connections between social science and biology into a field of inquiry now called sociobiology. However, most have sought to distance themselves from the implication that natural selection can be a justification for social inequality, which they consider a gross distortion of Darwin's message. Instead, the new sociobiologists are now focusing their energies on the more scientific principles associated with evolution and its connection to social development.

All of these areas of social science—sociology, political science, economics, and the several subdisciplines within each—are, in one sense, only different platforms from which to think about one large question: how human beings form themselves into groups, or societies, and how those groups behave. The study of political science gives us insight into how people create governments; the study of economics helps us understand how they produce and exchange goods; and so on. Of course each individual simultaneously participates in several groups, and so the larger concern for those who wish to understand behavior is how the pieces fit together and influence one another.

Although the idea of a unified theory of social science faded in the late nineteenth century, here at the beginning of the twenty-first century there has been a growing interest in what we might think of as a new unified approach. Scientists have now begun to study the behavior of whole systems—not only the behavior of individuals and groups but the interactions between them and the ways in which this interaction may in turn influence subsequent behavior. Because of this reciprocal influence, our social system is constantly engaged in a socialization process the consequence of which not only alters our individual behavior but often leads to unexpected group behavior.

Granted, this is a complicated perspective from which to investigate humankind. But man is a complex being, and those who would understand human behavior must find a way to work within the complexity. Fortunately, guidance is at hand in the scientific area of inquiry known as *complexity theory*.

In earlier chapters, we have identified economies and stock markets as complex systems. The term *complexity* is derived etymologically from the Latin word *plexus*, which means interwoven. When we think about complexity we intuitively understand the difficulty of separating the individual from the whole. Furthermore, separating individuals in order to study them singularly negates the observation, for we know individual behavior is highly influenced by its interactions with other individuals in the collective. We have come to understand that economies and stock markets are *adaptive* systems. As such, their behavior constantly changes as individuals in the system interact with other individuals and within the system itself.

Many social scientists now start with the same assumption. They recognize that human systems, whether economic, political, or social, are complex systems. Furthermore, sociologists now recognize that a universal trait of all social systems is their adaptability.

From these pioneering scientists now studying complex adaptive systems, we can gain insights into that great social system called humankind and, by extension, into the functioning of specific systems like the stock market.

One aspect of these systems is the formation process. How do people come together to form complex systems (social units) and then further organize themselves into some sense of order? This question has led to a new hypothesis that may provide a common framework to describe the behavior of all social systems. It is called the theory of self-organization.

The term "self-organization" refers to a process whereby structure appears in a system that does not have a central authority or some other element that imposes its will by preplanning. We can observe self-organization in chemistry, biology, mathematics, and computer science. It also occurs in human networks or societies.

The term was first used by Immanuel Kant in his *Critique of Judgment* (1790). Kant referred to an entity whose parts or "organs" are able to behave as if it had a mind of its own and was capable of governing itself. He writes, "Every part is thought as owning its presence to the agency of all the remaining parts, and also for existing for the sake of others . . . only under these conditions and upon these terms can such a product be an *organized* or a *self-organized* being [italics original]."

Self-organization as a theory, although associated with general systems theory in the 1960s, did not become a part of the mainstream academic literature until the late 1970s and early 1980s when physicists began to explore complex systems. Ilya Prigogine, the Russian chemist, is credited with popularizing self-organization theory. He was awarded the Nobel Prize in 1977 for his thermodynamic concept of self-organization.

The economist Paul Krugman, author of twenty books, over two hundred scholarly articles, and winner of the 2008 Nobel Prize for Economics, began a systematic inquiry into the theory of self-organization, particularly as it related to the economy (*The Self-Organizing Economy*, 1996). To illustrate how it works, Krugman asks us to imagine the city of Los Angeles. Today, we know that Los Angeles is not one homogeneous landscape but a collection of different socioeconomic, racial, and ethnic neighborhoods including Koreatown, Watts, and Beverly Hills. Surrounding the city is a further collection of many business districts. Now each of these distinct spaces was formed not by urban planners drawing lines on a map but by the spontaneous process of self-organization. Koreans moved to Koreatown to be closer to other Koreans. As the population increased, still more Koreans were drawn to the neighborhood, and thus a self-organized community also became self-reinforcing. No central controller made this decision for everyone, explains Krugman; the city just spontaneously evolved and organized itself in this fashion.

The evolution of a large city is a relatively simple example of self-organizing and self-reinforcing systems, but we can observe similar behavior in economic systems. Setting aside for the moment the occasional recessions and recoveries caused by exogenous events such as oil shocks or military conflicts, Krugman believes that economic cycles are in large part caused by self-reinforcing effects. During a prosperous period, a self-reinforcing process leads to greater construction and manufacturing until the return on investment begins to decline, at which point an economic slump begins. The slump in itself becomes a self-reinforcing effect, leading to lower production; lower production, in turn, will eventually cause return on investment to increase, which starts the process all over again. Some might argue that the Federal Reserve, by altering interest rates and making open market purchases and sales, acts as the central controller for the economy, but as we all know the Fed is not omnipotent. If we stop and think, we realize that the equity and debt markets have no central controller, and both are excellent examples of self-organizing, self-reinforcing systems.

It is important for us to keep in mind that the theory of self-organization is just that—a theory. Although it appears to be a plausible explanation of how social systems work, there are no models yet built that can test the theory, much less predict its future behavior. In search for unified theories of how social systems behave, however, the self-organizing theory appears to be a legitimate candidate.

The second characteristic of complex adaptive systems—their adaptivity—is embedded within what is known as the theory of emergence. This refers to the way individual units—be they cells, neurons, or consumers—combine to create something greater than the sum of the parts. Paul Krugman suggests that Adam Smith's "invisible hand" is a perfect example of emergent behavior. Many individuals, all of them trying to satisfy their own material needs, engage in buying and selling with other individuals, thereby creating an emergent structure called the market. The mutual accommodation of its individual units coupled with the self-organizing behavior of the system creates a behavioral whole, an emergent property that transcends its individual units.

Just like the concept of self-organization, emergence is also a theory. However, it appears to be a thoughtful explanation of what actually occurs when individual units come together and organize. Although scientists have had difficulty modeling the phenomenon of self-organization, they have made excellent progress modeling emergent behavior.

The Los Alamos National Laboratory (LANL) is the largest U.S. Department of Energy laboratory in the country and one of the biggest multi-disciplinary research institutions in the world. It covers forty-three square miles and employs almost ten thousand people, including physicists, engineers, chemists, biologists, and geoscientists.

Most people know Los Alamos as the facility that developed the first atomic bomb, but today the laboratory's vision has widened and now includes several scientific programs that are directed at preserving and improving the quality of life on earth. The research projects underway at Los Alamos are too numerous to list here. But to you give you a sense of the breadth of research, LANL includes the Center for Integrated Nanotechnologies; the Energy Security Center, which is exploring reliable, secure, and sustainable carbon-neutral energy solutions; the Institute of Geophysics and Planetary Physics; the Neutron Scattering Center; and a High Magnetic Field Laboratory.

At the top of the list is the Center for Bio-Security Science (CBSS). Founded in 2008, the CBSS works to achieve science and technology breakthroughs in understanding and mitigating threats to national security, public health, and agriculture from natural, emerging, and engineered infectious agents. Inside the CBSS resides the Biological Threat Reduction Program led by Dr. I. Gary Resnick and Dr. Norman L. Johnson, the assistant director.

Johnson studied chemical engineering at the University of Wisconsin, where he soon gained a reputation for tackling problems most people put in the "too hard to do" box. Johnson's success, he claimed, came from assembling heterogeneous teams that were able to break through the intellectual barriers by fostering synergistic solutions developed from diverse contributions.

After joining Los Alamos National Laboratory, Johnson founded the Symbiotic Intelligence Project (SIP). Its purpose was to study the unique abilities of information systems, such as the Internet, as well as human problem-solving teams to create a capability that is greater that the sum of the parts. This newly created knowledge is an emergent property of the collective. Although the term "emergent" may be new to laypeople, Johnson points out that the experience is commonplace. For thousands of years, societal structures have been able to collectively solve problems that have threatened their very existence.

Self-organized systems, explains Johnson, have three distinct characteristics. First, the complex global behavior occurs by simple connected local processors. In a social system, the local processors are individuals. Second, a solution arises from the diversity of the individual inputs. Third, the functionality of the system, its robustness, is far greater than any one of the individual processors. Johnson believes that the symbiotic combination of humans and networks (Internet) will generate, in a collective, far better results that any one individual can do acting alone. He envisions an "unprecedented capability in organizational and societal problem solving will result from increased human activity on smart distributed information systems."[2]

One of the great advantages of the Internet is how it helps us manage information; in this, explains Johnson, the Internet has three significant advantages over prior systems. First, it is able to integrate a wide breadth of knowledge compared to other systems whose information was often physically separated. Second, the Internet is able to capture and display depth of information. With digitization, systems are able to produce volumes of data on a single topic without significant additional cost. Third, the Internet is able to process information correctly. As we will learn in the next chapter on psychology, communication missteps between individuals sometimes result in the loss of vital information. Information exchanged via the Internet is delivered accurately, in much the same way that books and documents are able to transmit information. It is Johnson's belief that these three advantages, along with the interconnectivity of millions of individuals, will greatly enhance the collective problem-solving ability of self-organized systems.

To illustrate the phenomenon of emergence, let's look in on a familiar social system: an ant colony. Because ants are social insects (they live in colonies, and their behavior is directed to the survival of the colony rather than the survival of any one individual ant), social scientists have long been fascinated by their decision-making process.

One of the ant's most interesting behaviors is the process of foraging for food and then determining the shortest path between the food source and the nest.[3] While walking between the two, ants lay down a pheromone trail that allows them to trace the path and also show other ants the location of the new food source.

At the beginning, the search for food is a random process, with ants starting out in many different directions. Once they locate food, they return to the nest, laying down the pheromone trail as they go. But now comes the very sophisticated aspect to collective problem solving: the colony, acting as a whole, is able to select the shortest path. If one ant randomly finds a shorter path between the food source and the nest, its quicker return to the nest intensifies the concentration of pheromone along the path. Other ants tend to choose the path with the strongest concentration of pheromone and hence set off on this newly discovered short path. This increased number of ants along the trail deposits even more pheromone, which further attracts more ants until this path becomes the preferred line. Scientists have been able to demonstrate experimentally that the pheromone-trail behavior of the ant colony solves for the shortest path. In other words, this optimal solution is an emergent property of the collective behavior of the ant colony.

Norman Johnson, who like many is fascinated by ant behavior, set out to test humans' ability to solve collective problems. He constructed a computer version of a maze with countless paths but only a few that are short. The computer simulation consists of two phases: a learning phase and an application phase. In the learning phase, a person explores the maze with no specific knowledge of how to solve the maze until the goal is found. This is identical to the process an ant follows when it begins to look for food. In the application phase, people simply apply what they learned. Johnson discovered that people need an average of 34.3 steps to solve the maze in the first phase and 12.8 steps in the second phase. Then, to find the collective solution, Johnson combined all the individual solutions and applied the application phase. He found that if at least five people were considered, their collective solution was better than the average individual solution. It took a collective of only twenty to find the very shortest path through the maze, even though they had no global sense of the problem. This collective solution, argues Johnson, is an emergent property of the system.

Although Johnson's maze is a simple problem-solving computer simulation, it does demonstrate emergent behavior. It also leads us to better understand the essential characteristic a self-organizing system must contain in order to produce emergent behavior. That characteristic is diversity. The collective solution, Johnson explains, is robust if the individual contributions to the solution represent a broad diversity of experience in the problem at hand. Interestingly, Johnson discovered that the collective solution is actually degraded if the system is limited to only high-performing people. It appears that the diverse collective is better at adapting to unexpected changes in the structure.[4]

To put this in perspective, Johnson's research suggests that the stock market, theoretically, is more robust when it is composed of a diverse group of agents—some of average intelligence, some of below-average intelligence, and some very smart—than a market singularly composed of smart agents. At first, this discovery appears counterintuitive. Today, we are quick to blame the amateur behavior of uninformed individual investors and day traders for the volatile nature of the market. But if Johnson is correct, the diverse participation of all investors, traders and speculators—smart and dumb alike—should make the markets stronger, not weaker.

Another important insight from Norman Johnson was his discovery that the system, as long as it is adequately diverse, is relatively insensitive to moderate amounts of noise (by which he means any sort of discordant, disruptive activity). To prove the point, Johnson intentionally degraded an individual contribution; he learned his action had no effect on participants' finding the shortest path out of the maze. Even at the highest levels of disruption, the collective behavior, after a brief postponement, was able to discover the minimal path. Not until the system reached its highest noise level did the collective decision-making process break down.

The work of Norman Johnson appears to contradict the classical views of crowd behavior. From Henry David Thoreau to Thomas Carlyle to Friedrich Nietzsche, the nineteenth century's great intellectuals were highly suspicious of collective judgment. It was Thoreau who said "as a member of a crowd, he at once becomes a blockhead." Nietzsche tells us "the mass never comes up to the standard of its best member," and Carlyle wrote, "I do not believe in the collective wisdom of individual ignorance."[5] But no one was a more vocal critic of the intellect of crowds than Gustave Le Bon.

A French sociologist and psychologist, Le Bon spent his career studying herding behavior and crowd psychology. The culmination of his work was published in 1895 under the title *La psychologie des foules* (The Psychology of Crowds); the English version was titled *The Crowd: A Study of the Popular Mind.* On first reading, it appears Le Bon has foreseen Norman Johnson. He writes that the crowd is an independent organism greater than the sum of its parts. It has the ability to operate independently and as such forms its own identity and will. But whereas Johnson tells us the emergent property of the crowd is superior reasoning, Le Bon reached the opposite conclusion. Like Thoreau, Carlyle, Nietzsche, and Mackay, Le Bon believed that crowds "can never accomplish acts demanding a high degree of intelligence" and "they are always intellectually inferior to the isolated individual."[6]

Who is right?

The answer lies in an outstanding book titled, *The Wisdom of Crowds: Why the Many Are Smarter Than the Few and How Collective Wisdom Shapes Business, Economies, Societies, and Nations.* Written by James Surowiecki, the business columnist for *The New Yorker*, it purposefully takes aim at Mackay's idea of "the madness of crowds" with a simple, powerful thesis: "*under the right circumstances* [italics mine], groups are remarkably intelligent and are often smarter than the smartest people in them."[7]

Surowiecki begins by telling the story of Francis Galton, the English Victorian-era polymath. In a 1907 article in *Nature*, Galton describes a contest he promoted at the West of England Fat Stock and Poultry Exhibition. In that contest, 787 people paid sixpence for the opportunity to guess the weight of a rather large ox at the exhibition. A few of the guessers were farmers and butchers, people who might be classified as experts, but a far greater number had no specialized knowledge of farm animals. Based on this information, Galton surmised the mix of participants contained a few very smart guessers, a few who were totally clueless, and the rest—the largest number—being mediocre guessers at best. Based on that formula, he anticipated his 787 participants would most likely end up with a dumb answer. He was wrong.

The ox actually weighed 1,198 pounds. Galton took all the guesses and plotted a distribution curve. He found that the median guess was within 0.8 percent of the correct weight and the mean guess was within 0.1 percent. Put differently, the average guess was 1,197 pounds. What Galton had discovered was the errors in the left and right tail cancelled each other out and what remained was the distilled information.

According to Surowiecki, the two critical variables necessary for a collective to make superior decisions are *diversity* and *independence*. If a collective is able to tabulate decisions from a diverse group of individuals who have different ideas or opinions on how to solve a problem, the results will be superior to a decision made by a group of like-minded thinkers.

Independence, the second critical variable, does not mean each member of the group must remain in isolation but rather each member of the group is basically free from the influence of other members. Independence is important to the collective decision-making process for two reasons, explains Surowiecki. "First, it keeps the mistakes that people make from becoming correlated. Errors in individual judgment won't wreck the group's collective judgment as long as those errors aren't systematically pointing in the same direction. Second, independent individuals are more likely to have new information rather than the same old data everyone is already familiar with."[8]

Building on the work of Surowiecki and the science of Norman Johnson, Scott Page at the University of Michigan is working to continually press forward the theory of smart collectives.[9] Page is the Leonid Hurwicz Collegiate Professor of Complex Systems, Political Science and Economics, and also the current director for the Study of Complex Systems at the university.

Like Johnson, Page set up a series of computer-simulated problem-solving agents to demonstrate the emergent outcome of a diverse group attempting to solve a problem. For example, Page put together groups of ten to twenty agents, each with a different set of skills, and then had each group solve relatively difficult problems. In each group there were some who were excellent at solving the specific problem and others that were less effective. What Page discovered was a group composed of very smart agents and less-smart agents always did better at solving the problem than a segregated group of smart agents only. Furthermore, you could do just as well at solving the problem by randomly selecting any combination of agents as you could if you spent time isolating which were the smart agents and putting them to work on the problem.

In his book, *The Difference: How the Power of Diversity Creates Better Groups, Firms, Schools, and Societies,* Page firmly says, "Diverse perspectives and tools enable collections of people to find more and better solutions." He goes further: "Diverse predictive models enable crowds of people to predict values accurately."[10]

What does he mean by "predictive models"? Examples would include the Hollywood Stock Exchange (future predictions of ticket sales of movies), Iowa Electronics Market (future predictions on political contests), and Intrade (which claims to be the world's leading prediction market and will let you bet on pretty much anything you can imagine). Each of these predictive markets is composed of a *diverse* group of agents acting *independently* to make decisions. There are incentives to make the correct decision, and each of these markets aggregates the collective decisions.

How efficient are these predictive markets? In other words, how successful are they at correctly predicting outcomes? Remarkably successful, the evidence shows.

There is another predictive market we can observe. It is called the stock market.

So now we come to the crossroads. Is the stock market Charles Mackay's unruly mob of irrational investors who constantly unleash booms and busts or is it Francis Galton's county fair attendees who can miraculously make the right prediction? The answer is context dependent. In other words, it depends.

We know the stock market is an incentive-based system that can aggregate investor decisions. What we need to understand is the market's level of diversity and the independence of its participants. If the stock market is adequately diversified and, most importantly, if the decisions of its participants have been reached independently, then it is likely the market is efficient. Surowiecki reminds us that just because we can observe some irrational investors, that does not necessarily mean the market is inefficient. Indeed, proponents of the efficient market hypothesis have latched onto the "wisdom of the crowds" as a plausible explanation for market efficiency.[11]

But what if independence is lost? What if the decisions of the market's participants are not independent but are now coalesced into one opinion? When this occurs, the system has effectively lost its diversity and along with it any chance of generating an optimal solution. If diversity is the key to how collectives can best reach solutions, then diversity breakdowns are the cause of suboptimal outcomes—or in the case of the stock market, diversity breakdowns cause the market to become inefficient.

Scientists are now turning their attention to understanding what causes diversity breakdowns. Michael Mauboussin, author of two very important books, *More Than You Know: Finding Financial Wisdom in Unconventional Places* and *Think Twice: Harnessing the Power of Counterintuition*, tells us "information cascades (which can lead to diversity breakdowns) occur when people make decisions based on the actions of others rather than on their own private information. These cascades help explain booms, fads, fashions, and crashes."[12] Social network theorists, who view social relationships in terms of nodes and ties, whereby nodes are the individual actors and ties are the relationships between the actors, consider this to be the proper framework for understanding how information cascades can sweep across large populations.

Mauboussin also reminds us diversity breakdowns are not just a large group phenomenon but can also occur in smaller groups. Whether it be a committee, jury, or small working team, information cascades, which lead to diversity breakdowns, are often the result of a dominant leader operating with limited facts, sometimes even with no facts.

To illustrate his point, Mauboussin cites the work of Cass Sunstein, a professor at Harvard Law School. Sunstein first separated liberals and conservatives into like-minded groups and then asked them to debate controversial issues ranging from same-sex marriage to affirmative action. Sunstein then rearranged the groups so that each was an equal mix of liberal and conservative and asked them to repeat the same debates. One might think the new heterogeneous group would reach a more moderate conclusion. But in fact, because a strong leader emerged in all of these diverse groups, the groups ultimately settled on one view—the leader's—that was more extreme than the opinions held before the debate began. The strong leader, whether liberal or conservative, influenced the rest of the group to move completely to his position.

Much has been written about social conformity of groups over the years. Perhaps the most famous social psychology experiments were Solomon Asch's 1940s studies of individual conformity under group pressure, also described by Mauboussin.

Asch first assembled several groups of eight individuals. Each group was then asked to complete a very easy task. Several poster boards were divided in half. On the left-hand side was a single line. On the right-hand side were three unequal lines of which one was identical in length to the line on the left. The groups then had to match the length of the single line to one of the three unequal lines. The first few experiments went smoothly. Then on cue, seven of the eight members (who had been told about the experiment beforehand) purposely matched a noticeably shorter line from the right side to the test line on the left side. Asch wanted to gauge the response of the lone true subject.

What happened? Although several of the subjects did hold fast to their initial decision—they remained independent—about one-third of the test

subjects altered their decisions so they would conform to the group's decision. What Asch discovered was that group decisions, even noticeably
poor ones, have a profound influence over individual decisions.[13]

When catastrophes occur, we naturally seek to identify the principal cause
so we can avoid another disaster or at least derive some comfort from
knowing what happened. We like it best when we can point to one specific,
easily identifiable cause, but that is not always possible. Many scientists
believe that large-scale events in biology, geology, and economics are not
necessarily the result of a single large event but rather of the unfolding of
many smaller events that create an avalanche-like effect. Per Bak, a Danish
theoretical physicist (1948–2002), developed a holistic theory of how systems behave called "self-organized criticality."

     According to Bak, large complex systems composed of millions of in-
teracting parts can break down not only because of a single catastrophic
event but also because of a chain reaction of smaller events. To illustrate
the concept of self-criticality, Bak often used the metaphor of a sand pile.
Imagine an apparatus that drops one single grain of sand on a large flat
table. Initially, the sand spreads across the table and then begins to form a
slight pile. As one grain rests on top of another grain, the pile of sand rises
until it forms a gentle slope on each side. Eventually, the pile of sand cannot
grow any higher. At this point, sand trickles down the slope as fast as the
grains are added to the top. In Bak's analogy, the sand pile is self-organized
in the sense that it has formed without anyone placing the individual
grains. Each grain of sand is interlocked in countless combinations. When
the pile has reached its highest level, we can say the sand is in a state of
criticality. It is just on the verge of becoming unstable.

     When one more grain of sand is added to the pile at that point, that
single grain of sand can start an avalanche, with sand rolling down the
side slope of the pile. Each rolling grain of sand will stop if it happens to
fall into a stable position; otherwise, it continues to fall and possibly hits
other grains of sand that may also be unstable, knocking even more grains
farther down the side. The avalanche ceases when all unstable grains have
fallen as far as they are going to fall. If the shape of the pile of sand has flat-
tened from the avalanche, we can say the pile is in a subcritical phase and
will remain there until more sand is added, once again raising the sides of
the slope.

     Per Bak's sand pile metaphor is a powerful tool that helps us under-
stand the behavior of many different systems. In both natural and social

systems, we can see the dynamic: the systems become a class of interlocking subsystems that organize themselves to the edge of criticality and, in some cases, break apart violently only to reorganize themselves at a later point. Is the stock market such a system? Absolutely, said Per Bak.

In a joint paper written with two colleagues titled, "Price Variations in a Stock Market with Many Agents," Bak defended his thesis.[14] The three scientists constructed a very simple model that sought to capture the behavior of two types of agents operating in a stock market. They called the two types *noise traders* and *rational agents*. With apologies to the authors, I will instead use the more familiar terms of *fundamentalists* and *trend followers*. Trend followers seek to profit from changes in the market by either buying when prices go up or selling when prices go down. Fundamentalists buy and sell based not on the direction of the price changes but rather because of the difference between the price of a security and its underlying value. If the value of the stock is higher than the current price, fundamentalists buy shares; if the value is lower than the current price, they sell.

Most of the time, the interplay between trend followers and fundamentalists is somewhat balanced. Buying and selling continue with no discernible change in the overall behavior of the market. We might say the sand pile is growing without any corresponding avalanche effects. Put differently, diversification is present in the market.

But when stock prices climb, the ratio of trend followers to fundamentalists begins to grow. This makes sense. As prices increase, a larger number of fundamentalists decide to sell and leave the market and are replaced by a growing number of trend followers who are attracted to rising prices. When the relative number of fundamentalists is small, stock market bubbles occur, explained Bak, because prices have moved far above the fair price a fundamentalist would pay. Extending the sand pile metaphor further, as the number of fundamentalists in the market declines, and the relative number of trend followers increases, the slope of the sand pile becomes ever steeper, increasing the possibility of an avalanche. Once again, we can put this differently by saying that when the mix of fundamentalists and trend followers becomes unbalanced, we are heading toward a diversity breakdown.

It is important for us to remember at this point that while Per Bak's self-organizing criticality explains the overall behavior of avalanches, it does nothing to explain any one particular avalanche. When we ultimately are able to predict the behavior of individual avalanches, it will not be because of self-organized criticality but because of some other science yet to be discovered.

That in no way diminishes the significance of Bak's ideas. Indeed, several notable economists have acknowledged Per Bak's work on self-organized criticality as a credible explanation for how complex adaptive systems behave, including the Nobel physics laureate Phil Anderson and the Santa Fe Institute's Brian Arthur. Both recognize that self-organizing systems tend to be dominated by unstable fluctuations and that instability has become an unavoidable property of economic systems.

Instability in the stock market is, of course, painfully familiar to everyone involved. It is the treacherous threshold upon which we all too often stub our toes. Surely it would ease our frustration if we understood it better. To get a better fix on the dynamics of instability, we will need to venture back into the social sciences.

Diana Richards, a political scientist, is investigating what causes a complex system of interacting agents to become unstable. Or, in Per Bak's terms, she is trying to determine how a complex system of individuals reaches self-organized criticality.

According to Richards, a complex system necessarily involves aggregation of a wide number of choices made by the individuals in the system.[15] She calls this "collective choice." Of course, combining all the individuals' choices does not always result in a straightforward collective choice; nor should we assume the aggregate choice, which is the sum of individual choices, always leads to stable outcomes. Collective choice, says Richards, occurs when all the agents in the system aggregate information in a way that allows the system to reach a single collective decision. To reach this collective decision, it is not necessary that all the agents hold identical information but that they share a common interpretation of the different choices. Richards believes that this common interpretation, which she calls mutual knowledge, plays a critical role in the stability of all complex systems. The lower the level of this mutual knowledge, the greater the likelihood of instability.

An obvious question at this point is how people select from a collection of choices. According to Richards, if there is no clear favorite, the tendency of the system is to continually cycle over the possibilities. You might think this cyclical outcome would lead to instability, but according to Richards, it need not if the agents share similar mental concepts (that is, mutual knowledge) about the various choices. It is when the agents in the system do not have similar concepts about the possible choices that the system is in danger of becoming unstable. And that is clearly the case in the stock market.

If we step back and think about the market, we can readily identify a number of groups that exhibit different meta-models. We already know that fundamentalists and trend followers possess different meta-models. What about macro-traders who are not interested in individual companies but are interested only in directional changes in the overall market? What about long-short hedge funds? What about statistical arbitrageurs versus entrepreneurs? What about quantitatively driven strategists that seek low volatility-absolute return strategies? Each of these groups works from a different reality, a different sense of how the market operates and how they should operate within it. In reality, there are many different meta-models at work in the stock market, and if Richards's theory is correct, this all but guarantees periodic instability.

The value of this way of looking at complex systems is that if we know why they become unstable, then we have a clear pathway to a solution, to finding ways to reduce overall instability. One implication, Richards says, is that we should be considering the belief structures underlying various mental concepts and not the specifics of the choices. Another is to acknowledge that if mutual knowledge fails, the problem may center on how knowledge is transferred in the system. In the next chapter on psychology, we will turn to our attention to those two points: how individuals form belief structures and how information is exchanged in the stock market.

At this point, we have a fixed compass on how to analyze social systems. Whether they are economic, political, or social, we can say these systems are complex (they have a large number of individual units), and they are adaptive (the individual units adapt their behavior on the basis of interactions with other units as well as with the overall system). We also recognize that these systems have self-organizing properties and that, once organized, they generate emergent behavior. Finally, we realize that complex adaptive systems are constantly unstable and periodically reach a state of self-organized criticality.

We come to these conclusions by studying a large number of complex adaptive systems across a wide variety of fields in both the natural and the social sciences. In all our study, we are currently limited to understanding how the systems have behaved so far. We have not made the scientific leap that will enable us to predict the future behavior, particularly in complex social systems involving the highly unpredictable units known as human beings. But we may be on the track of something even more valuable.

What separates the study of complex natural systems from complex social systems is the possibility that in social systems we can alter the behavior of their individual units. Whereas we cannot as of yet change the trajectory of hurricanes, where groups of people are concerned we may be able to affect the outcome by influencing how individuals respond in various situations. To say this another way, although self-organized criticality is an inherent property of all complex adaptive systems, including economic systems, and although some degree of instability is unavoidable, we may be able to alter potential landslides by better understanding what makes criticality inevitable.

5

Psychology

In 2002, the Nobel Prize in Economics was shared by two people: Vernon Smith, for having "established laboratory experiments as a tool in empirical analysis, especially in the study of alternative market mechanisms," and Daniel Kahneman, for "having integrated insights from psychological research into economic science, especially concerning human judgment and decision-making under uncertainty." It was a remarkable achievement for both men, of course, but especially for Kahneman. For you see, Kahneman is not an economist—he is a psychologist.

Psychology studies how the human mind works. At first glance it may seem far removed from the world of investing, a world of impersonal balance sheets and income statements, especially since the very mention of psychology so frequently calls up an image of a tortured soul stretched out on the therapist's couch. But mental dysfunction is only one small part of what psychology entails. The word itself means "study of the mind," and thus psychologists are concerned with understanding all workings of the brain—the part that controls cognition (the process of thinking and knowing), as well as the part that controls emotion. This leads them to investigate how we learn, how we think, how we communicate, how we experience emotions, how we process information and make decisions, and how we form the core beliefs that guide our behavior.

The idea that individuals are not perfect thinkers is nothing new. The history of psychology dates back to the ancient civilizations of Egypt, Greece, China, and India, predating the work of Sigmund Freud and Carl Jung by over one thousand years. We have evidence of Islamic physicians treating individuals with mental illness as early as the eighth century in Fez, Morocco. But what is new, as of the late twentieth century, is the notion that psychology has a role in economic decision making. It was a radical idea that soon upset the apple cart of how the classical models were thought to work. Because modern portfolio theory rested on the assumption of rationality, the suggestion that individuals made decisions irrationally was revolutionary. It took a new generation of thinkers to help us reorient our perspective, a new group of thinkers who came not from the economic department but from psychology classrooms.

Daniel Kahneman grew up in Paris as a French Jew during the German occupation of World War II. Fortunately, Kahneman and his family were able to relocate to British Palestine, which later became the state of Israel. There, Kahneman studied psychology and mathematics at the Hebrew University of Jerusalem. After graduation, he served in the psychology department of the Israeli defense forces, where his responsibilities included developing psychological tests to evaluate candidates for officer's training school. After earning his PhD in psychology at the University of California, Berkeley, Kahneman returned to Israel and began his academic career as a lecturer in psychology at the University of Jerusalem.

In 1968, Kahneman invited Amos Tversky to give a guest lecture at one of his seminars. Tversky was a mathematical psychologist and considered, at the time, to be a pioneer in cognitive science. It was the beginning of a deep working relationship between the two that lasted for almost thirty years and ultimately led to the Nobel Prize. What made their research approach unique was the joint decision to not study any specific errors in human judgment unless they first detected the idiocy in themselves. "People thought we were studying stupidity," said Kahneman. "But we were not. We were studying ourselves." Kahneman has a memorable phrase to describe what they did: "Ironic research."[1]

Sadly, Tversky passed away in 1996, just six years prior to the Nobel Prize announcement. Because the Nobel Prize is not awarded posthumously, Tversky's name was not added. In his acceptance, Kahneman pointed out that the work was "done jointly with the late Amos Tversky during a long and unusually close collaboration."

Behavioral finance, which seeks to explain market inefficiencies using psychological theories, was born of the academic work of Kahneman and Tversky. If I tried to list and discuss all their research papers, it would overwhelm this chapter—it would overwhelm this book. Fortunately, much of their research is included in a wonderful collection of essays titled *Judgment under Uncertainty: Heuristics and Biases* (1982). Here you will find all the customary behavioral finance terms we have come to know and understand: anchoring, framing, mental accounting, overconfidence, and overreaction bias. But perhaps the most significant insight into individual behavior was the concept of *loss aversion*.

In 1979, Kahneman and Tversky wrote a paper titled "Prospect Theory: An Analysis of Decision under Risk." It would later become the most cited paper ever to appear in *Econometrica,* the prestigious academic journal of economics. Up until this point, the utility theory popularized by John von Neumann and Oskar Morgenstern (*The Theory of Games and Economic Behavior,* 1944) was the accepted dogma of how individuals made economic decisions. Utility theory postulates that it should not matter to an individual how the alternatives are presented. What matters most is concluding what is best for oneself—an individual's total satisfaction based on the judgment of the risks involved. Kahneman and Tversky were not so sure. Perhaps in an idealized world the utility theory is a valid concept, but they also knew individuals do not always act in an idealized fashion.

Kahneman and Tversky's research demonstrated that how alternatives are framed can make a significant difference in how individuals reach conclusions. In one of their most famous research studies they asked groups of people to decide between two programs that addressed the public health of 600 people. In the first case, people were asked to choose between (a) saving 200 lives for sure, or (b) a one-third chance of saving 600 lives with a two-thirds chance to save no one. The respondents overwhelmingly chose option a. Next the group was asked to decide between (a) 400 people dying for sure, or (b) a two-thirds chance of 600 people dying with a one-third chance of no one dying. Here the respondents chose option b. The math quickly tells you that the two versions are identical. The number of people who are saved in one version is the same as the number of people who will not die in the other version.

In essence, Kahneman and Tversky had discovered that people are generally risk averse when making a decision that offers hope of a gain but risk seeking when making a decision that will lead to certain loss. Under utility theory, value is assigned to the final asset. Under prospect theory, resting on its core notion of loss aversion, value is assigned to gains and losses. What Kahneman and Tversky were able to prove is that people do not look just at the final level of wealth but rather at the incremental gains and losses that contribute to this wealth.

The most important discovery in prospect theory was the realization that individuals are, in fact, loss averse. Kahneman and Tversky were able to prove mathematically that individuals regret losses more than they welcome gains of the exact same size—two to two and one-half times more. It was a stunning revelation. The now-popular concept of loss aversion, embedded in prospect theory, ultimately forced economists to rethink their basic assumptions of how people make decisions.

Even though behavioral finance is a relatively new field of study, its popularity has spread to almost every business school worldwide. Ironically, some of the better thinking comes from the economics department at the University of Chicago—an institution known for its Nobel laureates who postulate the efficient market theory of rational investors. Richard Thaler, a former Cornell economist, is now a professor of behavioral science and economics at the Chicago Booth School of Business. His research focus is questioning the rational behavior of investors.

Over the years, Thaler has had the good fortune of studying and collaborating with Kahneman and Tversky as well as many other colleagues in the behavioral finance field. Several of Thaler's research articles can be found in his popular book, *The Winner's Curse: Paradoxes and Anomalies of Economic Life* (1992). However, Thaler is perhaps best known among investors for his 1995 article titled "Myopic Loss Aversion and the Equity Risk Premium Puzzle" cowritten with Shlomo Benartzi. Benartzi is professor and cochair of the behavioral decision-making group at the UCLA Anderson School of Management. In their article, Thaler and Benartzi took loss aversion described in prospect theory and connected it directly to the stock market.

The title of this groundbreaking article guides us to two related ideas that call for some discussion: First, that the equity risk premium is puzzling, and second, that loss aversion, unequivocally identified by Kahneman and Tversky, is illogical and prevents investors from seeing long term; that is, it makes them myopic.

Equity risk premium is a term many investors have heard but few actually understand. It refers to the potential for higher returns represented by the inherently risky stock market compared to the risk-free rate, defined as the rate of a ten-year U.S. Treasury bond in effect at whatever point you're considering. (It is called the risk-free rate because up until now the government has never defaulted on its loans.) Whatever return an individual stock or the overall stock market earns beyond that rate is the investor's compensation for taking on the higher risk of the stock market—the equity risk. For example, if the return on a stock is 10 percent and the risk-free rate is 5 percent over the same period, the equity risk premium would be 5 percent. The size of the risk premium will vary based on the perceived riskiness of a particular stock or the stock market as a whole. According to Aswath Damodaran, professor of finance at the Stern School of Business at New York University, the implied equity risk premium has vacillated between less than 3 percent in 1961 and 6.5 percent in the early 1980s.

Thaler and Benartzi were puzzled by two questions. One, why is the equity risk premium so high; and two, why is anyone willing to hold bonds when we know that over the years, stocks have consistently outperformed? The answer, they believed, rested upon two central concepts from Kahneman and Tversky. The first was loss aversion. The second was a behavioral concept called *mental accounting*.

Mental accounting, explains Thaler, refers to the methods people use to code financial outcomes. To help make the connection, Thaler revisited an older problem first proposed by Paul Samuelson. In 1963, Samuelson asked a colleague if he would be willing to accept the following bet: a 50 percent chance of winning $200 or a 50 percent chance of losing $100. The colleague politely turned down the bet but then announced he would be happy to play the game 100 times so long as he did not have to watch each individual outcome. That counterproposal sparked an idea for Thaler and Benartzi.

Samuelson's colleague was willing to accept the wager with two qualifiers: lengthen the time horizon for the game and reduce the frequency in which he was forced to watch the outcomes. Moving that observation into investing, Thaler and Benartzi reasoned the longer the investor holds an asset, the more attractive the asset becomes but only if the investment is *not* evaluated frequently. If you don't check your portfolio every day, you will be spared the angst of watching daily price gyrations; the longer you hold off, the less you will be confronted with volatility and therefore the more attractive your choices seem. Put differently, the two factors that contribute to an investor's unwillingness to bear the risks of holding stocks are loss aversion and a frequent evaluation period. Using the medical word for shortsightedness, Thaler and Benartzi coined the term *myopic loss aversion* to reflect a combination of loss aversion and the frequency with which an investment is measured.

Thaler and Benartzi next considered whether myopic loss aversion could help explain the equity risk premium. They wondered what combination of loss aversion and evaluation frequency would explain the historical pattern of stock returns. How often, they asked, would an investor need to evaluate a stock portfolio to be indifferent to the historical distribution of returns on stocks and bonds? The answer: one year.

Never mind whether evaluating a stock portfolio once a year is plausible or not, the science for determining the crossover point of one year is straightforward. Thaler and Benartzi examined the return, standard deviation, and positive return probability for stocks with time horizons of 1 hour, 1 day, 1 week, 1 month, 1 year, 10 years, and 100 years. Next they employed a utility function based on a loss-aversion factor of 2 (utility = probability of price increase – probability of a decline × 2). Based on the historical returns, the utility function did not cross over to a positive number until a 1-year holding period.

Thaler and Benartzi argue that any discussion of loss aversion must be accompanied by a specification of the frequency by which returns are calculated. Clearly, investors are less attracted to high-risk investments like stocks when they evaluate their portfolio over shorter time horizons. "Loss aversion is a fact of life," explain Thaler and Benartzi. "In contrast, the frequency of evaluations is a policy choice that presumably could be altered, at least in principle."[2]

In my opinion, the single greatest psychological obstacle that prevents investors from doing well in the stock market is myopic loss aversion. In my twenty-eight years in the investment business, I have observed firsthand the difficulty investors, portfolio managers, consultants, and committee members of large institutional funds have with internalizing losses (loss aversion), made all the more painful by tabulating losses on a frequent basis (myopic loss aversion). Overcoming this emotional burden penalizes all but a very few select individuals.

Perhaps it is not surprising that the one individual who has mastered myopic loss aversion is also the world's greatest investor—Warren Buffett. I have always thought that much of Buffett's success is a result of his hybrid investment vehicle, Berkshire Hathaway. Because Berkshire owns both common stocks and wholly owned businesses, Buffett has benefited greatly from this unique perspective. Paraphrasing his teacher and mentor Benjamin Graham, Buffett has claimed he is "a better investor because he is a businessperson and a better businessperson because he is an investor."[3]

By way of example, Buffett the businessperson understands that so long as the economics of his companies continue to advance in a steady manner, the value of his investment will continue to march upward. He does not need the market's affirmation to convince him of this. As he often states, "I don't need a stock price to tell me what I already know about value."

In 1988, Buffett invested $1 billion in The Coca-Cola Company (KO). At the time it was the single largest investment Berkshire had ever made in a stock. Over the next ten years, the stock price of KO went up ten times while the S&P 500 Index went up three times. However, it wasn't a consistent pattern. During that ten-year period, KO outperformed the market six years and underperformed four years.[4] By the mathematics of loss aversion, investing in KO over the ten-year period was a negative emotional utility (six emotional positive units – four emotional negative units × 2).

Perhaps Buffett had read Joseph de la Vega's fourth principle in *Confusion of Confusions*: "He who knows how to endure blows without being terrified by the misfortune resembles the lion who answers the thunder with a roar and is unlike the hind who, stunned by the thunder, tries to flee."

Benjamin Graham, through two classic texts—*Security Analysis* (1934) and *The Intelligent Investor* ([1949] 1973—has taught three generations of investors how to navigate the stock market. His value-investing approach has helped, without exaggeration, hundreds of thousands of people pick stocks. But often overlooked are his ideas on the psychology of investing.

Graham devoted much of his teaching and writing to getting people to understand the critical distinction between investment and speculation. But his message went much deeper than one of mere definitions. We must all come to terms, he insisted, with the idea that common stocks have both an investment characteristic and a speculative characteristic. That is, we know the direction of stock prices is ultimately determined by the underlying economics but we must also recognize that "most of the time common stocks are subject to irrational and excessive price fluctuations in both directions, as the consequence of the ingrained tendency of most people to speculate or gamble—i.e., to give way to hope, fear, and greed."[5]

Investors must be prepared, he cautioned, for ups and downs in the market. And he meant prepared psychologically as well as financially–not merely knowing intellectually that a downturn will happen, but having the emotional wherewithal to react appropriately when it does. And what is the appropriate reaction? In his view, an investor should do just what a business owner would do when offered an unattractive price—ignore it.

"The investor who permits himself to be stampeded or unduly worried by unjustified market declines in his holdings is perversely transforming his basic advantage into a basic disadvantage," said Graham. "That man would be better off if his stocks had no market quotation at all, for he would then be spared the mental anguish caused him by another person's mistakes of judgment."[6]

With his eloquent comment about "mental anguish," Graham is speaking directly to the debilitating effects of myopic loss aversion. It would be another forty-five years before Thaler and Benartzi would write their paper.

Thus far we have examined psychology and investing from a theoretical viewpoint (Graham), an academic investigation (Kahneman, Tversky, Thaler, Benartzi) and from practical application (Buffett). Clearly, Buffett is a special case—an individual who has successfully risen above the psychological missteps to enjoy a celebrated career. However, as we know, he is the exception, not the rule.

In 1997, Terence Odean, a behavioral economist at the University of California, published a paper titled *Why Do Investors Trade Too Much?* To answer his question, he reviewed the performance of 10,000 anonymous investors.

Over a seven-year period (1987–1993), Odean tracked 97,483 trades among ten thousand randomly selected accounts of a major discount brokerage. The first thing he learned was that the investors sold and repurchased almost 80 percent of their portfolio each year (78 percent turnover ratio). Then he compared the portfolios to the market average over three different time periods (4 months, 1 year, and 2 years). In every case, he found two amazing trends: (1) the stocks that the investors bought consistently trailed the market, and (2) the stocks that they sold actually *beat* the market.[7]

Odean wanted to look deeper, so he next examined the trading behavior and performance results of 66,465 households. In a paper titled "Trading Is Hazardous to Your Wealth" (2000), Odean, along with Brad Barber, professor of finance at University of California, Davis, compared the records of people who traded frequently versus people who traded less often. They found that, on average, the most active traders had the poorest results, while those who traded the least earned the highest returns.[8] The implication here is that people who might have suffered the most from myopic loss aversion and acted upon it by selling stocks did less well—much less well— than those who were able to resist the natural impulse and instead hold their ground.

Unfortunately, the problem facing investors may only get worse. In an article titled "The Internet and the Investor" (2001), Odean and Barber postulate that the Internet may be doing more harm to investors than good. At first that seems counterintuitive when we think of all the informational benefits. But Odean and Barber suggest that the vast amount of information online enables investors to easily locate evidence that confirms their hunches, which in turn leads them to become overconfident in their ability to pick stocks.

"The Internet has brought changes to investing which may bolster the overconfidence of on-line investors by providing an illusion of knowledge and an illusion of control," they explain. "When people are given more information on which to base a forecast or assessment, their confidence in the accuracy of their forecasts tends to increase more quickly (and this is the important part) than the accuracy of the forecasts."[9] Information overload, they claim, can lead to an *illusion of knowledge.*

One other concern: because of the Internet, investors are now in a position to check their stock positions in real time. In the past, investors might have checked stock prices daily or weekly. Now with online trading, investors can monitor their portfolios by clicking on their computer or simply by walking down the street, staring at their smartphones.

Think back to the 1995 study conducted by Thaler and Benartzi, which gave us the term "myopic loss aversion." They found that measuring stock performance in one-hour increments generated the worse negative utility for investors. I can only imagine the myopic loss aversion penalty for investors who measure their portfolio every sixty seconds.

Investment professionals put strong emphasis on helping investors accurately assess their tolerance for risk. Seeing their clients boldly add stocks to their portfolio when the market rises only to watch helplessly as they sell stocks and buy bonds when the market swoons has frustrated advisors whose primary responsibility is to properly determine asset allocation. This flipping back and forth between aggressive and then conservative has prompted many to rethink how they should approach the study of risk tolerance.

Traditionally, calculating risk tolerance was simple and direct. Through a series of interviews and questionnaires, advisors would ask their client how they would feel about their portfolio under different scenarios. For example, if the stock market went down 20 percent and half the portfolio was invested in stocks, how would you feel if there was a temporary loss of 10 percent of your capital? Then they would pose another hypothetical scenario, and then another. The theory is that, by studying different market scenarios and adjusting the asset allocation, we can perfectly construct a portfolio that matches the client's risk profile. The problem with this approach is no matter how many different scenarios are examined, the estimation of a client's risk tolerance will be wrong more times than it will be right.

How can that be? According to the distinguished social psychologist Dean G. Pruitt, investors are acting out what is called the "Walter Mitty" effect."[10]

Walter Mitty is a fictional character in James Thurber's wonderful short story "The Secret Life of Walter Mitty." It was first published in the *The New Yorker* in 1939 and later made into a movie (1947) starring Danny Kaye. Walter Mitty was a meek fellow totally intimidated by his overbearing wife. He coped by daydreaming he was magically transformed into a courageous hero. One minute he was dreading facing his wife's sharp tongue; the next, he was a fearless bomber pilot undertaking a dangerous mission alone.

Pruitt believes investors react to the stock market the way Walter Mitty reacted to life. When the market is doing well, they become brave in their own eyes and eagerly accept more risk. But when the market goes down, they rush for the door. So when you ask an investor directly to explain their risk tolerance, the answer comes from either a fearless bomber pilot (in a bull market) or a henpecked husband (in a bear market).

How do we overcome the Walter Mitty effect? By finding ways to measure risk tolerance indirectly. You have to look below the surface of the standard questions and investigate the underlying psychological issues.

Working with Dr. Justin Green at Villanova University, I was able to develop a risk analysis tool that focused on an individual's personality rather than asking about risk directly. We identified important demographic factors and personality orientations that, taken together, might help people measure their risk tolerance more accurately.

Comfort with risk, we found, is connected to two demographic factors: age and gender. Older people are more cautious than younger people, and women more than men. Personal wealth does not seem to be a factor; having more money or less money does not seem to affect one's level of risk tolerance.

Two personality traits are also important: *personal control orientation* and *achievement motivation*. The first refers to people's sense that they are in control of their environment and decisions about their life. People who believe they have this control are called "internals." In contrast, "externals" think they have little control; they see themselves as being like a leaf blown about by the wind. According to our research, high risk takers were overwhelmingly classified as internals. Achievement motivation, the second important trait, describes the degree to which people are goal oriented. We found that risk takers are also goal oriented, even though a strong focus on goals may lead to sharp disappointments.[11]

Understanding your own comfort level for risk is more complicated than simply measuring personal control orientation and achievement motivation. To unlock the real relationship between these personality characteristics and risk taking, you also need to understand how you view the risk environment.[12] Do you think of the stock market as (1) a game you can win only with luck, or (2) an undertaking whose success depends on accurate information combined with rational choices?

Psychological research clearly demonstrates that "whether a person believes the outcomes of [their] decision are dependent upon skill or chance influences the riskiness of their choices."[13] On average, people will consistently select options of moderate to high risk when they perceive the outcome is dependent on skill. But if they think the outcome is governed largely by chance, they will limit themselves to a much more conservative array of choices.

In summary, let us look at how all these personality elements work together. Assuming age and gender variables are equal, we can identify risk-tolerant investors with three traits: They set goals, they believe they control their environment and can affect its outcome, and most important, they view the stock market as a contingency dilemma in which information, combined with rational choices, will produce winning results.

Psychologists tell us that our ability to understand abstract or complex ideas depends on carrying in our mind a working model of the phenomena. These mental models represent a real or hypothetical situation in the same way that an architect's model represents a planned building and that a colorful doodad made of Tinkertoy pieces can represent a complicated atomic structure.[14] To understand inflation, for example, we use mental models that represent what inflation means to us—experiencing higher gasoline or food prices, perhaps, or paying higher wages to our employees.

The first person to propose this thesis was the Scottish psychologist Kenneth Craik. In a short but extraordinary work titled *The Nature of Explanation* ([1943] 1952), Craik wrote that people are processors of information and that they construct mental models of reality to help anticipate events. With a "small-scale model of external reality and of possible actions" in our head, he believed, we are able to "try out various alternatives, conclude which is the best of them, react to future situations before they arise, utilize the knowledge of past events in dealing with the present and the future, and in every way react in a much fuller, safer, and more competent manner to the emergencies which [we] face."[15] The great exploration in psychology, said Craik, is to discover how individuals go about constructing these mental models.

Tragically, Craik's life was cut short by a bicycle accident when he was only thirty-one years old. Since then, much of the research on mental models has been led by Philip N. Johnson-Laird, psychology professor at Princeton University. Through a series of controlled experiments examining how people construct mental models, detailed in his book *Mental Models* (1983), Johnson-Laird observed several ways that people perform systematic errors in their thinking.

First, we tend to assume that each model is equiprobable. That is, given a list of mental models, we are more likely to weight all mental models equally in our thoughts than to adjust the potential contribution of each model differently. It can be said that humans are not mentally wired to perform Bayesian inferences. Johnson-Laird also discovered that when people possess a set of mental models about a particular phenomenon, they often focus on only a few, sometimes only one; obviously relying on a limited number of mental models can lead to erroneous conclusions. We also learn from Johnson-Laird that mental models typically represent what is true but not what is false. We find it much easier to construct a model of what inflation is rather than what it is not.

Ongoing research has shown that, overall, our use of mental models is frequently flawed. We construct incomplete representations of the phenomena we are trying to explain. Even when they are accurate, we don't use them properly. We tend to forget details about the models, particularly when some time has passed, and so our models are often unstable. Finally, we have a distressing tendency to create mental models based on superstition and unwarranted beliefs.

Because mental models enable us to understand abstract ideas, good models are particularly important for investors, many of whom consider the underlying concepts that govern markets and economies dauntingly abstract. And, because mental models determine our actions, we should not be surprised that poorly crafted mental models, built on weak information, lead to poor investment performance.

What drives people to accept and act on questionable information? Why, for instance, when it is clear no one has the ability to predict what is going to happen in the stock market in the short run, are investors mesmerized by the predictions of market forecasters? Otherwise intelligent people stop dead in their tracks to hear what forecasters have to say about the market and sometimes even make investment decisions based on these prognostications. What makes these people so gullible? The answer, according to Michael Shermer in *How We Believe* (2000), lies in the power of the belief system.

We must start with the premise, generally accepted by psychologists, that people are pattern-seeking creatures. Indeed, our survival as a species has depended on this ability. Shermer writes, "Those who are best at finding patterns (standing upwind of game animals is bad for the hunt, cow manure is good for the crops) left behind the most offspring [and] we are their descendants."[16] Through the forces of evolution we are hardwired to seek patterns to explain our world, and those patterns form the foundation of our belief systems, even when they are inherently specious.

Shermer suggests that we can better appreciate the role of the belief system when we think back to the Middle Ages. During this period, 90 percent of the population was illiterate. What little scientific information was available was possessed by only a few—the intellectual elite. Everyone else relied on black magic, sorcery, and monsters to explain the workings of their world. The Plague was caused by the misalignment of the stars and planets. The death of a child was caused by vampires or ghouls who lived in caves. A man who saw a shooting star or heard the howl of a wolf in the night would be dead by morning.

The Newtonian revolution accompanied by the overall rise of literacy worked to reduce outlandish superstition. Chemistry replaced alchemy. Pascal's math explained bad luck. Social hygiene reduced disease, and improved medicine prolonged life. Overall, we can say the Age of Science worked to reduce the errors in thinking and irrational beliefs. But it did not, Shermer believes, eliminate magical thinking entirely. Many athletes maintain bizarre rituals to keep their winning streak alive. Lottery players rely on astrological signs. Many people are petrified by the number 13, and countless others refuse to break chain letters for fear of dire consequences. Magical thinking invades all people regardless of education, intelligence, race, religion, or nationality.

We were not born in the prehistoric period, argues Shermer, but our minds were built there, and we function largely as we have throughout human history. We still succumb to magical thinking because as pattern-seeking animals we need explanations even for the unexplainable. We distrust chaos and disorder, so we demand answers, even if they are a product of magical rather than rational thinking. That which can be explained scientifically, is. That which cannot is left to magical thinking.

In his newest book, *The Believing Brain* (2011), Shermer tells us our superstitions are a product of the spurious identification of patterns. As such, beliefs precede reasoning. Our brains are belief engines that naturally look for patterns, which are then infused with meaning. Not surprisingly, we look for information that confirms our beliefs while ignoring information that contradicts them. Shermer calls this "belief dependent reality." We have all heard the well-worn phrase "seeing is believing"; according to Shermer, our beliefs dictate what we see.

Once I became aware of Shermer's ideas of magical thinking and belief engines, the attraction of market forecasters began to make sense. We are, through a long process of evolution, acutely uncomfortable and anxious in the face of uncertainty, so much so that we are willing to listen to those who promise to alleviate that anxiety. Even though we know in the rational part of our minds that market forecasters cannot predict what will happen tomorrow or next week, we want to believe they can, because the alternative (not knowing) is too uncomfortable.

Remember the observation at the beginning of this chapter that the study of psychology divides itself into two large domains: emotion and cognition. The cross-play between psychology and investing involves both domains, sometimes at the same time. Up to this point we have been considering individual, separate aspects of human psychology from both domains and their interplay with investing. We have seen, courtesy of Ben Graham, how we make a serious error of cognition by confusing investing with speculating; he also warns against investing errors made from emotion. We reviewed the many foibles of human nature in handling money that exist under the rubric of behavioral finance. We took a hard look at our comfort level with risk. We saw how mental models help us grasp abstractions and how shaky models can produce disappointing investment returns.

Finally, we looked back at humanity's proclivity toward finding patterns to explain the world, even if those patterns are based not on actual information but on magical thinking feeding the believing brain.

We must of necessity discuss these items one at a time, in linear fashion, but we know that in reality things are not nearly so tidy. Nothing is more complex than the human brain, nothing messier than the actions of human beings. We think we are investing, but we continue to act speculatively. We have a clear plan for what to do with our money, but let us read just one magazine article and we decide to scuttle that plan and do what everyone else is doing instead. We do serious and prolonged research into specific stocks, *and* we listen to specious advice from so-called market forecasters. And all this is going on at the same time. This chaotic environment, with so much rumor, miscalculation, and bad information swirling around with the good, has been dubbed "noise" by Fischer Black, a man I consider an extraordinary investment professional.

Black was professor of finance at both the University of Chicago and MIT before joining Goldman Sachs. He is perhaps best remembered in the profession for developing, along with Myron Scholes and Robert Merton, the formula we now use for pricing options, but I remember him most for his presidential address to the American Finance Association in 1986. In his talk, titled simply "Noise," this well-respected academician fearlessly took exception with his academic colleagues and challenged the widely accepted thesis that stock prices are rational. Rather than pure information leading to rational prices, Black believed that most of what is heard in the market is noise, leading to nothing but confusion. Investor confusion, in turn, further escalates the noise level. "Noise," said Black, "is what makes our observations imperfect."[17] The net effect of noise that builds in the system, he explained, makes prices less informative for the producers and consumers who use them to guide their economic decisions.

Is there a solution for noise in the market? Can we distinguish between noise prices and fundamental prices? The obvious answer is to know the economic fundamentals of your investment so you can rightly observe when prices have moved above or below your company's intrinsic value. It is the same lesson preached by Ben Graham and Warren Buffett. But all too often, deep-rooted psychological issues outweigh this commonsensical advice. It is easy to say we should ignore noise in the market but quite another thing to master the psychological effects of that noise. What investors need is a process that allows them to reduce the noise, which then

makes it easier to make rational decisions. That process is nothing more—
and nothing less—than the accurate communication of information.

In July 1948, the mathematician Claude E. Shannon published a groundbreaking paper for *The Bell Systems Technical Journal* titled "A Mathematical Theory of Communication." "The fundamental problem of communication," he wrote, "is that of reproducing at one point either exactly or
approximately the message selected at another point."[18] In other words,
communication theory is very much about getting information, accurately
and completely, from point A to point B. It is both an engineering and a
psychological challenge.

A communication system consists of five parts:

1. An *information source*, which produces a message or a sequence
   of messages.
2. A *transmitter*, which operates on the message to produce a signal
   that can be transmitted over the channel.
3. A *channel*, the medium used to transmit the signal from the transmitter to the receiver.
4. The *receiver*, which reconstructs the message (the inverse operation
   of the transmitter).
5. The *destination*, the person for whom the message is intended.

What is the communication system of investing? Our information
source is the stock market or the economy; both continually produce messages or sequencing of messages. The transmitters of the information include writers, reporters, company management, brokers, money managers, analysts, and anyone else who is moved to convey information: taxicab
drivers, doctors, next-door neighbors. The channel might be television,
radio, newspapers, magazines, journals, Web sites, analysts' reports, and
all manner of casual conversations. The receiver is a person's mind, the
place where the information is processed and reconstructed. The final destination is the investor who takes the reconstructed information and acts
on it.

Shannon cautioned that there are several points at which information
from the source can be degraded before it reaches its destination. The biggest danger, he warned, is noise in the system, whether during delivery
over the channel or at either the transmitting or receiving terminal. We
should not automatically assume that the transmitters have correctly

assembled the information from the source (the market) before the information is placed in the channel. Similarly, the receiver can incorrectly process the information, which can lead to errors at the final destination. We also know that the simultaneous delivery of multiple bits of information over the same channel can raise the noise level.

To overcome noise in a communication system, Shannon recommended that what he called a "correction device" be placed between the receiver and the destination. This correcting device would take the information from the receiving terminal, separate out the noise, and then reconstruct the messages so the information arrived correctly at its final destination.

Shannon's correction system is a perfect metaphor for how investors should process information. We must mentally place a correcting device in our information channel. The first task for this correcting device is to maintain integrity of the information coming from the source. The device must filter out incorrect source information and reconfigure the signal if it has become garbled. The process for doing this is within our control. To do so means improving our ability to gather and analyze information and use it to further our understanding.

The other side of our correcting device, the side that faces the receiving terminal, is responsible for verifying that the information is properly passed through and accurately received, without interference of psychological biases. The process for doing this is also within our control, but it is challenging. We must make ourselves aware of all the ways that emotion-based errors and errors of thinking can interfere with good investing decisions, as described in this chapter, and we must constantly be on guard against our own psychological missteps.

Charlie Munger, who gave us the concept of mental models, has spent much time thinking about how we accumulate bits of knowledge from various fields to achieve worldly wisdom. In investing, he says, obviously we need to understand basic accounting and finance. And as we will see in our chapter on mathematics, it is equally important to understand statistics and probabilities. But he believes one of the most important fields is psychology, especially what he calls the psychology of misjudgment.

Charlie warns us against taking mental shortcuts. He thinks we jump too easily to conclusions, we are easily misled and prone to manipulation. "Personally, I've gotten so that I now use a kind of two-track analysis," says Charlie. "First, what are the factors that really govern the interests involved, rationally considered? And second, what are the subconscious influences where the brain at a subconscious level is automatically doing these things—which by and large are useful, but often misfunction."[19] In his own way, Charlie has developed the kind of "correcting device" that Claude Shannon recommends.

Psychology—the study of what makes us tick—is endlessly fascinating. I'm especially intrigued that it plays such a strong role in investing, an arena generally thought to be made up of cold numbers. When making investment decisions, our behavior is sometimes erratic, often contradictory, occasionally goofy. Sometimes our illogical decisions are consistently illogical, and sometimes no pattern is discernible. We make good decisions for inexplicable reasons and bad decisions for no good reason at all.

What all investors need to internalize is that they are often unaware of their bad decisions. To fully understand the markets and investing, we now know we have to understand our own irrationalities. The study of the psychology of misjudgment is every bit as valuable as the thoughtful analysis of a balance sheet. Possibly more so.

6

Philosophy

Of all the different areas of knowledge surveyed in this book, philosophy is both the easiest and the most difficult. It is the easiest because it deals with familiar issues that affect every single one of us on a daily basis, and every single one of us comes into the world equipped with what we need to consider it: a brain, a heart, and a soul.

It is, at the same time, the most difficult discipline for one simple reason: it requires us to think. Unlike the sciences, philosophy does not come prepackaged with absolute answers. Whereas many of us find quantum mechanics extremely difficult to learn, for instance, if we are able to master its fundamentals, then we can proceed with confidence that, unless some future science reveals a new truth, we already know the essence of what there is to know. Similarly, once we understand the concepts of natural selection and genetics, we know the essence of evolution. But philosophy has no such absolutes. Whatever truth it holds is inherently personal and individual and exists only for those who have worked for it.

That is not to say we cannot study philosophy. Learning the ideas of the world's greatest philosophers is the best way—some would say the only way—to achieve clarity about what we ourselves believe. But philosophy, by its very nature, cannot be transferred intact from one person's mind to another's. No matter who first said it, a tenet of philosophy does not exist for us until it passes through the cognitive filter of our interpretation, experience, and beliefs.

The word *philosophy* is derived from two Greek words, usually translated as "love" and "wisdom." A philosopher, then, is a person who loves wisdom and is dedicated to the search for meaning. The pursuit of wisdom is an active, unending process of discovery. The true philosopher is filled with the passion to understand, a process that never ends.

In one sense philosophy began with the earliest forms of human life, as prehistoric societies struggled to make sense of their world. But as a formal area of study, we can say with reasonable certainty that the field of philosophy began, in the Western world at least, around 600 B.C.E., when serious-minded people in ancient Greece began to think about the universe in a way that was separate from the dictates of religious beliefs. In the ensuing twenty-six hundred years, the field of philosophy has been peopled by many hundreds of individuals, some well-known and others less so, and with almost as many different beliefs and perspectives. *The Oxford Companion to Philosophy*, a comprehensive reference work, comprises more than a thousand pages of listings of individual philosophers, concepts, and related topics. For present purposes, we will quickly reduce this vast body of knowledge down to the working parts that are most relevant to our needs.

Strictly for organizational simplicity, we can separate the study of philosophy into three broad categories. First, critical thinking as it applies to the general nature of the world is known as *metaphysics*. Physics, we have learned, is the study of the physical world, tangible objects and forces in nature. It is the study of tables and chairs and their molecular components, of inclined planes and free-falling balls, and of the laws of motion that control the sun and the moon. Metaphysics means "beyond physics." When philosophers discuss metaphysical questions, they are describing ideas that exist independently from our own space and time. Examples include the concepts of God and the afterlife. These are not tangible events like tables and chairs but rather abstract ideas that exist apart from our natural world. Philosophers who debate metaphysical questions readily concede the existence of the world that surrounds us but disagree about the essential nature and the meaning of that world.

The second body of philosophical inquiry is the investigation of three related areas: aesthetics, ethics, and politics. Aesthetics is the theory of beauty. Philosophers who engage in aesthetic discussions are trying to ascertain what it is that people find beautiful, whether it be in the objects they observe or in the state of mind they achieve. This study of the beautiful should not be thought of as a superficial inquiry, because how we conceive beauty can affect our judgments of what is good and bad. Ethics is the philosophical branch that studies the issues of right and wrong. It asks what is moral and what is immoral, what behavior is appropriate and what behavior is inappropriate. Ethics makes inquiries into the activities people undertake, the judgments they make, the values they hold, and the character they aspire to achieve. Closely connected to the idea of ethics is the philosophy of politics. Whereas ethics investigates what is right or wrong at the societal level, political philosophy is a debate over how societies should be organized, what laws should be passed, and what connections peoples should have to these societal organizations.

Epistemology, the third body of inquiry, is the branch of philosophy that seeks to understand the limits and nature of knowledge. The term itself comes from the Greek words *epiteme*, meaning "knowledge," and *logos*, which literally means "discourse" and more broadly refers to any kind of study or intellectual investigation. Epistemology then is the study of the theory of knowledge. To put it simply, when we make an epistemological inquiry, we are thinking about thinking.

When philosophers think about knowledge, they are trying to discover what kinds of things are knowable, what constitutes knowledge (as opposed to beliefs), how it is acquired (innately or empirically, through experience), and how we can say that we know a thing. They also consider what kinds of knowledge we can have of different things. For example, we have learned that our knowledge of physics is different from our knowledge of biology, which is different from our knowledge of sociology, which is different from our knowledge of psychology.

In one way or another, all these branches of philosophy touch our lives every day. We all have a view of the world and probably some idea of the world beyond. For this, metaphysics replaces uncontested assumptions with rationally organized investigation into some understanding of the whole world. Likewise, all of us have our own ideas of beauty and waste, of right and wrong, and of justice and injustice. For these issues, the philosophy of aesthetics, ethics, and politics provides a systematic inquiry into the rules and principles individuals and societies should embrace. Lastly, we all have at some point expressed doubts and questioned our own way of thinking. For those questions, epistemology seeks to clarify the process by which we form our beliefs and to eliminate confusions that can occur when errors creep into our thinking.

Now, without question, each of these three major bodies of philosophical inquiry is a worthy intellectual pursuit. But in this chapter we will focus solely on epistemology. Although some may argue that socially responsible investing links perfectly to the philosophy of aesthetics, ethics, and politics, I do not wish to debate here the right and wrong of individual companies. Neither do I wish to consider the connection between investing and religion. Although these topics are undoubtedly worthwhile, they are best served by others. I am, however, deeply interested in the epistemological questions. I am interested in learning how the process of thought formations occurs and how good thinking skills can be acquired.

Thinking is much more than just acquiring knowledge, and the process of thinking can be done badly or well. By learning to think well, we can better avoid confusion, noise, and ambiguities. Not only will we become more aware of possible alternatives, we will be more capable of making reliable arguments. How we think about investing ultimately determines how we do it. If we can consciously adopt an epistemological framework, always considering at some level whether our thinking process is rigorous and cohesive, we can go a long way toward improving our investment results.

One of the underlying themes that runs throughout this book is the idea that the market is a complex adaptive system, which reflects all the characteristics of such a system. Thus far, our study of complex adaptive systems has had a mostly scientific orientation. We have studied market behavior from the point of view of physicists, biologists, sociologists, and psychologists. In that we are trying to uncover the science of complexity, you might think philosophy has very little to offer. But Lee McIntyre, research fellow at the Center for Philosophy and History of Science at Boston University, disagrees. He believes that philosophy is the critical variable for understanding complexity and that any investigation of the science of complexity must also address philosophical implications.[1]

The first question McIntyre asks is whether the study of complex adaptive systems is epistemological or ontological in nature. Ontology is best understood as a branch of metaphysics. Ontological questions are questions of being, for example: What is the nature of reality? Now it may be that the nature of reality is so complex we will never be able to understand it. If that is so, our inability to understand is an ontological issue. But it may also be that our inability to understand the nature of reality is caused by our own lack of knowledge about it, which makes it an epistemological issue. Ontological limits are caused by the nature of things; epistemological limits are caused by limited understanding.

Are scientific mysteries an artifact of the nature of things or of our limited understanding of the world? At the beginning of each new scientific exploration, scientists are confronted with the ultimate questions: Is the world indeterminable, or are these only hidden, as-yet-undiscovered variables? The study of complex adaptive systems immediately raises that question. We know that these systems, because they are nonlinear, cannot be studied with traditional linear methods. We also know that the emergent properties of these systems all but disappear when they are simplified or reduced into individual parts, which also alleviates reductionist methods of study. Complex adaptive systems must be studied at the level of description that preserves the whole system. "Thus," explains McIntyre, "a central idea behind complexity theory is that there are limits to our knowledge of some systems, even though they are ordered, because we must study this order only at a level of inquiry at which the complexity of the system is ineliminable."[2]

But what is underneath these limits to understanding? Are complex adaptive systems really unexplainable (ontological) or are they only unexplainable because of our limited ability to understand them (epistemological)? That question is a fundamental issue in philosophy, and it is identical to the one asked more than three hundred and fifty years ago. Until Newton proposed his laws of planetary motion (epistemological), the workings of nature and the heavens were considered so perplexing as to be unexplainable (an ontological limitation).

It is McIntyre's belief that complex adaptive systems are not inherently enigmatic but rather appear so only because of our limited descriptive abilities. "Once one accepts that complex systems are only complex as described, there is always the possibility that some alternative description— some *redescription* [italics mine]—of the system will yield regularities that are simpler and can be handled by science," he explains. "If there is order behind complex systems, and if complexity is remediable by alternative descriptions, doesn't it follow that some redescription will make that order apparent while others will not?"[3] McIntyre thus asks us to consider that complexity is not an innate feature of the world, but rather a derivative of how we think. To paraphrase the poet Alexander Pope, disorder is nothing more than order misunderstood.

McIntyre points out that the sense of disorder that appears on the surface is less confusing underneath and that the mandate for scientists is therefore to search for different descriptions that get beneath the surface. This is, if we stop and think for a minute, the very heart of scientific investigation: finding new ways to describe observed phenomena.

Redescription is not, however, the sole province of science. It is also a critical tool for nonscientists who search for understanding. If things remain a mystery, our job then is to shuffle our descriptions and offer redescriptions. Think of it this way: redescriptions are very powerful tools capable of breaking gridlock that sometimes occurs in the pursuit of understanding. I firmly believe, for instance, that one reason we have such difficulty understanding markets is that we have been locked into an equilibrium description of how they should behave. To reach a higher level of understanding, we must remain open-minded to accepting new descriptions of systems that appear complex, whether they are financial markets, social and political systems, or the physical world.

Do not, however, assume that I advocate a kind of intellectual free-for-all. The goal of scientists is to explain nature in descriptive terms that do not violate the basic assumptions of nature itself. The goal of investors is to explain the market in terms that accommodate its basic principles. We cannot slap together any description or combination of descriptions that on the surface appear to offer some legitimate explanation. We cannot create order where there is none. Nature is not so obliging and neither are markets. Naïve correlations will quickly be dissipated.

"Failure to explain is caused by failure to describe!"

His voice was so loud it exploded, booming throughout the room. There was no mistaking its intent. Someone was angry and frustrated. Stunned, we all sat frozen in our seats. The audience went silent. Slowly a few turned around to see who had the fired the vocal bazooka—it was Benoit Mandelbrot.

The topic that night was a big one: is the stock market efficient—or not? It was part of a three-day seminar at the Santa Fe Institute titled "Beyond Equilibrium and Efficiency," organized by J. Doyne Farmer, a research professor at the institute, and John Geanakoplos of the Cowles Foundation at Yale. In attendance was a diverse group of physicists, economists, mathematicians, finance professors, and money managers, including some of the best investment minds in the world.

The attendee list included, among others, Robert Shiller (Yale University), Franco Modigliani (MIT), Richard Thaler (University of Chicago), Richard Roll (UCLA), Steve Ross (MIT), Michael Mauboussin

(Credit-Suisse/Legg Mason Capital Management), Sandy Grossman (Princeton/Penn/Quantitative Financial Strategies), Bill Miller (Legg Mason Capital Management), Brian Arthur (Stanford), Murray Gell-Mann (winner of the 1969 Nobel Prize in Physics), and, of course, Mandelbrot.

Benoit Mandelbrot (1924–2010) was a maverick mathematician. He spent thirty-five years at IBM's Thomas J. Watson Research Center before moving to Yale, where, at the age of seventy-five, he became the oldest professor in the university's history to receive tenure. Along the way he received more than fifteen honorary doctorates. Mandelbrot developed the field of fractal geometry (he coined the term) and applied it to physics, biology, and finance. A *fractal* is defined as a rough or fragmented shape that can split into parts, each of which is at the least a close approximation of its original self. This is a property called *self-similarity*.

About now you might be thinking, "I wouldn't know a fractal if one hit me in the head." But you may be surprised to learn that fractals are easily found in nature; they surround us, and we observe them every day. Examples include clouds, mountains, trees, ferns, river networks, cauliflower, and broccoli. The recursive nature of each of these is somewhat obvious. The branch from a tree or a frond from a fern is a miniature of its whole. Below the surface we have discovered that blood vessels and pulmonary vessels are a fractal system. And from thirty thousand feet looking down, we can see that a coastline, once thought to be impossible to measure, is one of nature's fractals. For those who are now intrigued, Mandelbrot's *The Fractal Geometry of Nature* (1982) is considered the seminal book that brought fractals into the mainstream of professional mathematics.

What I find fascinating about Mandelbrot is not the mathematical rigor of fractals (which is obviously impressive) but the realization that he looked at nature's constituents, as we all have, but saw something different. "Clouds are not spheres, mountains are not cones, coastlines are not circles, and bark is not smooth, nor does lightning travel in a straight line."[4] Because his description of clouds and lightning is different from ours, it should not be surprising his explanation differed. Now we can better appreciate his late-night pronouncement that "failure to explain is caused by failure to describe."

Are descriptions important in investing? You bet they are. But our study of descriptions will not take us to the mathematics department; that part will come later. Rather, we will stay with the philosophy curriculum and next meet someone who is arguably the most distinguished philosopher of the twentieth century. Bertrand Russell described him as "the most perfect example I have ever known of genius as traditionally conceived, passionate, profound, intense, and dominating."[5]

Ludwig Josef Johann Wittgenstein (1889–1951) was an Austrian philosopher who worked primarily in logic, philosophy of mathematics, philosophy of mind, and the philosophy of language. Widely known as a deep thinker and a prodigious writer, surprisingly enough he published just one book review, one article, a children's dictionary, and one very short book, a seventy-five-page volume titled *Tractatus Logico-Philosphicus* (1921).

Wittgenstein wrote the notes for *Tractatus* while serving as an officer on the front lines during the First World War and completed the book while on leave in August 1918. It was an ambitious book that sought to identify the relationship between language and reality. In the first half of his academic life, largely defined by the *Tractatus*, Wittgenstein was primarily concerned with the logical relationship between propositions (formal statements of truth) and the world he observed, believing that if he could provide an account of logic underlying this relationship he would be able to solve all philosophical problems.

In a stunning reversal, Wittgenstein spent the last twenty-two years of his life disputing the very conclusions he had written in *Tractatus*. "I have been forced to recognize the grave mistakes in what I wrote in that first book," he confessed. Starting over, Wittgenstein began by writing down his thoughts as remarks—short paragraphs. His mind jumped from one topic to another: the "concepts of meaning, of understanding, of a proposition, of logic, the foundations of mathematics, states of consciousness, and other things." He said he had first tried to "weld [his] thoughts into a whole" but realized early on he would never succeed. "My thoughts were soon crippled if I tried to force them on in any single direction against their natural inclination. The very nature of the investigation compels us to travel over a wide field of thought crisscrossing in every direction."[6]

Although Wittgenstein never published the new writings, his remarks were assembled, after his death, in a book titled *Philosophical Investigations* (1953). Many thoughtful scholars consider it the most important book of the twentieth century, standing out as "the one crossover masterpiece, appealing across diverse specializations and philosophical orientations."[7]

Wittgenstein came to believe that the meaning of words is constituted by the very function they perform within any language-game. Instead of believing there was some kind of omnipotent and separate logic to the world independent of what we observe, Wittgenstein took a step back and argued instead that the world we see is defined and given meaning by the words we choose. In short, the world is what we make of it.

To help us better understand how this new philosophy of meaning actually worked, Wittgenstein drew a very simple three-sided figure.

He then writes, "Take as an example the aspects of a triangle. This triangle can be seen as a triangular hole, as a solid, as a geometrical drawing, as standing on its base, as hanging from its apex; as a mountain, as a wedge, as an arrow or pointer, as an overturned object, which is meant to stand on the shorter side of the right angle, as a half parallelogram, and as various other things. . . . You can think now of *this* now of *this* as you look at it, can regard it now as *this* now as *this,* and then you will see it now *this* way, now *this*." It is a compelling, even poetic way to describe his belief that reality is shaped by the words we select. Words give meaning.[8]

How does this relate to investing? As we will see, stocks have a lot in common with Wittgenstein's triangle.

On May 15, 1997, Amazon.com (Amazon) became a publicly traded company.[9] The target price set by the underwriters was $18 per share. It finished its first full day of trading at $23—a 28 percent one-day gain. By December 1999, in the midst of the technology bubble, the stock traded over $100 per share. Unfazed, a few analysts predicted Amazon.com would soon be a $300 stock.

The company was founded in 1994 by Jeff Bezos. One year later, Amazon went live on the Internet as an online bookstore. During the technology bubble and the collapse afterwards, so many Internet companies were born and soon buried that it was hard to keep track. But Amazon made it through to the other side. When the NASDAQ Composite, home for many of the Internet newborns, finally bottomed on October 9, 2002, down 78 percent from its 1999 high, Amazon was still standing.

You might think investors would have congratulated the company for surviving the tech crash. But soon analysts were claiming Amazon was still massively overpriced. Although the company had sidestepped the guillotine, they said, its days were numbered. By year-end 2002, Amazon was trading ninety times cash flow and posted a $2.4 million earnings loss.

The bear case rested on the fact that as a book retailer, Amazon appeared massively overpriced relative to brick-and-mortar bookstores. Even when the company diversified into DVDs, CDs, computer software, video games, electronics, apparel, furniture, toys, and food, the brick-and-mortar description stuck. The bears first compared Amazon to Barnes & Noble then later to Wal-Mart. In both cases, Amazon's price to earnings and price to cash flow were significantly higher than the traditional retailers.

Conversely, the Amazon bulls looked at the company and saw something different. To them Amazon did not look like Barnes & Noble or Wal-Mart but instead resembled Dell Computer (Dell). Initially, the bears were shocked by the comparison. Dell was a direct distributor of personal computers and computer products. It was one of the best-performing stocks during the 1990s. Between 1995 and 1999, the stock was up 7,860 percent compared to the S&P 500 Index, which gained 250 percent. The bears quickly chided the Amazon bulls for latching on to a proven winner.

But if you step back and look at Amazon, the company's business operations are more similar to Dell than Wal-Mart. Dell assembles and ships personal computers from various distribution centers located around the country. Orders for computers taken online negate the need for a large and costly sales force. Amazon, like Dell, takes orders online. Also like Dell, Amazon ships products to their customers from one of their distribution centers, bypassing expensive brick-and-mortar retail stores. The business model allows both companies to operate with negative working capital (they get money from customers before they have to pay suppliers/manufacturers), and thus both companies are able to achieve returns on capital above 100 percent.

Does it make sense to compare Amazon to Wal-Mart? It is true that they sell essentially the same merchandise to customers, but the similarities stop there. Wal-Mart has 9,500 brick-and-mortar stores with over 2.1 million employees, each of whom helps to generate about $200,000 in sales. Amazon has 69 distribution centers with 51,000 employees, each of whom helps to generate over $950,000 in sales.

As a side note, Wal-Mart is expected to grow sales annually at 9 percent over the next five years. Over the same time period, Amazon is expected to grow sales annually at 28 percent.

Cyber Monday, the Monday after Thanksgiving when online retailers offer discounts to lure holiday shoppers, is now the biggest shopping day of the year. Online sales on Cyber Monday completely overwhelmed the sales figures racked up by the brick-and-mortar retail stores three days earlier on Black Friday.[10]

Is Amazon best described as Barnes & Noble? As Wal-Mart? Or as Dell?

Mandelbrot was right. Failure to explain is caused by failure to describe.

Wittgenstein lives.

The words we choose give meaning (description) to what we observe. In order to further explain and/or defend our description, we in turn develop a story about what we believe is true. There is nothing wrong with story-telling. In fact, it is a very effective way of transferring ideas. If you stop and think, the way we communicate with each other is basically through a series of stories. Stories are open-ended and metaphorical rather than determinate. Think back to our first chapter where Lakoff and Johnson (*Metaphors We Live By*) remind us that we fundamentally think and act metaphorically.

Today, scientists and philosophers have dropped the word "storytelling" and instead use the word "narrative." Indeed, it appears that "narrative" has now slipped into the mainstream. Philosophers, doctors, and scientists speak of "narrative knowledge" as "what one uses to understand the meaning and significance of stories through cognitive, symbolic, and effective means."[11] Journalists and politicians also use the word. During elections we are told about a candidate's "narrative" or the need for the candidates to "change their narrative." And yes, investors use narratives. There is a narrative about the economic recovery following the financial crisis. There is a narrative about inflation following the massive printing of money used to combat the financial crisis. There is a narrative for deflation, which tells the depressing story of how the massive debt levels accumulated over the past decade will take years to pay down, causing prices and wages to fall.

However, even though narratives are commonly used by almost everyone, narrative knowledge as a means for communication is not without its critics. Indeed, there is a long-standing tension between storytellers and statisticians. On May 7, 1959, C. P. Snow (1905–1980), the noted English physicist and novelist, delivered a lecture called "The Two Cultures." (The lecture was later published as *The Two Cultures and the Scientific Revolution.*) Snow argued that the breakdown in communication between the "two cultures" of society—humanists and scientists—was the major obstacle to solving many of the world's problems. He believed that the quality of education was on the decline because scientists were ignorant of great literature while humanists were equally uninformed about science.

Snow writes, "A good many times I have been present at gatherings of people who, by standards of the traditional culture, are thought highly educated and who have with considerable gusto been expressing their incredulity at the illiteracy of scientists. Once or twice I have been provoked and have asked the company how many of them could describe the Second Law of Thermodynamics. The response was cold: it was negative. Yet I was asking something which is about the scientific equivalent of 'Have you read a work of Shakespeare's?' "[12]

Why should investors care about a half-century-old debate between humanists and scientists? Because the narratives investors use to explain the market or economy sometimes lack the statistical rigor required for a proper description. And as we have learned, if the description is faulty the explanation is likely wrong.

An individual who has given this subject a great deal of thought is John Allen Paulos, professor of mathematics at Temple University. Paulos is a best-selling author, best known for *Innumeracy* (1988) and *A Mathematician Reads the Newspaper* (1995). Both books are enjoyable reads, but it was his 1998 book, *Once Upon a Number: The Hidden Mathematical Logic of Stories,* that is best connected to our philosophy chapter.

Paulos tells us people are very good at storytelling. They are also decent at statistics. But rarely does the storyteller import a statistical defense for the story. Likewise, people are capable of citing good statistics but rarely can they put the statistical revelation into proper context. "Unfortunately, people generally ignore the connections between the formal notions of statistics and the informal understanding and stories from which they grow," says Paulos. "They consider numbers as coming from a different realm than narratives and not as distillations, complements, or summaries of them. People often cite statistics in bald form, without the supporting story and context needed to give them meaning."[13]

When we listen to stories we have the tendency to suspend disbelief in order to be entertained, says Paulos. But when we evaluate statistics, we are less willing to suspend disbelief in order that we are not duped. Paulos goes on to describe the two types of errors in formal statistics. Type I error occurs when we observe something that is not really there. A Type II error occurs when we fail to observe something that is actually there. According to Paulos, those who like to be entertained and wish to avoid making a Type II error are more likely to prefer stories over statistics. Those who do not necessarily yearn for entertainment but are desperate to avoid Type I errors are apt to prefer statistics to stories.[14]

For investors it is important to realize the slippery slope of narratives. Storytelling inadvertently increases our confidence in propositions as the story itself becomes its own proof. "The focus of stories is on the individual rather than the averages, on motives rather than movements, on context rather than raw data," explains Paulos.[15] Because investors primarily use storytelling to explain markets and economies, the absence of statistical evidence weakens the description. Quoting James Boswell, best known as the biographer of Samuel Johnson: "A thousand stories which the ignorant tell, and believe, die away at once when the computist takes them in his gripe [sic]."[16]

The lessons we have learned thus far from Benoit Mandelbrot, Ludwig Wittgenstein, C. P. Snow, and John Allen Paulos are all connected. The right description is critical for providing the right explanation. However, there is often more than one obvious description. Even so, we go to great lengths to defend our chosen description, constructing elaborate and entertaining stories in order to make our point despite the risk of statistical inconsistencies.

One of the most difficult intellectual confessions is to admit you are wrong. Behaviorally we know we are subject to confirmation bias. Eagerly we wrap our minds around anything and everything that concurs with our statement. Too often, we misjudge stubbornness for conviction. We are willing to risk the appearance of being wrong long before a willingness to personally confess our own errors.

In investing, no one is perfect. Some of our mistakes will be minor and easy to overcome. Others will be intransigent. It is difficult to navigate our faults, particularly if they are steadfast and deeply held beliefs. To be a successful investor we must be prepared for redescriptions. Fortunately there is a philosophical guidepost that will make our journey easier and more sensible. We find such a guidepost in the philosophy of pragmatism.

As a formal branch of philosophy, pragmatism is only about one hundred years old; it was first brought to public attention by William James in an 1898 lecture at the University of California, Berkeley. In his lecture, "Philosophical Conceptions and Practical Results," James introduced what he called "the principle of Peirce, the principal of pragmatism." It was a clear homage to his friend and fellow philosopher Charles Sander Peirce.

Some twenty years earlier, a small group of scientists, philosophers, and other intellectuals in Cambridge, Massachusetts, including James, Peirce, and Oliver Wendell Holmes, had formed themselves into the Metaphysical Club for the purpose of critically discussing the metaphysical questions about beliefs and reality. Stimulated by the club discussions, Peirce found himself increasingly moving away from the metaphysical abstractions and toward a different way of defining reality. Originally trained as a mathematician, he came to believe that reality is a function not of abstract absolutes but of the practical relationships between entities (he referred to them as symbols or signs, a reflection of his algebraic work).

Through lively discussions at the Metaphysical Club, Peirce refined his theories and eventually came to this proposition: It is through thinking that people resolve doubts and form their beliefs, and their subsequent actions follow from those beliefs and become habits. Therefore anyone who seeks to determine the true definition of a belief should look not at the belief itself but at the actions that result from it. He called this proposition "pragmatism," a term, he pointed out, with the same root as *practice* or *practical*, thus cementing his view that the meaning of an idea is the same as its practical results. "Our idea of anything," he explained, "is our idea of its sensible effects." In his classic 1878 paper, "How to Make Our Ideas Clear," Peirce continued: "The whole function of thought is to produce habits of action. To develop its meaning, we have, therefore, simply to determine what habits it produces, for what a thing means is simply what habit it involves."[17]

When originally published, "How to Make Our Ideas Clear" caused few ripples outside Peirce's small circle. But another club member, William James, was profoundly influenced by Peirce's ideas, and twenty years later brought them to the attention of the general public, beginning with the Berkeley lecture in 1898.

Peirce, we should point out, was concerned with developing a logical way of solving philosophical problems—specifically, a method for establishing the meaning of things. He intended this concept to be applied principally to scientific inquiry. James, for his part, took Peirce's method and applied it to thinking in general. He moved away from the narrow question of both meaning and truth. A belief is true, James said, not because it can stand up to logical scrutiny but rather because holding it puts a person into more useful relations with the world.

Like Peirce, James concluded that philosophers had wasted far too much time debating abstract principles (metaphysical issues) and trying to prove or disprove various philosophical tenets. Instead, he argued, they should ask what practical effects come from holding one philosophical view over another. More bluntly, James asks, in his famous statement, "what is the cash-value" of the belief in terms of a person's practical experience?

James, a popular and charismatic lecturer, soon became much better known than Peirce as the chief proponent of pragmatism. Eventually, Peirce distanced himself from James's work and even gave his own theory a slightly different name: *pragmaticism,* a term he called "too ugly to be kidnapped." In his later years Peirce became an eccentric, poverty-stricken recluse. William James contributed to his financial support and never failed to acknowledge Peirce as the founder of the philosophical movement for which he, James, became famous.

William James was born in 1842 into a boisterous, unconventional family of intellectuals. His father, Henry James, was a theologian and minor philosopher who educated his children principally by having them sit in on discussions of invited adult guests, and by relentlessly moving the family from one European capital to another in search of intellectual stimulation. William's younger brother, named Henry after their father, became a famous novelist.

As a youngster, William wanted to become a professional artist, but he soon admitted he lacked the level of talent needed for success. At the age of eighteen, he entered the Lawrence Scientific School of Harvard University and then went on to earn a medical degree from Harvard Medical School, with a concentration in psychology. He joined the Harvard faculty and attained a significant reputation as a psychologist, highlighted by the 1890 publication of his classic text, *Principles of Psychology.* At the same time he was, as we have seen, devoting more and more of his considerable intellectual gifts to the study of philosophy.

James's perspective was uncommonly broad. He read widely in classical philosophy and maintained lively personal contacts with several contemporary philosophers, particularly Peirce. His training in psychology gave him a fuller understanding of the workings of the human mind than most philosophers enjoyed. He was also captivated by the theory of evolution, which was then still quite new and causing much excitement among scientists in America (Darwin's *The Origin of Species* was published about the time James entered Harvard as an undergraduate). Blending all these influences along with his personal reflections, James gradually developed his own style of pragmatism. Because he devoted most of his professional energy to writing and lecturing on the subject, and because both were well received by the public, James became the best-known proponent of this philosophy, and his ideas became accepted as the popular understanding of pragmatism.

To state the matter as simply as possible, pragmatism holds that truth (in statements) and rightness (in actions) are defined by their practical outcomes. An idea or an action is true, and real, and good, if it makes a meaningful difference. To understand something, then, we must ask what difference it makes, what its consequences are. "Truth," James wrote, "is the name of whatever proves itself to be good in the way of belief."[18]

If truth and value are determined by their practical applications in the world, then it follows that truth will change as circumstances change and as new discoveries about the world are made. Our understanding of truth evolves. Darwin smiles.

In this, pragmatism is the exact opposite of most earlier schools of philosophic thought, which hold that their version of truth (however they theorize it) is absolute and unchangeable. But James believed that we can never expect to receive absolute proof of anything. Asking, for example, whether God's existence can be proved is a waste of time because the answer is irrelevant. We need only ask ourselves what difference believing or not believing in God makes in our life. This attitude became central to James's pragmatic approach.

James promulgated his ideas in a series of lectures designed for, and attended by, the general public. He addressed his speeches to a popular audience because he believed that they, not philosophers, were the ultimate authority over philosophical questions. In those pre-television days, such events were quite popular, and James was very well received. His speaking style was dynamic, and his articulate and stylish use of language showed some of the same gifts as his brother, the novelist.

One typical lecture, given in 1907 to a large audience in New York, was entitled "What Pragmatism Means." James began by asking his listeners to observe how science had evolved over the years. When the first laws of mathematics and physics were discovered, he said, people believed they had "deciphered authentically the eternal thoughts of the Almighty" and that such laws were therefore absolute. But as science developed, he continued, it became clear that our basic laws are only approximations, not absolutes. Furthermore, the laws themselves had grown in number, with many different rival formulations proposed within each discipline. Scientists, he said, had come to realize that no one theory is the "absolute transcript of reality, but any one of them may from some point of view be useful."[19]

The great use of beliefs, James pointed out, is to help summarize old facts and then lead the way to new ones. After all, he reminded the audience, all our beliefs are man-made. They are a conceptual language we use to write down our observations of nature, and as such, they become the choice of our experience. Thus, he summarized, "ideas (which themselves are but parts of our experience) become true just in so far as they help us get into satisfactory relation with other parts of our experience."[20]

How do we get from old beliefs to new beliefs? According to James, the process is the same as that followed by any scientist.

> An individual has a stock of old opinions already, but he meets a new experience that puts them to strain. Somebody contradicts them; or in a reflective moment he discovers that they contradict each other; or he hears of facts with which they are incompatible; or desires arise in him which they cease to satisfy. The result is inward trouble to which his mind till then had been a stranger and from which he seeks to escape by modifying his previous mass of opinions. He saves as many of them as he can, for in this matter of belief we are all extreme conservatives. So he tries to change first that opinion and then that (for they resist change very variously), until at least some idea comes up that he can graft upon the ancient stock with a minimum of disturbances of the latter, some idea that mediates between the stock and the new experience and runs them into one another most felicitously and expediently.[21]

(If that description of how our minds handle evolving ideas strikes you as familiar, you are right. James has quite eloquently previewed Thomas Kuhn's ideas [Chapter 3] by some fifty years.)

What happens, to summarize James, is that the new idea is adopted while the older truths are preserved with as little disruption as possible. The new truths are simply go-betweens, transition-smoothers, that help us get from one point to the next. "Our thoughts become true," says James, "as they successfully exert their go-between function."[22] A belief is true and has "cash-value" if it helps us get from one place to another. Truth then becomes a verb, not a noun.

So we can say that pragmatism is a process that allows people to navigate an uncertain world without becoming stranded on the desert island of absolutes. Pragmatism has no prejudices, dogmas, or rigid canons. It will entertain any hypothesis and consider any evidence. If you need facts, take the facts. If you need religion, take religion. If you need to experiment, go experiment. "In short, pragmatism widens the field of search for God," says James. "Her only test of probable truth is what works best in the way of leading us."[23]

Pragmatism has been called a uniquely American philosophy. Its heyday (the early part of the twentieth century) coincided with the great westward expansion, and in many ways it echoes the pioneering spirit we associate with that movement. It also coincided with a time of tremendous economic and industrial expansion in our country, when a sense of optimism and New World success seemed to call for a new philosophy. In more recent times, the essence of pragmatism has often been distorted into an opportunistic approach wherein any means, even corrupt ones, are justified by a satisfactory end. This is not James's intention at all. His foremost concern was with morality; he proposed a philosophical method for living well and honorably with our fellow human beings and with our environment.

Pragmatism, in summary, is not a philosophy as much as it is a way of *doing philosophy*. It thrives on open minds and gleefully invites experimentation. It rejects rigidity and dogma; it welcomes new ideas. It insists that all possibilities should be considered, without prejudice, for important new insights often become disfigured as frivolous, even silly notions. It seeks new understanding by redefining old problems. You may recall from the earlier part of this chapter Lee McIntyre's words about the importance of redescribing things we do not understand. Although William James did not use the word, redescription is very much at the heart of his message. We learn by trying new things, by being open to new ideas, by thinking differently. This is how knowledge progresses. In short, pragmatism is the perfect philosophy for building and using a latticework of mental models.

For the pragmatist, the reliance is not on absolute standards and abstract ideals but rather on results—those things that are actually working and that help you reach your goals. Investors are acutely interested in understanding what is working in the market so they too can reach their goals. They recognize the limitations of investment models and are quick to recognize that any model is highly sensitive to the purposes for which it was developed.

For example, consider the classic "value stock" strategy built on selecting stocks with a low price-to-earnings ratio, low price-to-hard-book value, and above-average dividend yield. This model was based on academic studies that demonstrated that the strategy could provide above-average market returns. What we know about modeling is that models have a tendency to work for a while and then unexpectedly stop working. Suddenly, the model no longer has an explanatory value, but some people still insist it is an accurate representation of how the world works. How are we to know?

If you hold a correspondence theory of truth, then it is likely you will hold on to your model, whether it is working or not, for a lot longer because you believe it *corresponds* to some deep structure in markets. This correspondence of truth is equivalent to the use of absolutes. Now contrast this to a pragmatic approach. If you are a pragmatist, you typically have a shorter time period in which you will hold an ineffectual model. Pragmatists realize the model, any model, is there only to help you with a certain task.

What is the best measure of value? Most believe John Burr Williams's theory of discounted cash flow (DCF) is the best model for determining economic value. We should think of Williams's DCF model as being a "first-order model." However, many investors shy away from its inherent difficulties.[24] Instead, they drop down one level of explanation and select one of the second-order models—perhaps low price-to-earnings ratios or some other accounting factor-based measure—which they rigidly hold up as the only correct approach.

The stock market is a giant discounting mechanism that is constantly repricing stocks. There are occasions when the stocks that offer the greatest discount to the company's cash flows (the DCF model) are stocks with low price-to-earnings ratios; at other times the greatest discounts can be found in those stocks with high price-to-earnings ratios. No one metric is absolute; none is always right. Pragmatic investors can, and should, apply any second-order model that is fruitful and discard any that are worthless, all without violating the first order.

Remember, James tells us that even "the most violent revolutions in an individual's beliefs leave most of his old order standing." Even when we adopt a new idea, we can still preserve the older ones with minimum modification. From a pragmatist's point of view, it is permissible, even advisable, to search for those explanations that work. "Stretch them enough to make them admit the novelty," James said, "but conceiving in ways as familiar as the case leaves possible."[25]

The philosophic foundation of successful investors is twofold. First, they quickly recognize the difference between first- and second-order models, and as such they never become a prisoner of the second-order absolutes. Second, they carry their pragmatic investigations far from the field of finance and economics. It can be best thought of as a Rubik's Cube approach to investing. The successful investor should enthusiastically examine every issue from every possible angle, from every possible discipline, to get the best possible description—or redescription—of what is going on. Only then is an investor in a position to accurately explain.

The only way to do better than someone else, or more importantly, to outperform the stock market, is to have a way of interpreting the data that is different from other people's interpretations. To that I would add the need to have sources of information and experiences that are different.[26] In studying the great minds in investing, the one trait that stands out is the broad reach of their interests. Once your field of vision is widened, you are able to understand more fully what you observe, and then you use those insights for greater investment success.

We live and work in a world in which the pace of change is staggering; just when you think things can't possibly move any faster, the pace once again accelerates. In such a world, successful performance demands flexible thinking. In an environment of rapid change, the flexible mind will always prevail over the rigid and absolute.

The "cash-value" of studying philosophy is very real. Put quite simply, it teaches you to think better. Once you commit yourself to philosophy, you find that you have set yourself on a course of critical thinking. You begin to look at situations differently and to approach investing in a different manner. You see more, you understand more. Because you recognize patterns, you are less afraid of sudden changes. With a perpetually open mind that relishes new ideas and knows what to do with them, you are set firmly on the right path.

7

Literature

Charlie Munger, whose concept of a latticework of mental models inspired this book, is sometimes asked, when he describes his concept to audiences, how a person goes about learning those models. They may use different words to frame their question, but essentially those in the audience are asking, "I certainly understand the value of knowing key ideas from different disciplines and building my own latticework, but I didn't learn any of that in school, and I'd be starting from ground zero. Frankly, it seems overwhelming. How do I cultivate the kind of depth and breadth of knowledge that leads to worldly wisdom?"

Charlie is not known for pulling his punches; his answer is blunt. Most people didn't get the right kind of education, he says; too many academic departments are too narrow, too territorial, too self-absorbed with parochial issues to focus on what they should be about, which is helping students become truly educated people. Even earning a degree from a prestigious university is no guarantee that we have acquired what he calls worldly wisdom or even started on the path toward it.

If that is the case, he says with a smile, then the answer is simple: we must educate ourselves. The key principles, the truly big ideas, are already written down, waiting for us to discover them and make them our own.

The vehicle for doing so is a book—or rather, a whole library of books—supplemented with all other media both traditional and modern: newspapers, magazines, broadcast commentaries, technical journals, analyst's reports, and all the digital material on the Internet, to name the most obvious. It's not merely a question of quantity. No one would be foolish enough to suggest that you try to read everything ever written on physics, biology, or other areas addressed in this book. Even if you could somehow manage to do so, I'd be willing to wager that from the sheer volume of ideas, you would end up more confused than enlightened. So we are talking about learning to be discriminating readers: to analyze what you read, to evaluate its worth in the larger picture, and to either reject it or incorporate it into your own latticework of mental models.

Yes, I know; you already have too much to read as it is. But I ask you to consider for a moment whether you might be emphasizing the wrong material. I suspect much of what you currently read regularly (the material about which you think "but I *have* to read that") is about adding facts rather than increasing understanding. In this chapter we are more concerned with the latter than the former. We can all acquire new insights through reading if we perfect the skill of reading thoughtfully. The benefits are profound: Not only will you substantially add to your working knowledge of various fields, you will at the same time sharpen your skill at critical thinking.

In this chapter you will learn ways to analyze a book (or other material) and critically evaluate its contents. That will tell you whether the material has value and whether it is worth your time to study it in depth. The process is not unlike analyzing a potential investment and has similar goals: to facilitate an informed, clear-headed decision. You will recall that both Charlie Munger and Warren Buffett stress the importance of understanding the fundamentals of a company—the business model you invest in. And they mean *real* understanding, not mere data gathering; the sort of understanding that comes only from careful study and intelligent analysis. Thoughtfully choosing investments requires the same mental skills as thoughtfully reading a book.

But what books, on what topics, and it what order? How do we choose, and how can we be sure we are reading appropriately to make the ideas our own? That is what we shall consider in this chapter: what to read, and how, and why.

Let us start by dropping in on a college campus.

*   *   *

On Friday evenings, the entire student body at St. John's College in Annapolis, Maryland, along with all the members of the faculty, assembles in the Francis Scott Key auditorium for a formal lecture. The lecture, delivered by a faculty member or an invited speaker, may be about a great book or a famous author or perhaps a topic such as judgment, love, or wisdom. This is, the college wryly notes, the only time its students are lectured to. After the presentation, members of the audience engage the speaker in an extended conversation about the topic, contributing their comments and asking in-depth questions. For the first half hour, only students may ask questions. The college believes the format serves two important purposes: it reinforces the habit of listening steadily to material that may be unfamiliar, and it gives students an opportunity to polish their public-speaking skills.

But all this on a Friday night, the time usually dedicated to serious partying on most college campuses? Suffice to say that St. John's is not like most college campuses. In fact, it is unlike any other college in the country.[1] St. John's is a coeducational, four-year liberal arts college known for its Great Books program. The entire curriculum is devoted to reading and discussing the great books of Western civilization; there are no separate disciplines or departments, no electives. Over the four years, the Johnnies, as St. John's students are called, will read classic works in literature, philosophy, theology, psychology, physics, biology, government, economics, and history, and discuss them intensively in seminars of eighteen to twenty students. In smaller classes, they also study music, the visual arts, languages (Greek in the freshman and sophomore years, French the final two years), mathematics, and laboratory science.

The curriculum design follows an approximate chronological sequence (see St. John's College reading list in the appendix). In the freshman year, students focus their attention exclusively on the great thinkers of ancient Greece. The second year covers the Roman, medieval, and Renaissance periods and includes classical music and poetry. In the third year, students read the major works of seventeenth- and eighteenth-century thinkers. Seniors move on to the nineteenth and twentieth centuries.

Through the intensive, formalized process of reading significant works and talking together about them, the students at St. John's receive the kind of broad liberal arts education that Benjamin Franklin promoted 250 years ago in the famous 1749 pamphlet that we first met in Chapter 1.[2]

In the course of developing this chapter, I talked to several "Johnnies" who after graduation entered the investment world. All of them said that the number one thing they learned in college was how to be a better thinker rather than a better trader, investment banker, financial advisor, or analyst—and that being a better thinker invariably made them better at their jobs.[3]

"My education at St. John's gave me a sense of perspective, a broader view of the world," said Lee Munson, who manages Portfolio LLC in Albuquerque. "It was very clear that to be successful I would have to consider all the possibilities not just the tunnel vision you get from standard finance classes. As a trader I rely on the idea that I'm seeing the same pattern over and over again; it may look somewhat different, but it's really all the same thing. I have a much better perspective than people who think this is the first time these things have happened.

"At business school they teach you *things*—formulas, theorems, charts. But that's just punching in numbers in a calculator. What's worse, you learn just one way to do things, and then you can't change your thinking fast enough to keep up with the market. Of course, it's important to do all the research and do it thoroughly, but after that, don't just look to the market or the industry to help you with your decisions. Look outside, at the broader picture; that is what lets you think freely. If you don't know how to think, you'll always lose money."

Don Bell, senior vice president at IPC Acquisition, added: "One other thing I learned at St. John's that was immensely helpful was how to have a meaningful discussion with others on sensitive topics in a constructive fashion rather than just launching opinions back and forth. You can see that skill develop right in front of you. As freshmen, everyone is eager to make their own points, they don't really listen; they just wait for someone to take a breath so they can jump in. But by the third and fourth year, we all learned how to listen carefully, to weigh what someone else is saying, and to explain our viewpoint in a respectful, nonconfrontational way. I use that every day of my life."

Steve Bohlin, who graduated from St. John's Santa Fe campus, echoes the value of studying the first sources. "When you study the original work," said Bohlin, "you are never reading the derivative. At St. John's, we learned to break down the original argument into its basic principles then rebuild from there." It is a type of reverse engineering, or what Bohlin calls "learning to learn." Bohlin is currently the head of the investment committee at St. John's, which means he has interviewed countless investment professionals eager to manage part of the college's endowment. Did his unique education help? "The same methods we used at St. John's to break down arguments are the same methods I use to examine money managers," he says. "Most managers that generate alpha are just leveraging beta. What I want to understand is the manager's core principles and how those core principles work to generate excess returns."

When Greg Curtis joined the board of St. John's College in 1990, he began to attend classes and seminars. Because of his tireless dedication to studying the Great Books, St. John's made him an honorary alumnus. Today, Curtis is an emeritus board member, and his passion for St John's and the Great Books program has never wavered. "The education at St. John's is the same today as it was in the 1930s. It's a principle-based education that requires a rigorous examination of the original text. Other colleges may teach a liberal arts education but not with the same intensity found at St. John's," said Curtis. "Being at St. John's is both exhilarating and terrifying because you are required to engage rigorously with the greatest minds of Western civilization. Once you are trained in this manner you are perfectly prepared to take on the world. However, once you leave St. John's you also begin to observe with frustration the slippery work of others who have not taken their education as seriously."

You will recall from Chapter 5 that one way through the psychological quicksand threatening our ability to make good investment decisions is communication—the transmittal of accurate and complete information, free of noise. The entire communication chain must be noise-free, starting with the original information being transmitted. Ideally, that information will be accurate and true (otherwise all we are doing is correctly transmitting error), it will be reasonably relevant to the matter at hand (otherwise we are spinning our wheels), and it will address the underlying question (otherwise we are merely regurgitating data and not increasing insight).

One way to make sure that the original information is accurate and relevant is to apply a correcting device, something we also learned about in Chapter 5. In electronic communications systems, the correcting device is a literal, tangible piece of equipment. For our mental communications systems, a correcting device is whatever cognitive mechanism we can devise to authenticate the information. One very powerful such device—at least for the transmitting end—is the ability to read analytically and think critically.

Once we develop the skills of a discerning reader, we will be able to decide whether what we are reading is worth passing through the communication channel. This is extremely important for those of us involved with investing and finance, for the sheer volume of reading material all but guarantees that some of it will be of marginal value. For simple self-preservation, we must be able to winnow out the good from the not so good.

For us to be able to start the communication chain with good information, we need to develop the skill of discrimination: learning to select, from the sea of information that threatens to drown us, that which will truly add to our knowledge. That is the focus of this chapter: making good choices about what to read and reading in an intelligent, perceptive way so as to enhance knowledge. And here the students of St. John's give us a very valuable tool.

In addition to the complete reading list of Great Books over a four-year period, nearly every St. John's student becomes intimately familiar with one book that is *not* on the list: *How to Read a Book*, by Mortimer J. Adler.[4] Scores of dog-eared, highlighted, margin-scribbled copies circulate among the students, many of whom consider it an indispensable tool for getting the most from their reading. A surprise bestseller when first published in 1940, this remarkable book was revised in 1972 and is still in print, still carefully passed around at St. John's.[5]

There are other books describing a "how to read" system, some more recent than Adler's (see the reading list for this chapter at the end of the book), but I know of none better. My copy of *How to Read a Book* is yellow-highlighted to a fare-thee-well and the margins are filled with notes, arrows, and exclamation points—and every time I open it I find something new. Even though the original concept of Adler and Van Doren's book is seventy years old, the lessons it holds for us as investors are timeless, and I believe it is well worth our time to explore them in depth.

The central purpose for reading a book, Adler believes, is to gain understanding. (For the time being we will set aside the idea of reading for pleasure.) That is not the same as reading for information. The distinction is extremely important, and I believe it is especially important for investors.

Much of what we read each day (unless we deliberately choose material outside our field, which is a very worthwhile thing to do) is for collecting information. The *Wall Street Journal, Financial Times,* the *New York Times, Fortune, Forbes,* and *The Economist,* as well as all the other newspapers, magazines, professional journals, and analysts' reports that cross our desks, contain new information but not necessarily new insights. When we read this material, we collect more data, but our understanding of the matter does not generally increase. Clearly, information is a prerequisite for enlightenment, but the trick, says Adler, is not to stop at just being informed.

There is a simple way to tell the difference between collecting information and gaining understanding. Any time you read something and find you can easily "get it," chances are you are just cataloging information. But when you come across a work that makes you stop, think, and reread for clarification, chances are this process is increasing your understanding. Using this as a litmus test, think about how much of the reading you have done over the past year was for information and how much was for increased understanding.

The process of moving from understanding less to understanding more is a critical journey for anyone who wishes to gain wisdom. It is not a simple matter of reading one book, setting it aside, and reaching for the next one. Achieving real understanding requires you to work, to think. To the degree that your reading involves subjects that are new to you, you as a reader start out on unequal footing with the writer—the writer knows more about the subject than you do. The more unfamiliar you are with the material, the more effort you will need to overcome this inequality.

Also, some writers are, by their style of writing, simply more difficult to grasp; their works, too, take more effort on our part. Adler compares it to the relationship between a pitcher and a catcher in baseball. Pitchers, like some writers, can be wild and out of control, which requires the catcher (the reader) to work harder. Therefore, if you are going to become a good reader, you will sometimes have to make an extra effort to catch a loosely pitched idea.

Adler proposes that all active readers need to keep four fundamental questions in mind:[6]

1. What is the book about as a whole?
2. What is being said in detail?
3. Is the book true, in whole or part?
4. What of it?

No matter how long the material, its format (fiction or nonfiction), or the immediate purpose for reading it (to gain information, to enhance broader knowledge, or for sheer pleasure), you should always be evaluating the material from the perspective of these four fundamental questions if you want to read intelligently.

To determine, as quickly as possible, what the book is about (question 1), Adler suggests a fast review. First, read the preface. Here the author typically gives a brief explanation of the book, the rationale for writing it, and perhaps an outline of what to expect. Next, look carefully at the table of contents; it will give you a good overview of what the book is about. Then turn to the back and run through the index, looking for familiar as well as unfamiliar terms. This will give you a sense of the book's major topics. You can also learn much about the book from its bibliography. Do you recognize the names of the authors referenced and have you read any of their work? Then read a few paragraphs here or there, perhaps from a section that discusses a topic you are somewhat familiar with. After that systematic skimming, turn to the very end and read the author's summation of the book, if there is one.

This entire exercise, from reading the preface, table of contents, index, and bibliography to systematically skimming, should take at most thirty minutes to an hour. You can do this standing in a brick-and-mortar bookstore or online, taking advantage of the "peek inside" benefit available from many online booksellers. At the end, you should know what the book is about as a whole, and that will tell you whether you wish to take your valuable time to read it.

If you do, Adler suggests you start with a complete but somewhat superficial reading. Here you will begin to answer the second fundamental question: What is the book about in detail? That will tell you whether you want to invest the time for a serious, analytical read. The goal now is to get through the book without getting bogged down in small distractions such as unfamiliar vocabulary. Pay attention to what you understand, and skip over the parts that are difficult. Caution: This requires concentration. Even though you are skimming the book, you should not let yourself daydream. Stay alert and focus on what you are reading so that you can comprehend the basics of the material. Adler suggests we adopt the role of a detective, constantly looking for clues that will tell us if the book deserves a deeper examination.

If it does, you move to what Adler calls analytical reading, the most thorough and complete way to absorb a book. Through analytical reading, you will reinforce your answers to the first two fundamental questions (what the book is about as a whole and in detail), and you will begin to answer the third question: Is the book true?

Analytical reading has three goals: (1) to develop a detailed sense of what the book contains, (2) to interpret the contents by examining the author's own particular point of view on the subject, and (3) to analyze the author's success in presenting that point of view convincingly.

You may find it helpful at first to approach analytical reading the way you would approach assigned reading in a college class. Have a notepad at hand, and make your own outline of the key topics, chapter by chapter. Write down, in your own words, what you deduce is the author's main purpose in writing the book. List what you think are the author's main primary arguments, and then compare that list against the outline of contents. Decide for yourself whether the author has fulfilled the original goals, defended the arguments, and convinced you of the main thesis. Ask yourself whether the author seems illogical or presents material that you know from other sources is inaccurate. If something seems incomplete or unsatisfactory, does the author candidly acknowledge that a full answer was not possible, rather than trying to bluff the readers?

After you have read several books in this detailed way, you will very likely find that your analytical skills are improving and that you can proceed without the notepad by your side. You will, however, always be concerned with answering these fundamental questions: What is the book about in detail, and is it true?

The detailed examination of the book that you perform with analytical reading will also begin to answer the fourth fundamental question: What of it? That is to say, what is the significance of this material? A full answer to that question, however, comes only at a still-deeper level of reading, what Adler calls synoptical reading, or comparative reading. (We'll use the latter term here, for I believe it is more descriptive.) In this level of reading, we are interested in learning about a certain subject, and to do so we compare and contrast the work of several authors rather than focusing on just one work by one author. Adler considers this the most demanding and most complex level of reading. It involves two challenges: first, searching for other possible books on the subject and then deciding, after finding them, which books should be read.

Once you have identified the subject you wish to study, the next step is to construct a bibliography. Depending on the subject, the bibliography might include a few books or many. To read that number of books analytically would take months, maybe years. Comparative readers must use shortcuts, inspecting each book to ensure it has something important to say about the subject and then discarding less relevant ones. Once you have decided which books to include, you are ready to begin.

The first step in comparative reading is to locate the relevant passages in each book. You are not doing a full analysis of each book individually but finding the important parts of each separate book that relate to what you need to know. This is a fundamentally different approach from analyzing a book in its entirety. In analytical reading, you accept information from the author as it is given; in comparative reading, your investigation must serve your own needs.

Develop your list of questions, expressed in your own language, and analyze how well the selected books answer those questions. Do not be dismayed if the authors give different answers to your questions, but do take the time to determine the context for each author's answer.

The final step in comparative reading is analyzing the discussion among all the authors. Be careful not to take sides but to let the debate between authors unfold with some objectivity. Of course, perfect objectivity is rarely possible, but the more you can resist jumping to conclusions, the better will be your overall understanding. At the end, you will have answered the last of Adler's fundamental questions: What of it? Is this material important to me, and does it require me to learn more?

Looking back over Adler's complete program, we take note of the connections he has carefully built. Each level of reading is connected to the next, and the process is cumulative. We cannot hope to reach the highest level of reading until we master the earlier ones.

It is important to note that the techniques we have discussed thus far apply to nonfiction books, or what Adler calls expository work. (We shall consider fiction a bit later.) Adler defines as *expository* any book that conveys knowledge, and subdivides those books into two categories: practical and theoretical.

Theoretical books are concerned with ideas—history, mathematics, science, and social sciences. Practical books, in contrast, suggest action. Whatever truth is contained within them becomes real only when you take action; merely reading the book is not sufficient. Any book that lists a set of rules or steps that you should follow to reach a goal is a practical book; how-to books are the most familiar example. Of course, many practical books also have a theoretical component. Typically, they first present general principles that are then transformed into action steps.

Practical books are very much about a process—step-by-step rules— and an end result. To analyze a practical book, you must focus on both the set of rules (the means) and the goal (the end). The rules have to make sense to you, and they have to appear doable.

Reading a theoretical book is an entirely different matter. Here we are not concerned with rule sets and end results; we simply want to learn something about history, or science, or philosophy, or some other discipline where we believe our knowledge is incomplete. The author's goal is also different: not to provide an action road map but, by explanation and reason, to convey knowledge.

The challenge for us as readers is to receive that knowledge and integrate it into our latticework of mental models. How well we are able to do so is a function of two very separate considerations: the author's ability to explain, and our skills as careful, thoughtful readers. We have little control over the first, other than to discard one particular book in favor of another, but the second is completely within our control.

As we have already learned, our challenge as readers is far greater when the material is unfamiliar to us. For most of us, that challenge is particularly acute in books on science and mathematics, where simply understanding the material can be daunting. This is often the case because most scientists write specifically for other scientists; lay readers are not their first priority.

This is markedly different from scientific writing of one hundred years ago. Even today, those of us who are not scientists can read Newton's *Principia* or Darwin's *The Origin of Species* and understand the material. Although Newton and Darwin certainly wanted their ideas to reach other scientists, they were especially interested in explaining their thinking to the general public.

However, today there are some scientists and science writers who have successfully bridged the gap between deep science and popular reading. Richard Dawkins, James Gleick, Stephen Jay Gould, Stephen Hawking, George Johnson, Scott Page, Mitchell Waldrop, and others have written books on science that can be read by the average person. Richard Feynman wrote several books on physics that are accessible for nonphysicists, and Murray Gell-Mann's *The Quark and Jaquar* manages to deal with physics and complexity without intimidating the rest of us.

Reading philosophy is similar to other kinds of expository material in that it requires us to become actively involved in the material by carefully considering Adler's four fundamental questions. But it is also different in that this detailed thinking is the only way we can truly read philosophy. Unlike a work of science, we cannot independently verify whether the book is true. We can only consider whether the writer's ideas ring true to us in accord with our own consideration of the same questions.

How, then, should we approach the reading of philosophy? First, using Adler's principles, you must do everything you can to uncover the author's perspective, the basic assumptions that undergird his or her ideas. If they are not explicitly stated, you will have to do some detective work. This may mean reading several of the author's works, looking for clues. It may mean learning more about the history and culture of the times. It may mean reading other philosophers who are concerned with the same questions. Next, decide whether the writer adheres to his own assumptions.

Then, try to understand the vocabulary used to describe the questions. This can sometimes be tricky because the words are usually in common language but may have been given special meaning. Finally, and most importantly, make up your own mind using common sense and your own observations of the world around you. "It is, indeed, the most distinctive mark of philosophical questions that everyone must answer them for himself," Adler points out. "Taking the opinions of others is not solving them, but evading them."[7]

To illustrate the process, I'll use myself as an example. Chapter 6 of this book is about philosophy, a topic on which I was not particularly knowledgeable. When thinking about how to approach such a vast subject in just one chapter, I first had to educate myself on the basic concepts of philosophy and then determine which might be especially relevant to investors. My first step was to do general overview reading about the discipline of philosophy as efficiently as possible. To this end, *The Oxford Companion to Philosophy* and *The Cambridge Dictionary of Philosophy* were both valuable in helping me navigate the discipline. I turned to the Index and List of Entries, running my finger quickly down each page, looking for any notation that at first might appear relevant to the world of investing. I soon spotted William James, the Harvard psychologist and philosopher. You may remember we briefly met James in the first chapter, along with his graduate student Edward Thorndike.

The William James entry included several notations about "pragmatism" and the "pragmatic theory of truth." A quick reading of both of these topics led me to believe pragmatism was something worthwhile to study. So I quickly read through several books that dealt with pragmatism specifically, including highlights of its most significant practitioners (*The Revival of Pragmatism* and *The Metaphysical Club*). To learn about the circumstances of William James's life and the times in which he lived, I analytically read two well-reviewed biographies (*Genuine Reality: A Life of William James* and *William James: In the Maelstrom of American Modernism*). I then systematically skimmed a collection of James's own writings, including some of his personal letters. Several touching letters written to his brother Henry helped me appreciate the challenge James faced promoting his new philosophy. Lastly, I read, analytically, James's famous treatise *Pragmatism*.

Finally, I gave myself time to sit quietly and review what I had read, thinking it through in the context of some of my own life experiences. As everything I had learned gradually sorted itself out in my mind, I concluded that pragmatism is an area of philosophy that seems to have important lessons for investors.

Generally speaking, the most popular and easily understood expository books can be found in the social sciences. Oftentimes, the experiences described in these works are familiar to us all, and we have already formed our beliefs about them. But paradoxically, it is these same beliefs that make reading social science difficult. Don't forget that your goal as a reader is to determine whether the book is true, not whether it supports what you already think. "You must check your opinions at the door," says Adler. "You cannot understand a book if you refuse to hear what it is saying."[8]

When we read social sciences, it is important that we separate our front-loaded opinions from the author's. Even more important is the technique of comparative reading. People who purchase social science books are most often interested in learning about the topic, not the reputation of any particular author. For this reason, instead of analytically reading just one book, it may be more beneficial to complete a comparative reading of several.

Let's take a moment to put into perspective what we have been learning in this chapter. We start with this irrefutable point: The mental skill of critical analysis is fundamental to success in investing. Perfecting that skill—developing the mind-set of thoughtful, careful analysis—is intimately connected to the skill of thoughtful, careful reading. Each one reinforces the other in a kind of double feedback loop. Good readers are good thinkers; good thinkers tend to be great readers and in the process learn to be even better thinkers.

So the very act of reading critically improves your analytical skills. At the same time, the content of what you read adds to your compendium of knowledge, and this is enormously valuable. If you decide to expand your knowledge base by reading in areas outside finance, including some of the other disciplines presented in this book, you are assembling the individual elements to construct your own latticework of mental models.

Or, to put the matter more directly, learning to be a careful reader has two enormous benefits to investors: it makes you smarter in an overall sense, and it makes you see the value of developing a critical mind-set, not necessarily taking information at face value.

This critical mind-set, in turn, has two aspects that relate to the reading process: (1) evaluate the facts, and (2) separate fact from opinion. To see the process at work, let us briefly consider an analyst's report. I chose this as a specific example because we all spend so much time reading them, but of course the general approach can be, and should be, used universally.

First, look at the facts in the report. It is not unknown for analysts to make ordinary mistakes in their math. That's a simple way to start double-checking facts. Then look at other facts in the report, and think of ways that you could independently verify them—perhaps by comparing the facts against those in an independent source such as Value Line or by comparing the report against similar reports by other analysts. Better yet, the St. John's "Johnnies" would tell you to go and study the original source—the company's own financial documents.

Finally, you must consciously try to discern how much of what you are reading is fact and how much is opinion. If you have already found that some of the facts are shaky, that's a good clue that much of what you're reading might be opinion. But even if the facts are correct, it's quite possible that much of the other commentary is one person's opinion. Then you must stop and think about what is behind that opinion. Is there some vested interest at work? Does the analyst have a long-standing personal bias that creeps in? Has the analyst's opinion changed from opinions expressed in prior reports, and if so, is there is a legitimate reason for the change? Every time you read a report in this fashion you are perfecting your critical-thinking skills.

So far we have been learning about doing careful reading of expository works, but knowledge, insight, and wisdom are not limited to works of nonfiction. Novels, poetry, essays, plays, short stories, even so-called popular fiction can nurture and replenish our understanding of the world we live in.

Noting that they appeal more to our imagination than to our intellect, Adler puts all these types of books under the all-inclusive label of imaginative literature. Although in a very real sense the four fundamental questions apply with equal significance to all kinds of books, reading imaginative material is, Adler believes, far more difficult than reading expository books.

Expository books convey knowledge, he explains. When we are reading them, our goal is to determine their truth. Imaginative books, on the other hand, convey an experience. The beauty of a book relates to that experience. However, this experience is highly subjective and therefore impossible to analyze. Our challenge as readers is to welcome this experience, to open wide our senses and our imagination. "Don't try to resist the effect that a work of imaginative literature has on you," says Adler. "Let it do whatever work it wants to do."[9]

To gain riches from imaginative literature takes different skills from those used in reading expository books. For starters, realize that fiction writers use language differently. Multiple metaphors and shades of meaning convey between the lines more than is stated explicitly; the entire story thus says more than the sum of its individual words. Our investigation of the truth of the work is also different. In an expository work, technical errors can diminish our confidence in the book. But in a work of fiction, whether the novelist depicts the character's actions and emotions in a way that seems believable is far more important than whether specific technical details are correct.

In other ways, however, critically reading fiction is like critically reading nonfiction. You must still attend to the content by understanding the characters and their relationships. You must still find the author's main points by fully inhabiting the imaginary world of the novel. You must still follow the author's "argument" by allowing yourself to experience what the characters experience. In the end, however, the basic question is not whether you agree or disagree with the book but whether you do or do not like it—and why.

Have you ever found, when reading a work of fiction or poetry, that you are stopped cold by a sentence that perfectly expresses something you have felt but have never been able to put so clearly into words? The thought is not new, but suddenly it seems stronger and more real. The recognition of truth can be as strong and sudden as a shot of electric current, and the insight you gain will stay with you. This is the power of imaginative literature: it helps us more poignantly know what we know, feel what we feel, believe what we believe.

Anyone who has read the work of Shakespeare has learned much about human nature while also being thrilled by the beauty and drama of words the characters speak. Modern novelists and playwrights challenge us to consider the great and awful issues of our day while at the same time entertaining us.

The more practical-minded among you may be wondering what investors can learn from imaginative literature. If it doesn't add any new insights about investing, why allocate your valuable time to it? My answer is simple: because we learn from experiences—and not only from our own. Just as we learn from our daily experiences how to become better mates, parents, citizens, and investors, so too can we learn from the fictional experiences that fine writers place in our imagination.

One individual who passionately believes in the power of imaginative literature is Benjamin Doty, senior investment director at Koss Olinger in Gainesville, Florida. He is one of those rare individuals in our business who, while making his living as an investment professional, can see the benefits of reading great literature. In addition to the informational tabloids we are all required to read, Doty's reading list includes William Shakespeare, F. Scott Fitzgerald, Sinclair Lewis, Joseph Conrad, William Dean Howells, and Philip Roth.

Doty's ability to connect investing to literature is a direct result of his combined graduate education in business and English. This would explain why, at the height of the dot-com bubble, he was reading Theodore Dreiser's *The Financier*, which follows the rise and fall of a gifted banker who made and lost several fortunes in the nineteenth century. According to Doty, the lesson of *The Financier* is very much about unchecked greed and extreme ambition. He remembers at the time thinking the moral of the story, which is an indictment of excess capitalism, was the perfect antidote to the philosophy of objectivism, a late twentieth-century idea developed by Ayn Rand and largely made popular by Alan Greenspan, who believed unfettered laissez-faire capitalism was the right moral compass for financial order.

Years later, Doty read Robert Shiller's *The Subprime Solution*, which examines the subprime mortgage crisis of 2007–2008. It started him thinking about the "human factor," the way the financial crisis permanently harmed so many people up and down the social strata. Doty believed the time was right to change the *zeitgeist*—the moral trend of our investing culture. The following year, as adjunct professor at the University of Minnesota, Benjamin Doty was teaching a new class called "The American Novel, Business and Financial Crisis."

In his class, Doty begins with Shiller's analysis of the financial crisis and then introduces *Macbeth, Richard III, The Great Gatsby, Oil!, The*

Heart of Darkness, The Rise of Silas Lapham, American Pastoral, and of course his favorite, *The Financier.* Doty believes that in writing *The Financier,* Dreiser was in effect trying to change the zeitgeist. "We shouldn't underestimate the power of literature in a world where most of the business reading consists of corporate profiles, technical manuals and self-help guides," says Doty. Literature adds what most business nonfiction cannot—it dramatizes the complexity of events. Perhaps most importantly, literature, by its writing magic, places you, the reader, alongside the characters as they confront the consequences of their actions. "Good literature often takes a critical stance," Doty explains, "and that may be what we need right now."[10]

Sometimes I wonder why my profession has not fully embraced literature. Perhaps it's because the rush for gaining information about trading outweighs the desire for longer-term understanding. Certainly other professions that deal with complexity and uncertainty (one that comes to mind immediately is the military) are avid readers of fiction. Perhaps it is because the stakes are much higher—not gains and losses but life and death.

Reading has always been a central tenet for the military ever since Alexander the Great slept with a copy of the *Iliad* under his pillow. When the U.S. Military Academy was founded in 1802, President John Adams advocated an ambitious reading program for the academy's officers. Today, each branch of the military has its own reading list. The Army has at least six, overseen by the Chief of Staff, the War College Library, and the Center for Army Leadership. The Marines have dozens of reading lists, and the Navy has its Professional Reading Program, which includes Melville's *Billy Budd.*[11]

Of course the military list of recommended books does have its fair share of nonfiction, but it also includes a rich library of some of the great works of literature, including Stephen Crane's *The Red Badge of Courage,* Fyodor Dostoyevsky's *The Brothers Karamazov,* Joseph Heller's *Catch-22,* E. M. Forster's *A Passage to India,* and *Snow* by Orhan Pamuk. For those of you who wish to dig deeper, I recommend *Soldier's Heart: Reading Literature Through Peace and War at West Point* by Elizabeth Samet, professor of English at West Point. In the appendix, Samet includes five pages of books and films that are a part of her course.

The great works of literature have enormous power to touch our hearts and expand our minds. But I don't want you to conclude that only serious literature is worth your time. There is much to be learned from popular fiction as well, especially from what is arguably the most popular of all: detective stories.

For me it all began with Rex Stout's Nero Wolfe. Between my freshmen and sophomore years in college, I worked the graveyard shift as bellhop in a hotel in downtown Nashville. The work of bellhop is not bad so long as you can stay busy. But between two and five in morning there is not much to do. Boredom quickly set in.

When my dad heard I was thinking about quitting this cushy and well-paying job, he tossed me a paperback book, suggesting it would help the time go by faster. The book was *Fer-de-lance*, the very first book featuring Nero Wolfe and his trusted assistant, Archie Goodwin. My dad had collected thirty-nine Nero Wolfe books, and by the end of the summer I had read them all.

After Nero Wolfe, I moved on to other detectives. I visited small English villages peering over the shoulders of Miss Jane Marple and Hercule Poirot. I drank elegant cocktails with Nick and Nora Charles, busted heads with Philip Marlowe, and prowled the late-night streets of San Francisco with Sam Spade. Later I endured grotesque autopsies with Dr. Kay Scarpetta and chased lunatics with Detective Alex Cross before returning to the English countryside with Commander Adam Dalgliesh.

Why this attraction to detective stories? Several reasons. At the surface level, a well-written detective story is terrific entertainment and provides a healthy escape from the stresses of work and hectic schedules. But for all the action that is packed into a detective story, what most grabs my attention is the challenge of solving the puzzle. In the beginning, each case seems baffling, with a long list of suspects. Yet as the story unfolds, the detective takes the pieces of evidence (pieces that were all laid before my eyes but were overlooked) and arranges them into a neat patchwork of undeniable guilt. To this day, whenever I start a new detective story I construct a mental list of the suspects and search intensely for clues. For me, the ultimate pleasure of reading a mystery is the chance to solve the crime before the detective does.

Looking back, I have often wondered whether my fascination with detective fiction led to my interest in investing. In a fundamental way, solving a mystery is similar to figuring out whether a security is priced accurately. Both are puzzles. The detective gathers clues to determine whether a suspect is guilty or innocent. A security analyst gathers financial data and industry facts to determine whether the market is accurately assessing a company's value, in the form of its stock price, that particular day.

Shortly after the 2000–2002 bear market, I decided to take an academic look at the genre of detective fiction to see if in fact there were lessons to be distilled for investors.[12] My first stop was the Mysterious Book Shop in midtown Manhattan. My objective was to meet Otto Penzler, proprietor—a legend in the world of mysteries. When I asked Otto who he considered to be the greatest detectives, his answer was concise and unhesitating: Auguste Dupin, Sherlock Holmes, and Father Brown. These three, said Otto, are considered to be the Great Detectives.

The Great Detectives are defined first and foremost by their superior intellect. They possess extraordinary mental acumen that puts them on a higher plane and distinguishes them from ordinary smart people who may be engaged in the same activities. They are, in a word, mental giants.

Great Detectives, in sum, outwit the criminal not because they work harder, not because they are luckier, not because they can run faster, hit harder, or shoot straighter, but because they *think* better. Let's take a look at each of three detectives and list individually their habits of mind.

Auguste Dupin is the creation of Edgar Allan Poe. He made his first appearance in *The Murders in the Rue Morgue* (1841), widely considered the first detective story (making Dupin the first detective). He reappears in Poe's *The Mystery of Marie Roget* (1842) and *The Purloined Letter* (1844).

If we carefully study Dupin's methods, what lessons can we learn?

1. Develop a skeptic's mindset; don't automatically accept conventional wisdom.
2. Conduct a thorough investigation.

Our second Great Detective, Sherlock Holmes, is without question the most popular and well-known detective in all of fiction. The creation of the Scottish author and physician Sir Arthur Conan Doyle, Holmes first appeared in 1887, in the novel *A Study in Scarlet.* All told, Doyle wrote fifty-six short stories and four novels featuring his enigmatic, brilliant detective.

What lessons can we learn by studying Holmes's methods?

1. Begin an investigation with an objective and unemotional viewpoint.
2. Pay attention to the tiniest details.
3. Remain open-minded to new, even contrary, information.
4. Apply a process of logical reasoning to all you learn.

Finally, Father Brown. Although not as well-known as Sherlock Holmes, Father Brown quickly became a favorite of literary critics, perhaps because he was the creation of the famous and respected English novelist, G. K. Chesterton. Father Brown was introduced to the world in a story titled *The Blue Cross* and ultimately starred in fifty-one others (later compiled into five books).

What does Father Brown have to teach us?

1. Become a student of psychology.
2. Have faith in your intuition.
3. Seek alternative explanations and redescriptions.

Entertainment *and* education. Relaxation *and* insight. An escape from stressful reality *and* a new way of thinking. That's what we get from these three and many others besides. Your own favorites may be different, and as I mentioned I also enjoy many modern authors of detective fiction. But no matter whom you like to read, I can't think of many other activities that provide so many strong benefits so painlessly.

If the SAT scores for the high-school graduating class is any indication, it looks like we may be losing a generation of readers. The reading scores of high school seniors is now the lowest ever recorded. Not only are students spending less time reading, they understand less of what they do read. It is hard to quantify what kind of intellectual disaster we are facing. Suffice to say, the penalty we face as individuals—as investors—will be harsh, both intellectually and financially.

But it doesn't have to be this way. Alan Jacobs, professor of English at Wheaton College in Illinois and author of *The Pleasures of Reading in an Age of Distraction*, argues, "The cause of reading is not a lost one." In his mind, reading ought to be a pleasurable activity. "We should be reading for the sake of reading," he exclaims, "rather than reading for the sake of having read."[13]

Reading is good for the mind. Even if you were fortunate enough to have the sort of broad education advocated by Benjamin Franklin and pursued at institutions like St. John's College, you will want to continue reading throughout your life. Exploring challenging ideas keeps your mind stimulated, open, and alive. And if your education gave you specific and "practical" knowledge but not broad understanding, then it is up to you to do the rest—to fill in the knowledge your education did not provide.

In either case, the process is easier, and more fruitful, if you learn the skills of an intelligent, analytical reader.

I wish I could guarantee that this approach to reading will automatically give you Charlie Munger's worldly wisdom. It will not. By itself, reading is insufficient. You must put yourself—your own good brain and some of your soul—into the process, by reflecting on what you read. Indeed, the harder you work to understand and absorb the material, the more deeply embedded it becomes. As Charlie himself puts it, "Good literature makes [you] reach a little. Then it works better. If you've reached for it, the idea's pounded in better."[14]

But if you are still skeptical about all of this and worried about taking on even more reading than you already have, especially reading that you fear will be too difficult, listen once more to Charlie:

> I believe in . . . mastering the best that other people have figured out [rather than] sitting down and trying to dream it up yourself. . . . You won't find it that hard if you go at it Darwinlike, step by step with curious persistence. You'll be amazed at how good you can get. . . . It's a huge mistake not to absorb elementary worldly wisdom. . . . Your life will be enriched—not only financially but in a host of other ways—if you do.[15]

8

Mathematics

Nightingale, perched upon an oak, was seen by Hawk, who swooped down and snatched him. Nightingale, begging earnestly, besought Hawk to let him go, insisting he wasn't big enough to satisfy the hunger of Hawk, who ought instead to pursue larger birds. Hawk replied, "I should indeed have lost my senses if I should let go food ready to my hand, for the sake of pursuing birds which are not even seen within sight."

Undoubtedly you recognize the fable of "The Hawk and the Nightingale," and you already know the moral of the story: "A bird in hand is worth two in the bush."

The fable is credited to Aesop, a slave and storyteller believed to have lived in ancient Greece between 620 and 560 B.C.E. Since then, countless versions have been told. In *The Boke of Nurture or Schoole for Good Maners* (1530), Hugh Rhodes mentions, "a byrd in hand—is worth ten flye at large." A few years later, John Heywood in his ambitiously titled *A dialogue conteinyng the number in effect of all the proverbes in the Englishe tongue* (1546) claims "Better one byrde in hand than ten in the wood." Finally, John Ray in *A Hand-book of Proverbs* (1670) gives us the first fully developed written version, which remains the definitive interpretation: "A bird in the hand is worth two in the bush." But my favorite version of Aesop's fable comes from Warren Buffett: "A girl in a convertible is worth five in the phone book."

I am quite sure that when Aesop wrote "The Hawk and the Nightingale" 2,600 years ago, he had no idea he was laying down one of the definitive laws of investing.

Listen to Buffett: "The formula we use for evaluating stocks and businesses is identical. Indeed, the formula for valuing *all* assets that are purchased for financial gain has been unchanged since it was first laid out by a very smart man in about 600 B.C.E. The oracle was Aesop and his enduring, though somewhat incomplete, insight was 'a bird in the hand is worth two in the bush.' To flesh out this principle, you must answer only three questions. How certain are you that there are indeed birds in the bush? When will they emerge and how many will there be? What is the risk-free interest rate? If you can answer these three questions, you will know the maximum value of the bush—and the maximum number of birds you now possess that should be offered for it. And, of course, don't literally think birds. Think dollars."[1]

Buffett goes on to say that Aesop's investment axiom is immutable. And it matters not whether you apply the fable to stocks, bonds, manufacturing plants, farms, oil royalties, or lottery tickets. Buffett also points out that Aesop's "formula" survived the advent of the steam engine, electricity, automobiles, airplanes, and the Internet. All you need to do, Buffett says, is insert the correct numbers and the attractiveness of all investment opportunities will be rank-ordered.

In this chapter we will take a close look at several mathematical concepts that are critical to smart investing: calculating cash flow discounts, probability theory, variances, regression to the mean, and uncertainty vis-à-vis risk. As in earlier chapters, we will peel back a few layers, learning where and how these concepts originated, how they have evolved over time, and how they contribute to an investor's latticework of ideas.

You may recall that in our chapter on philosophy, we described John Burr Williams's theory of discounted cash flow as the best model for determining value. We also acknowledged that applying the model is anything but easy. You have to calculate the future growth rate of the company. You have to determine how much cash the company will generate over its lifetime. And you have to apply the appropriate discount rate. (For the record, Buffett uses the risk-free rate, defined as the interest rate on the ten-year U.S. Treasury note, whereas modern portfolio theory adds an equity risk premium to this risk-free rate).

Because of these challenges, many investors drop down one level of explanation and select one of the second-order models, perhaps price-to-earnings ratios or price-to-book ratios or dividend yields. Buffett gives no weight to these common investment yardsticks. Although these are mathematical ratios, he says, they tell you nothing about value. They are, at best, relative markers of value used by investors who are unable, or unwilling, to work with discounted cash-flow models.

Buffett gives a great deal of thought about the company he is going to invest with as well as the industry the company operates within. He also closely examines the behavior of management, particularly how management thinks about allocating capital.[2] These are all important variables, but they are largely subjective measurements. As such, they do not easily lend themselves to mathematical computation. In contrast, Buffett's mathematical principles of investing are straightforward. He has often said he can do most business-value calculations on the back of an envelope. First, tabulate the cash. Second, estimate the growth probabilities of the cash coming and going over the life of the business. Then, discount the cash flows to present value.

For help with that last step, we start by looking backward to the Great Depression.

In 1923, a young John Burr Williams enrolled at Harvard University to study mathematics and chemistry. After graduation, he was snared by the stock market euphoria of the late 1920s and became a security analyst. Despite the bullish attitude of Wall Street, or perhaps because of it, Williams was puzzled by the lack of framework to determine a stock's intrinsic value. After the crash of 1929 and the Great Depression that followed, Williams returned to Harvard as a PhD candidate in economics. He wanted to understand what caused the crash.

When it came time to pick a thesis topic, Williams consulted his advisor, Joseph Schumpeter. You may recall we met Professor Schumpeter in our chapter on biology. Considering his background, Schumpeter suggested Williams study the question of how to determine the intrinsic value of a common stock. In 1940, Williams won faculty approval for his doctorate. Amazingly, his dissertation, titled *The Theory of Investment Value*, was published in book form by Harvard University Press two years before he received his doctorate.

Williams's first challenge was to counter the conventional view of most economists who believed financial markets and asset prices were largely determined by investors' expectations for capital gains—all investors, collectively. In other words, prices were driven by opinion, not economics. This was similar to John Maynard Keynes's famous "beauty-contest" doctrine. In Chapter 12 of *The General Theory of Employment, Interest and Money* (1936), Keynes offered his own explanation for the fluctuation of stock prices. He suggested investors pick stocks similarly to how a newspaper might run a beauty contest in which people are asked to pick the most beautiful woman from among six photographs. The trick to winning the contest, said Keynes, was not to pick the woman *you* thought was the most beautiful, but the one you thought everyone else would consider the most beautiful.

But Williams believed that prices in a financial market were ultimately a reflection of the asset's value. Economics, not opinion. In making this statement, Williams turned attention away from the time series of markets (technical analysis) and instead sought to measure the underlying components of asset value. Rather than forecasting stock prices, Williams believed investors should focus on a corporation's future earnings. He then proposed that the value of an asset could be determined using the "evaluation by the rule of present worth." In other words, the intrinsic value of a common stock, for example, is the present value of the future net cash flows earned over the life of the investment.

In his book, Williams acknowledged that his theory was built on a foundation laid down by others. The pioneering step in measuring intrinsic value, he said, was taken in a 1931 book titled *Stock Growth and Discount Tables* by Guild, Weise, Heard, and Brown. In addition, Williams had the benefit of studying the mathematical appendix in *The Nature of Dividends* (1935), by G. A. D. Preinreich. Following the same trail, Williams showed in particular how a company's dividends could be forecast using estimates of the company's future growth. Although Williams did not originate the idea of "present value," he is given credit for the concept of discounted cash flows, largely because of his approach to modeling and forecasting, an approach he called "algebraic budgeting."

For those who are still fuzzy about the discounted present value of future cash, think about how a bond is valued. A bond has both a coupon (cash flows) and a maturity date; together they determine its future cash flows. If you add up all the bond's coupons and divide the sum by the appropriate rate, the price of the bond will be revealed. You determine the value of a business the same way. But instead of counting coupons, you are counting the cash flows the business will generate for a period into the future and then discounting that total back to the present.

You may be asking yourself, if the discounted present value of future cash flows is the immutable law for determining value, why do investors rely on relative valuation factors, second-order models? Because predicting a company's future cash flows is so very difficult. We can calculate the future cash flows of a bond with near certainty—it's a contractual obligation. But a business does not have a contractual obligation to generate a fixed rate of return. A business does the best it can, but many forces—the vagaries of the economy, the intensity of competitors, and innovators who have the ability to disrupt an industry—combine to make predictions about future cash flows less than precise. That doesn't excuse us from making the effort, for as Buffett often quips, "I would rather be approximately right than precisely wrong."

Yes, forecasting growth rates and cash flows gives us only an approximation. But there are mathematical models that can help us navigate these uncertainties and keep us on course for determining the true value of assets. These models help us quantify risk and put us in a better position to navigate our approximations.

We can trace the fundamental concept of risk back eight hundred years to the Hindu-Arabic numbering systems. But for our purposes, we know the serious study of risk began during the Renaissance. In 1654, the Chevalier de Méré, a French nobleman with a taste for gambling, challenged the famed French mathematician Blaise Pascal to solve a puzzle: "How do you divide the stakes of an unfinished game of chance when one of the players is ahead?"

Pascal was a child prodigy educated by his father, himself a mathematician and tax collector in Rouen, the capital of Upper Normandy. Early on, it was clear the younger Pascal was special. He discovered Euclidean geometry on his own by drawing diagrams on the tiles of his playroom floor. When he was sixteen, Pascal wrote a paper on the mathematics of the cone, a paper so advanced and detailed that it was said Descartes himself was impressed. At eighteen, Pascal began tinkering with what was called a calculating machine. After three years of work and over fifty prototypes, Pascal invented a mechanical calculator. Over the next ten years, he built twenty machines he called the "Pascaline."

De Méré's challenge was already well-known. Two hundred years earlier, the monk Luca Pacioli had posed the same question, and for two hundred years the answer remained hidden. Pascal was not deterred. Instead, he turned for help to Pierre de Fermat, a lawyer who was also a brilliant mathematician. He invented analytical geometry and contributed to the early developments in calculus. In his spare time, he worked on light refraction, optics, and research that sought to determine the weight of the earth. Pascal could not have picked a better intellectual partner.

Pascal and Fermat exchanged a series of letters, which ultimately formed the basis of what today is called *probability theory*. In *Against the Gods,* the brilliant treatise on risk, Peter Bernstein writes that this correspondence "signaled an epochal event in the history of mathematics and the theory of probability."[3] Although they attacked the problem differently—Fermat used algebra whereas Pascal turned to geometry—each was able to construct a system for determining the probability of several possible but not yet realized outcomes. Indeed, Pascal's geometric triangle of numbers can be used today to solve many problems, including the probability that your favorite baseball team will win the World Series after losing the first game.

The contributions of Pascal and Fermat mark the beginning of what we now call *decision theory*—the process by which we can make optimal decisions even in the face of an uncertain future. "Making that decision," wrote Bernstein, "is the essential first step in any effort to manage risk."[4]

We now know probability theory is a potent instrument for forecasting. But, as we also know, the devil is in the details. In our case, the details are the quality of information, which forms the basis for the probability estimate. The first person to think scientifically about probabilities and information quality was Jacob Bernoulli, a member of the famed Dutch-Swiss family of mathematicians that also included both Johann and Daniel Bernoulli.

Jacob Bernoulli recognized the differences between establishing odds for a game of chance and odds for answering life's dilemmas. As he pointed out, you do not need to actually spin the roulette wheel to figure out the odds of the ball landing on the number seventeen. However, in real life, relevant information is essential in understanding the probability of an outcome. As Bernoulli explained, nature's patterns are only partly established, so probabilities in nature should be thought of as degrees of certainty, not as absolute certainty.

Although Pascal, Fermat, and Bernoulli are credited with developing the theory of probability, it was another mathematician, Thomas Bayes, who laid the groundwork for putting the theory into practical action.

Thomas Bayes (1701–1761) was both a Presbyterian minister and a talented mathematician. Born one hundred years after Fermat and seventy-eight years after Pascal, Bayes lived an unremarkable life in the British county of Kent, south of London. He was elected to membership in the Royal Society in 1742 on the basis of his treatise, published anonymously, about Sir Isaac Newton's calculus. During his lifetime, he published nothing else in mathematics. However, he stipulated in his will that at his death a draft of an essay he had written and one hundred pounds sterling was to be given to Richard Price, a preacher in neighboring Newington Green. Two years after Bayes's death, Price sent a copy of the paper, "Essay Towards Solving a Problem in the Doctrine of Chances," to John Canton, a member of the Royal Society. In his paper, Bayes laid down the foundation for the method of statistical inference—the issue first proposed by Jacob Bernoulli. In 1764, the Royal Society published Bayes's essay in its journal, *Philosophical Transactions.* According to Peter Bernstein, it was a "strikingly original piece of work that immortalized Bayes among statisticians, economists, and other social scientists."[5]

Bayes's theorem is strikingly simple: When we update our initial belief with new information, we get a new and improved belief. In Sharon Bertsch McGrayne's thoughtful book on Bayes, *The Theory That Would Not Die,* she succinctly lays out the Bayesian process. "We modify our opinions with objective information: Initial Beliefs + Recent Objective Data = A New and Improved Belief." Later mathematicians assigned terms to each part of the method. *Priori* is the probability of the initial belief; *likelihood* for the probability of a new hypothesis based on recent objective data; and *posterior* for the probability of a newly revised belief. McGrayne tells us "each time the system is recalculated, the posterior becomes the prior of the new iteration. It was an evolving system, with each bit of new information pushed closer and closer to certitude."[6] Darwin smiles.

Bayes's theorem gives us a mathematical procedure for updating our original beliefs and thus changing the relevant odds. Here's a short, easy example of how it works.

Let's imagine that you and a friend have spent the afternoon playing your favorite board game and now, at the end of the game, are chatting about this and that. Something your friend says leads you to make a friendly wager: that with one roll of the die you will get a "6." Straight odds are one in six, a 16 percent probability. But then suppose your friend rolls the die again, quickly covers it with her hand, and takes a peek. "I can tell you this much," she says; "it's an even number." With this new information your odds change to one in three, a 33 percent probability. While you consider whether to change your bet, your friend teasingly adds: "And it's not a 4." Now your odds have changed again, to one in two, a 50 percent probability. With this very simple sequence, you have performed a Bayesian analysis. Each new piece of information affected the original probability.

Bayesian analysis is an attempt to incorporate all available information into a process for making inferences, or decisions. Colleges and universities use Bayes's theorem to help students learn decision making. In the classroom, the Bayesian approach is more popularly called the "decision tree theory," in which each branch of the tree represents new information that, in turn, changes the odds in making decisions. "At Harvard Business School," explains Charlie Munger, "the great quantitative thing that bonds the first-year class together is what they call decision tree theory. All they do is take high school algebra and apply it to real-life problems. The students love it. They're amazed to find that high school algebra works in life."[7]

Now let's insert Bayes's theorem into Williams's discounted cash flow model (DCF). We already know one of the challenges of employing the DCF is the uncertainty of predicting the future. Probability theory and Bayes's theorem help us overcome this uncertainty. Still, another criticism of the DCF model is that it's a linear extrapolation of the economic return of a company operating in a nonlinear world. The model assumes the growth rate of cash will remain constant for the number of years you are discounting. But it is of course highly unlikely that any company will be able to produce a perfectly predictable and constant rate of return. The economy jumps up and down, consumers are fickle, and competitors are vigorous.

How does an investor compensate for all the possibilities?

The answer is to expand your decision tree to include various time horizons and growth rates. Let's say you want to determine the value of a certain company, and you know it has grown its cash at a rate of 10 percent in the past. You might reasonably start with an assumption that the company has a 50 percent chance of generating the same growth rate over the next five years, a 25 percent chance of a 12 percent rate, and a 25 percent chance of growing at 8 percent. Then, because the economic landscape invites competition and innovation, you might lower the assumptions for years six through eight, giving it a 50 percent probability of 8 percent growth, a 25 percent probability of 6 percent, and 25 percent probability of 10 percent. Then break the growth assumptions again for years nine and ten.

There are two broad categories of probability interpretations. The first is called *physical probabilities*, more commonly referred to as *frequency probabilities*. They are commonly associated with systems that can generate tons of data over very long periods. Think roulette wheels, flipping coins, and card and dice games. But frequency probabilities can also include probability estimates for automobile accidents and life expectancy. Yes, cars and drivers are different, but there are enough similarities among people driving in a particular area that tons of data can be generated over a multiyear period that in turn will give you frequency-like interpretations.

When a sufficient frequency of events, along with an extended time period to analyze the results, is not available, we must turn to *evidential probabilities*, commonly referred to as *subjective probabilities*. It is important to remember, a subjective probability can be assigned to any statement whatsoever, even when no random process is involved, as a way to represent the "subjective" plausibility. According to the textbooks on Bayesian analysis, "if you believe your assumptions are reasonable, it is perfectly acceptable to make your subjective probability of a certain event equal to a frequency probability."[8] What you have to do is to sift out the unreasonable and illogical in favor of reasonable.

A subjective probability, then, is not based on precise computations but is often a reasonable assessment made by a knowledgeable person. Unfortunately, when it comes to money, people are not consistently reasonable or knowledgeable. We also know that subjective probabilities can contain a high degree of personal bias.

Any time subjective probabilities are in use, it is important to remember the behavioral finance missteps we are prone to make and the personal biases to which we are susceptible. A decision tree is only as good as its inputs, and static probabilities—those that haven't been updated—have little value. It is only through the process of continually updating probabilities with objective information that the decision tree will work.

Whether or not they recognize it, virtually all decisions investors make are exercises in probability. To succeed, it is critical that their probability statements combine the historical record with the most recent data available. That is Bayesian analysis in action.

Eight years after Claude Shannon wrote "A Mathematical Theory of Communication" (Chapter 5), a young scientist at Bell Labs, James Larry Kelly Jr., took Shannon's celebrated paper and distilled from its findings a new probability theory.[9]

Kelly worked alongside Shannon at Bell Labs and thus had a close look at Shannon's mathematics. Inside Shannon's paper was a mathematical formula for the optimal amount of information that, considering the possibilities of success, can be pushed through copper wire. Kelly pointed out that Shannon's various transmission rates and the possible outcomes of a chance event are essentially the same thing—probabilities—and the same formula could optimize both. He presented his ideas in a paper called "A New Interpretation of Information Rate." Published in *The Bell System Technical Journal* in 1956, it opened a mathematical doorway that could help investors make portfolio decisions.[10]

The Kelly criterion, as applied to investing, is also known as the Kelly Optimization Model, which in turn is called the *optimal growth strategy*. It provides a way to determine, mathematically, the optimal size of a series of bets that would maximize the growth rate of a portfolio over time, and it's based on the simple idea that if you know the probability of success, you bet the fraction of your bankroll that maximizes the growth rate. It is expressed as a formula: $2p - 1 = x$; where 2 times the probability of winning minus 1 equals the percentage of one's bankroll that should be bet. For example, if the probability of beating the house is 55 percent, you should bet 10 percent of your bankroll to achieve maximum growth of your winnings. If the probability is 70 percent, bet 40 percent. And if you know the odds of winning are 100 percent, the model would say, bet your entire bankroll.

Ed Oakley Thorp, a mathematics professor, blackjack player, hedge fund manager, and author, was the pioneer in applying the Kelly criterion to gambling halls as well as to the stock market. Thorp worked at MIT from 1959 to 1961. There he met Claude Shannon and read Kelly's paper. He immediately set forth to prove to himself whether or not the Kelly criterion would actually work. Thorp learned Fortran so he could program the university's computer to run countless equations on the probabilities of winning at blackjack using the Kelly criterion.

Thorp's strategy was based on a simple concept. When the deck is rich with tens, face cards, and aces, the player has a statistical advantage over the dealer. If you assign a −1 for the high cards and +1 for the low cards, it's quite easy to keep track of the cards dealt; just keep a running tally in your head, adding or subtracting as each card shows. When the count turns positive, you know there are more high cards yet to be played. Smart players would save their biggest bets for the tipping point at which the card count reached a high relative number.

Thorp continued to devise card-counting schemes. He would tweak the computer programming language while using the Kelly criterion to determine the weight of each bet. He soon ventured to Las Vegas to test his theory in practice. Starting with $10,000, Thorp doubled his money in the first weekend. He claimed he could have won more but his winning streak caught the eye of the casino security, and he was tossed out.

Over the years, Thorp became a celebrity among the blackjack aficionados. His reputation skyrocketed when it was learned he actually used a wearable computer to play roulette. This device, codeveloped with Claude Shannon, was the first computer used in a casino and is now considered illegal. No longer able to apply his mathematical theories on gambling floors, Thorp tipped his hat to Las Vegas by writing *Beat the Dealer* in 1962, a *New York Times* best seller that sold over seven hundred thousand copies. Today, it is considered the original card-counting and betting-strategy manual.

Over the years, the Kelly criterion has become a part of the mainstream investment theory. Some believe that both Warren Buffett and Bill Gross, the famed bond portfolio manager at PIMCO, use Kelly methods in managing their portfolio. William Poundstone further popularized the Kelly criterion in his popular book, *Fortune's Formula: The Untold Story of the Scientific Betting System That Beat the Casinos and Wall Street* (2005). However, despite its academic pedigree and simplistic formulation, I caution that the Kelly criterion should be used by only the most thoughtful investors and even then with reservation.

In theory, the Kelly criterion is optimal under two criteria: (1) the minimal expected time to achieve a level of winnings and (2) the maximal rate of wealth increase. For example, let's say two blackjack players each have a $1,000 stake and twenty-four hours to play the game. The first player is limited to betting only one dollar on each hand dealt; player number two can alter the bet depending on the attractiveness of the cards. If the second player follows the Kelly approach and bets the percentage of the bankroll that reflects the probability of winning, it is likely that, at the end of twenty-four hours, he will have done much better than player number one.

Of course, the stock market is more complex than a game of blackjack, in which there is a finite number of cards and therefore a limited number of possible outcomes. The stock market has thousands of companies and millions of investors and thus a greater number of possible outcomes. Using the Kelly approach, in conjunction with the Bayes theorem, requires constant recalculations of the probability statement and adjustments to the investment process.

Because in the stock market we are dealing with probabilities that are less than 100 percent, there is always the possibility of realizing a loss. Under the Kelly method, if you calculated a 60 percent chance of winning you would bet 20 percent of your assets, even though there is a 2 in 5 chance of losing. It could happen.

Two caveats to the Kelly criterion that are often overlooked: You need (1) an unlimited bankroll and (2) an infinite time horizon. Of course, no investor has either, so we need to modify the Kelly approach. Again, the solution is mathematical in the form of simple arithmetic.

To avoid "gambler's ruin," you minimize the risk by underbetting—using a half-Kelly or fractional Kelly. For example, if the Kelly model were to tell you to bet 10 percent of your capital (reflecting a 55 percent probability of success), you might choose to invest only 5 percent (half-Kelly) or 2 percent (fractional Kelly). That underbet provides a margin of safety in portfolio management; and that, together with the margin of safety we apply to selecting individual stocks, provides a double layer of protection and a very real psychological level of comfort.

Because the risk of overbetting far outweighs the penalties of underbetting, investors should definitely consider fractional-Kelly bets. Unfortunately, minimizing your bets also minimizes your potential gain. However, because the relationship in the Kelly model is parabolic, the penalty for underbetting is not severe. A half-Kelly, which reduces the amount of the bet by 50 percent, reduces the potential growth rate by only 25 percent.

"The Kelly system is for people who simply want to compound their capital and see it grow to very large numbers over time," said Ed Thorp. "If you have a lot of time and a lot of patience, then it's the right function for you."[11]

At age 40, Stephen Jay Gould, the famous American paleontologist and evolutionary biologist, was diagnosed with abdominal mesothelioma, a rare and fatal form of cancer, and was rushed into surgery. After the operation Gould asked his doctor what he could read to learn more about the disease. She told him there was "not much to be learned from the literature."[12]

Undeterred, Gould headed to Harvard's Countway medical library and punched "mesothelioma" into the computer. After spending an hour reading a few of the latest articles, Gould understood why his doctor was not so forthcoming. The information was brutally straightforward: mesothelioma was incurable, with a median life expectancy of only eight months. Gould sat stunned until his mind began working again. Then he smiled.

What exactly did an eight-month median mortality signify? The median, etymologically speaking, is the halfway point between a string of values. In any grouping, half the members of the group will be below the median and half above it. In Gould's case, half of those diagnosed with mesothelioma would die in less than eight months and half would die sometime after eight months. (For the record, the other two measures of central tendency are mean and mode. Mean is calculated by adding up all the values and dividing by the number of cases—a simple average. Mode refers to the most common value. For example, in the string of numbers 1, 2, 3, 4, 4, 4, 7, 9, 12, the number 4 is the mode.)

Most people look on averages as basic reality, giving little thought to the possible variances. Seen this way, "eight months' median mortality" meant he would be dead in eight months. But Gould was an evolutionary biologist and evolutionary biologists live in a world of variation. What interests them is not the average of what happened but the variation in the system over time. To them, means and medians are abstractions.

Most of us have a tendency to see the world along the bell shape curve with two equal sides, where mean, median, and mode are all the same value. But as we have learned, nature does not always fit so neatly along a normal, symmetrical distribution but sometimes skews asymmetrically to one side or the other. These distributions are called either right or left skewed depending on the direction of the elongation.

Gould the biologist did not see himself as the average patient of all mesothelioma patients but as one individual inside a population set of mesothelioma patients. With further investigation, he discovered that the life expectancy of patients was strongly right skewed, meaning that those on the plus side of the eight-month mark lived significantly longer than eight months.

What causes a distribution to skew either left or right? In a word, variation. As variation on one or the other side of the median increases, the sides of the bell curve are pulled either right or left. Continuing with our example, in Gould's case, those patients who lived past the eight-month mark showed high variance (many of them lived not just more months but years), and that pulled the curve to form a right skew. In a right-skewed distribution, the measures of central tendency do not coincide; the median lies to the right of the mode and the mean lies to the right of the median.

Gould began to think about the characteristics of those patients who populated the right skew of the distribution, who exceeded the median distribution of life expectancy. Not surprisingly, they were young, generally in good health, and had benefited from early diagnosis. This was Gould's own profile, and so he reasoned there was a good chance he would live well beyond the eight-month mark. Indeed, Gould lived for another twenty years.

"Our culture encodes a strong bias either to neglect or ignore variation," Gould said. "We tend to focus instead on measures of central tendency, and as a result we make some terrible mistakes, often with considerable practical import."[13]

The most important lesson investors can learn from Gould's experience is to appreciate the differences between the trend *of* the system and trends *in* the system. Put differently, investors need to understand the difference between the average return of the stock market and the performance variation of individual stocks. One of the easiest ways for investors to appreciate the differences is to study sideways markets.

Most investors have experienced two types of stock markets—bull and bear—that go either up or down over time. But there is a third, less familiar type of market. It is called a "sidewinder" and it produces a sideways market—one that barely changes over time.

One of the more famous sideways markets occurred between 1975 and 1982. On October 1, 1975, the Dow Jones Industrial Average stood at 784. Nearly seven years later, on August 6, 1982, the Dow closed at the exact 784. Even though nominal earnings grew over the time period, the price paid for those earnings dropped. By the end of 1975, the trailing price-earnings multiple for the S&P 500 was almost 12 times. By the fall of 1982, it had declined to nearly 7 times.

Some stock market forecasters are drawing analogies to what happened then to what may be happening today. There are concerns about the rate of corporate profit growth against the backdrop of a weak global economic recovery. Others fear the massive stimulation provided by the monetary authorities will cause a rise in commodity prices, inflation, and decline in the dollar. This will, in turn, feed back into the stock market, causing price-earnings multiples to fall. Ultimately, investors could face a prolonged period when the market barely budges—and when they are best advised to avoid stocks.

When I first heard that argument—that we might be facing a sideways market similar to the late 1970s and it was best to avoid stocks—I was puzzled. Was it really true that sideways markets are unprofitable for long-term investors? Warren Buffett, for one, had generated excellent returns during the period; so did his friend and Columbia University classmate Bill Ruane. From 1975 through 1982, Buffett generated a cumulative total return of 676 percent at Berkshire Hathaway; Ruane and his Sequoia Fund partner Rick Cunniff posted a 415 percent cumulative return. How did they manage these outstanding returns in a market that went nowhere? I decided to dig a little.

First, I examined the return performance of the 500 largest stocks in the market between 1975 and 1982. I was specifically looking for stocks that had produced outsized gains for shareholders. Over the 8-year period, only 3 percent of the 500 stocks went up in price by at least 100 percent in any one year. When I extended the holding period to 3 years, the results were more encouraging: Over rolling 3-year periods, 18.6 percent of the stocks, on average, doubled. That equals 93 out of 500. Then I extended the holding period to 5 years. Here the returns were eye-popping. On average, an astonishing 38 percent of the stocks went up 100 percent or more; that's 190 out of 500.[14]

Putting it in Gould's terms, investors who observed the stock market between 1975 and 1982 and focused on the market average came to the wrong conclusion. They wrongly assumed that the direction of the market was sideways, when in fact the variation *within* the market was dramatic and led to plenty of opportunities to earn high excess returns. Gould tells us "the old Platonic strategy of abstracting the full house as a single figure (an average) and then tracing the pathway of this single figure through time, usually leads to error and confusion." Because investors have a "strong desire to identify trends," it often leads them "to detect a directionality that doesn't exist." As a result, they completely "misread the expanding or contracting variation within a system. "In Darwin's world," said Gould, "variation stands as the fundamental reality and calculated averages become abstractions."[15]

On the first page of their seminal book *Security Analysis*, Benjamin Graham and David Dodd included a quote from Quintus Horatius Flaccus, (65–8 B.C.E.) "Many shall be restored that now are fallen and many shall fall that are now in honor." Just as Aesop had no clue his fable about Hawk and Nightingale was the literary preamble to the discounted cash flow model, so too I am sure Horace had no idea he had just written down the narrative formula for regression to the mean.

Whenever you hear someone say, "It all averages out," that's a colloquial rendition of regression to the mean—a statistical phenomenon that, in essence, describes the tendency of unusually high or unusually low values to eventually drift back toward the middle. As used in investing, it suggests that very high or very low performance is not likely to continue and will probably reverse in a later period. (That's why it is sometimes called *reversion* to the mean.) Regression to the mean, Peter Bernstein points out, is the core of several homilies, including "what goes up must come down," "pride goeth before a fall," and Joseph's prediction to Pharaoh that seven years of famine would follow seven years of plenty. And, Bernstein tells us, it also lies at the heart of investing, for regression to the mean is a common strategy—often applied and sometimes overused—for picking stocks and predicting markets.

We can trace the mathematical discovery of regression to the mean to Sir Francis Galton, a British intellectual and cousin of Charles Darwin. (You may recall Galton and his ox-weighing contest in our chapter on sociology). Galton had no interest in business or economics. Rather, one of his principal investigations was to understand how talent persisted in a family generation after generation—including the Darwin clan.

Galton was the beneficiary of the work by a Belgian scientist named Lambert Adolphe Jacques Quetelet (1796–1874). Twenty years older than Galton, Quetelet had founded the Brussels Observatory and was instrumental in introducing statistical methods to the social sciences. Chief among his contributions was the recognition that normal distributions appeared rooted in social structures and the physical attributes of human beings.

Galton was enthralled with Quetelet's discovery that "the very curious theoretical law of the deviation from the average—the normal distribution—was ubiquitous, especially in such measurements as body height and chest measurements."[16] Galton was in the process of writing *Hereditary Genius*, his most important work, which sought to prove that heredity alone was the source of special talents, not education or subsequent professional careers. But Quetelet's deviation from the average stood in his way. The only way Galton could advance his theory was to explain how the differences within a normal distribution occurred. And the only way he could do this was to figure out how data arranged itself in the first place. In doing so, Galton made what Peter Bernstein calls an "extraordinary discovery" that has had vast influence in the world of investing.

Galton's first experiments were mechanical. He invented the Quincunx, an unconventional pinball machine shaped like an hourglass with twenty pins stuck in the neck. Demonstrating his idea before the Royal Society, Galton showed that when he dropped balls at random they tended to distribute themselves in compartments at the bottom of the hourglass in a classic Gaussian fashion. Next he studied garden peas—or more specifically, the peas in the pod. He measured and weighed thousands of peas and sent ten specimens to friends throughout the British Isles with specific instructions on how to plant them. When he studied the offspring of the ten different groups, Galton found that their physical attributes were arranged in normal, Gaussian distribution just as the Quincunx would have predicted.

This experiment, along with others including the study of height variation between parents and their children, became known as regression, or reversion, to the mean. "Reversion," said Galton, "is the tendency of the ideal filial type to depart from the parent type, reverting to what may be roughly and perhaps fairly described as the average ancestral type."[17] If this process were not at work, explained Galton, then large peas would produce ever-larger peas and small peas would produce ever-smaller peas until we had a world that consisted of nothing but giants and midgets.

J. P. Morgan was once asked what the stock market would do next. His response: "It will fluctuate." No one at the time thought this was a backhanded way of describing regression to the mean. But this now-famous reply has become the credo for contrarian investors. They would tell you greed forces stock prices to move higher and higher from intrinsic value, just as fear forces prices lower and lower from intrinsic value, until regression to the mean takes over. Eventually, variance will be corrected in the system.

It is easy to understand why regression to the mean is slavishly followed on Wall Street as a forecasting tool. It is a neat and simple mathematical conjecture that allows us to predict the future. But if Galton's Law is immutable, why is forecasting so difficult?

The frustration comes from three sources. First, reversion to the mean is not always instantaneous. Overvaluation and undervaluation can persist for a period longer—much longer—than patient rationality might dictate. Second, volatility is so high, with deviations so irregular, that stock prices don't correct neatly or come to rest easily on top of the mean. Last, and most important, in fluid environments (like markets) the mean itself may be unstable. Yesterday's normal is not tomorrow's. The mean may have shifted to a new location.

In physics-based systems, the mean is stable. We can run a physics experiment ten thousand times and get roughly the same mean over and over again. But markets are biological systems. Agents in the system—investors—learn and adapt to an ever-changing landscape. The behavior of investors today, their thoughts, opinions and reasoning, is different from investors of the last generation.

Up until the 1950s, the dividend yield on common stocks was always higher than the yield on government bonds. That's because the generation that lived through the 1929 stock market crash and Great Depression demanded safety in the form of higher dividends if they were to purchase stocks over bonds. They may not have used the term, but in fact they employed a simply strategy of regression to the mean. When common stock yields approached or dipped below government bond yields, they sold stocks and bought bonds. Galton's Law reset prices.

As economic prosperity returned in the 1950s, a generation removed from the painful stock market losses of the 1930s embraced common stocks. Had you held steadfast to the idea that common stock yields would revert back to levels higher than bond yields, you would have lost money. And an example from today's market: In a striking turn of events, the dividend yields on many common stocks in 2011 were higher than the yield on 10-year U.S. Treasury notes. Following the regression approach, you would have sold bonds in favor of stocks. Yet as we move into 2012, bonds have continued to outpace stocks. How long will this economic deviation from the mean last? Or has the mean now shifted?

Most people think the S&P 500 Index is a passively managed basket of stocks that rarely changes. But that is untrue. Each year the selection committee at Standard & Poor's subtracts companies and adds new ones; about 15 percent of the index, roughly 75 companies, is exchanged. Some companies exit the index because they have been taken over by another company. Others are removed because their declining economic prospects mean they no longer qualify for the largest 500 companies. The companies that are added are typically healthy and vibrant in industries that are having a positive impact on the economy. As such, the S&P 500 Index evolves in a Darwinian manner, populating itself with stronger and stronger companies—survival of the fittest.

Fifty years ago, the S&P 500 Index was dominated by manufacturing, energy, and utility companies. Today it is dominated by technology, health care, and financial companies. Because the return on equity for the latter three is higher than the first group of three, the average return on equity of the index is now higher today than it was thirty years ago. The mean has shifted. In the words of Thomas Kuhn, there has been a paradigm shift.

Overemphasizing the present without understanding the subtle shifts in composition can lead to perilous and faulty decisions. Although regression to the mean remains an important strategy, it is imperative that investors remember it is not inviolable. Stocks that are thought to be high in price can still move higher; stocks that are low in price can continue to decline. It is important to remain flexible in your thinking. Although reversion to the mean is the most likely outcome in markets, its presence is not sacrosanct.

Gottfried Leibniz (1646–1716), the German philosopher and mathematician, wrote, "Nature has established patterns originating in the return of events, but only for the most part."[18] The mathematics in this chapter is very much about helping investors better understand, so they can better anticipate, the "returning events." Still, we are left with uncertainties, discontinuities, irregularities, volatilities, and fat tails.

Frank H. Knight (1885–1972) was an American economist who spent his career at the University of Chicago and is credited with founding the Chicago School of Economics. His students included Nobel laureates James Buchanan, Milton Friedman, and George Stigler. Knight is best known as the author of *Risk, Uncertainty, and Profit,* in which he seeks to distinguish between economic risk and uncertainty. Risk, he said, involves situations with unknown outcomes but is governed by probability distributions known at the outset. We may not know exactly what is going to happen, but based on the past events and the probabilities assigned, we have a pretty good idea what is likely to happen.

Uncertainty is different. With uncertainty, we don't know the outcome, but we also don't know what the underlying distribution looks like, and that's a bigger problem. Knightian uncertainty is both immeasurable and impossible to calculate. There is only one constant: surprise.

Nassim Nicholas Taleb, in his best-selling book *The Black Swan: The Impact of the Highly Improbable* (2007), has done much to reconnect investors to Knight's notion of uncertainty. A "black swan," as described by Taleb, is an event with three attributes: (1) "it is an outlier, as it lies outside the realm of regular expectations, because nothing in the past can convincingly point to its possibility, (2) it carries an extreme impact, (3) in spite of its outlier status, human nature makes us concoct explanations for its occurrence *after* the fact, making it explainable and predictable."[19]

In *The Black Swan*, Taleb's goal was to help investors better appreciate the disproportionate role of events that are hard-to-predict, high-impact, and rare—a swan born black—events well beyond the normal expectations we have for history, science, technology, and finance. Second, he wanted to bring attention to the incomputable nature of these ultrarare events using scientific methods based on the nature of a small probability set. Lastly, he wanted to bring to light the psychological biases, the blindness, we have to uncertainty and history's rare events.

According to Taleb, our assumptions about what is going to happen grow out of the bell-shape curve of predictability—what he calls "Mediocristan." Instead, the world is shaped by wild, unpredictable, and powerful events he calls "Extremistan." In Taleb's world, "history does not crawl, it jumps."

The attack on Pearl Harbor in 1941 and the 9/11 terrorist attack on the World Trade Center are examples of black swan events. Both were outside the realm of expectation, both had extreme impact, and both were readily explainable after the fact. Unfortunately, the term black swan has become trivialized. Media is quick to attach the moniker to just about anything that is the least bit irregular, including freak snowstorms, earthquakes, and stock market volatility. It would be more appropriate to label these events "gray swans."

Statisticians have a term for black swan events; it is called a *fat tail*. William Safire, *New York Times* columnist, explains the terminology: In a normal distribution, the bell curve is tall and wide in the middle and drops and flattens out at the bottom. The extremities at the bottom, either on the right side or the left, are called tails. When the tails balloon instead of vanishing in a normal distribution, the tails are designated as "fat."[20] Taleb's black swan event shows up as a fat tail. In statistics, events that deviate from a normal distribution mean by five or more standard deviations are considered extremely rare.

Like the term black swan, fat tail has become a part of the investing nomenclature. We hear constantly that investors cannot suffer another "left-tail" event. Institutional investors are now buying "left-tail" insurance; hedge funds are selling "left-tail" protection. Here again, I believe we are misusing terms. Today, any mild deviation from the norm is quickly labeled as a black swan or a fat tail.

Mathematics, like physics, has a seductive quality about it. Math leads us toward precision and away from ambiguity. Still, there is an uneasy relationship between quantification of the past in order to predict versus subjective degrees of belief about what the future might hold. The economist and Nobel laureate Kenneth Arrow warns us that the mathematically driven risk management approach to investing contains the seeds of its own self-destructive technology. He writes, "Our knowledge of the way things work, in society or in nature, comes trailing clouds of vagueness. Vast ills have followed a belief in certainty."[21]

This is not to say probability, variance, regression to the mean, and fat tails are useless. Far from it. These mathematical tools have helped us narrow the cone of uncertainty that exists in markets—but not eliminate it. "The recognition of risk management as a practical art rests on a simple cliché with the most profound consequences: when our world was created, nobody remembered to include certainty," said Peter Bernstein. *"We are never certain; we are always ignorant to some degree.* Much of the information we have is either incorrect or incomplete."[22]

Gilbert Keith Chesterton, the English literary critic and author of the Father Brown mysteries, captured our dilemma perfectly:

> The real trouble with this world of ours is not that it is an unreasonable world, nor even that it is a reasonable one. The commonest kind of trouble is that it is nearly reasonable, but not quite. Life is not an illogicality; yet it is a trap for logicians. It looks just a little more mathematical and regular than it is; its exactitude is obvious, but its inexactitude is hidden; its wildness lies in the wait.[23]

9

Decision Making

A bat and ball cost $1.10.

The bat costs one dollar more than the ball.

How much does the ball cost?

You now have a number in your mind. I'm sorry to tell you this, but chances are excellent that your answer is wrong. Don't despair—over half the students at Harvard, MIT, and Princeton got it wrong too. And they didn't do any better on the next two problems.

If it takes 5 machines 5 minutes to make 5 widgets, how long would it take 100 machines to make 100 widgets?

In a lake, there is a patch of lily pads. Every day, the patch doubles in size. If it takes 48 days for the patch to cover the entire lake, how long will it take for the patch to cover half of the lake?[1]

These three problems—easy, in hindsight—were devised by Shane Frederick, associate professor of marketing at Yale University, as part of the Cognitive Reflection Test he created in 2005 while working at MIT. He was interested in measuring people's cognitive reasoning, and in particular how readily they could override the brain's reflexive decision-making center—what is commonly called intuition.

For years, psychologists have been interested in the idea that our cognitive processes are divided into two modes of thinking, traditionally referred to as *intuition,* which produces "quick and associative" cognition, and *reason,* described as "slow and rule-governed." Today, these cognitive systems are commonly referred to as System 1 and System 2. System 1 thinking is intuitive. It operates automatically, quickly, and effortlessly with no sense of voluntary control. System 2 is reflective. It operates in a controlled manner, slowly and with effort. The operations of System 2 thinking require concentration and are associated with subjective experiences that have rule-based applications.

Although we like to think of ourselves as having sturdy System 2 ability, in fact much of our thinking occurs in System 1. Let's return to Frederick's college students. More than half of them said the ball cost 10 cents. And what is most surprising, it is also the same answer most gave when they were asked, "Is that your final answer?"

It is clear the college students were stuck in System 1 thinking and could not, or would not, convert over to System 2. If they had taken even just one moment to think, Frederick said, they would have realized that the difference between $1 and 10 cents is 90 cents, not one dollar. The surprisingly high rate of errors among college students indicates two problems. First, people are not accustomed to thinking hard about problems and often rush to the first plausible answer that comes to mind. Second, the System 2 process does a bad job of monitoring System 1 thinking.

Frederick also discovered that people who did well on the Cognitive Reflection Test tended to be more patient in answering questions. System 2 thinking is a relatively slow process. When we are forced to answer quickly, we don't have enough time to engage the rationality that is at the heart of the reflective process.

This is not to say intuition does not have a role in our thinking—far from it. I dare say we could not get through the day without our basic intuitions. When you're driving a car, if the back end begins to slip sideways, intuition tells you to turn the wheel in the direction of the slide. You have no time to engage System 2 thinking and carefully ponder a list of different options.

Indeed, the role of intuition in our cognitive process has earned the attention of serious scientists. You may remember Daniel Kahneman from our chapter on psychology—the psychologist who won the Nobel Prize in Economics for his studies of human judgment and decision making.

Kahneman believes there are indeed cases where intuitive skill reveals the answer, but that such cases are dependent on two conditions. First, "the environment must be sufficiently regular to be predictable" second, there must be an "opportunity to learn these regularities through pro-longed practice." For familiar examples, think about the games of chess, bridge, and poker. They all occur in regular environments, and prolonged practice at them helps people develop intuitive skill. Kahneman also ac-cepts the idea that army officers, firefighters, physicians, and nurses can develop skilled intuition largely because they all have had extensive expe-rience in situations that, while obviously dramatic, have nonetheless been repeated many times over.

Kahneman concludes that intuitive skill exists mostly in people who operate in simple, predictable environments and that people in more com-plex environments are much less likely to develop this skill. Kahneman, who has spent much of his career studying clinicians, stock pickers, and economists, notes that evidence of intuitive skill is largely absent in this group. Put differently, intuition appears to work well in linear systems where cause and effect is easy to identify. But in nonlinear systems, includ-ing stock markets and economies, System 1 thinking, the intuitive side of our brain, is much less effectual.

Let's return to our college students for a moment. We can assume they're all smart, so why did they have trouble solving the problems? Why did they leap to a conclusion based totally on intuition (System 1 thinking), and why didn't System 2 thinking correct their faulty answers? Because, in a nutshell, they lacked adequate reservoirs of information.

In his own writing about intuition, Kahneman called on a definition developed by Herbert Simon—another psychologist who also won a Nobel Prize in Economics based on his studies of decision making. "The situa-tion has provided a cue; this cue has given the expert access to information stored in memory, and the information provides the answer. Intuition is nothing more and nothing less than recognition."[2] Thus, Kahneman be-lieves, increasing the amount of information stored in memory increases our skill at intuitive thinking. Further, he says, the failure of System 2 to override System 1 is largely a *resource* condition. "In some judgmental tasks, information (in System 2 thinking) that could serve to supplement or correct the heuristic (occurring in System 1 thinking) is not neglected nor underweighted, but simply lacking."[3]

Improving the resource condition of our System 2 thinking—that is to say, deepening and broadening our reserves of relevant information—is the principal reason this book was written.

*   *   *

College students are not investment professionals—at least not for a few more years. So we might say Shane Frederick's pessimistic view of the thinking talent among undergraduates is premature and will eventually be righted. If Kahneman's theory is correct, all that is needed is a bit more learning time with hands-on experience, and our young intellectuals will be able to calculate the cost of a baseball, how long it takes to make widgets, and how many days it takes lily pads to cover a lake. Soon these fresh-faced graduates, who are eager to slay the world, will become the next generation of investment experts.

Philip Tetlock, professor of psychology at the University of Pennsylvania, might also have had an optimistic view about their future had he not spent fifteen years (1988–2003) studying the decision-making process of 284 experts. He defined experts as people who appeared on television, were quoted in newspaper and magazine articles, advised governments and businesses, or participated in punditry roundtables. All of them were asked about the state of the world; all gave their prediction of what would happen next. Collectively, they made over 27,450 forecasts. Tetlock kept track of each one and calculated the results. How accurate were the forecasts? Sadly, but perhaps not surprisingly, the predictions of experts are no better than "dart-throwing chimpanzees."[4]

How can this be? According to Tetlock, "How you think matters more than what you think?"[5]

It appears experts are penalized, like the rest of us, by thinking deficiencies. Specifically, experts suffer from overconfidence, hindsight bias, belief system defenses, and lack of Bayesian process. You may remember these mental errors from our chapter on psychology.

Such psychological biases are what penalize System 1 thinking. We rush to make an intuitive decision, not recognizing that our thinking errors are caused by our inherent biases and heuristics. It is only by tapping into our System 2 thinking that we can double-check the susceptibility of our initial decisions.

Some 2,600 years ago, the Greek warrior poet Archilochus wrote, "The fox knows many tricks, the hedgehog only one." The quote was later made famous by Sir Isaiah Berlin in his popular essay, "The Hedgehog and the Fox: An Essay on Tolstoy's View of History." In it, Berlin divided writers and thinkers into two categories: hedgehogs, who viewed the world through the lens of a single defining idea, and foxes, who were skeptical of grand theories and instead drew on a wide variety of experiences before making a decision. Berlin was surprised by the controversy the essay created. "I never meant it very seriously," he said. "I meant it as a kind of enjoyable intellectual game, but it was taken seriously."[6]

Researchers were quick to grab the analogy to help explain their own research on decision making—Tetlock included. In his *Expert Political Judgment* study, Tetlock divided the forecasters into Hedgehogs and Foxes. Despite the overall dismal performance, he was able to discern differences. The aggregate success of the forecasters who behaved most like foxes was significantly greater than those who behaved like hedgehogs.

Why are hedgehogs penalized? First, because they have a tendency to fall in love with pet theories, which gives them too much confidence in forecasting events. More troubling, hedgehogs were too slow to change their viewpoint in response to disconfirming evidence. In his study, Tetlock said Foxes moved 59 percent of the prescribed amount toward alternate hypotheses, while Hedgehogs moved only 19 percent. In other words, Foxes were much better at updating their Bayesian inferences than Hedgehogs.

Unlike Hedgehogs, Foxes appreciate the limits of their own knowledge. They have better calibration and discrimination scores than Hedgehogs. (Calibration, which can be thought of as intellectual humility, measures how much your subjective probabilities correspond to objective probabilities. Discrimination, sometimes called justified decisiveness, measures whether you assign higher probabilities to things that occur than to things that do not.) Hedgehogs have a stubborn belief in how the world works, and they are more likely to assign probabilities to things that have not occurred than to things that actually occur.

Tetlock tells us Foxes have three distinct cognitive advantages.

1. They begin with "reasonable starter" probability estimates. They have better "inertial-guidance" systems that keep their initial guesses closer to short-term base rates.
2. They are willing to acknowledge their mistakes and update their views in response to new information. They have a healthy Bayesian process.
3. They can see the pull of contradictory forces, and, most importantly, they can appreciate relevant analogies.[7]

Hedgehogs start with one big idea and follow through—no matter the logical implications of doing so. Foxes stitch together a collection of big ideas. They see and understand the analogies and then create an aggregate hypothesis. I think we can say the fox is the perfect mascot for the College of Liberal Arts Investing.

Keith Stanovich, professor of human development and applied psychology at the University of Toronto, believes that intelligence tests (like the ACT and SAT) measure important qualities but do a very poor job of measuring rational thought. "It is a mild predictor at best," he says, "and some rational thinking skills are totally dissociated from intelligence."[8] Intelligence tests typically measure mental skills that have been developed over a long period. But remember, the most common thinking errors have less to do with intelligence and more with rationality—or, more accurately, the lack of it.

The idea that people with high IQs could be so bad at decision making at first seems counterintuitive. We assume that anyone with high intelligence will also act rationally. But Stanovich sees it differently. In his book, *What Intelligence Tests Miss: The Psychology of Rational Thought,* he coined the term "dysrationalia"—the inability to think and behave rationally despite having high intelligence.

Research in cognitive psychology suggests there are two principal causes of dysrationalia. The first is a processing problem. The second is a content problem.

Stanovich believes we process poorly. When solving a problem, he says, people have several different cognitive mechanisms to choose from. At one end of the spectrum are mechanisms with great computational power, but they are slow and require a great deal of concentration. At the opposite end of the spectrum are mechanisms that have low computational power, require very little concentration, and make quick action possible. "Humans are cognitive misers," Stanovich writes, "because our basic tendency is to default to the processing mechanisms that require less computational effort, even if they are less accurate."[9] In a word, humans are lazy thinkers. They take the easy way out when solving problems and as a result, their solutions are often illogical.

The second cause of dysrationalia is the lack of adequate content. Psychologists who study decision making refer to content deficiency as a "mindware gap." First articulated by David Perkins, a Harvard cognitive scientist, *mindware* refers to the rules, strategies, procedures, and knowledge people have at their mental disposal to help solve a problem. "Just as kitchenware consists in tools for working in the kitchen, and software consists in tools for working with your computer, mindware consists in the tools for the mind," explains Perkins. "A piece of mindware is anything a person can learn that extends the person's general powers to think critically and creatively."[10]

Mindware gaps, he believes, are generally caused by the lack of a broad education. In Perkins's view, schools do a good job of teaching the facts of each discipline but a poor job of connecting the facts of each discipline together in such a way to improve our overall understanding of the world. "What is missing," he says, "is the *metacurriculum*—the 'higher order' curriculum that deals with good patterns of thinking in general and across subject matters."[11]

How to fix this? At first, Perkins envisioned special courses that focused on the art of thinking. But he realized that adding courses to an already crowded curriculum would prove difficult. Instead, he thought what was needed with each subject matter was a direct injection of thoughtfulness— what he called a mindware booster shot. "I am an advocate of what is often called infusion," he wrote, "integrating the teaching of new concepts in a deep and far-reaching way with subject matter instruction."[12]

So now we come around to the heart of the matter. Perkins's hope for a new way of learning perfectly aligns with the underlying principle of this book—that people studying the art and science of investing are best served by incorporating the "rules, strategies, procedures, and knowledge" from several different disciplines. In this regard, *Investing: The Last Liberal Art* is a direct example of a mindware booster shot.

It is rare when the *Wall Street Journal* and the *New York Times* reach the same conclusion. But they both agreed Daniel Kahneman's new book, *Thinking Fast and Slow,* was one the top five nonfiction books in 2011. As of this writing (September 2012), it has appeared on the *Times* best seller list for twelve weeks and counting—a remarkable feat for a 500-page book on decision making. I take it as a positive sign. Finally, behavioral finance has become a part of the mainstream.

Kahneman tells us much of the book is about the biases of intuition. "However," he writes, "the focus on error does not denigrate human intelligence any more than the attention to diseases in medical texts denies good health. Most of us are healthy most of the time, and most of our judgments and actions are appropriate most of the time. As we navigate our lives, we normally allow ourselves to be guided by impressions and feelings, and the confidence we have in our intuitive mind beliefs and preferences are usually justified. But not always. We are confident even when we are wrong and an objective observer is more likely to detect our errors than we are." The goal of the book, says Kahneman, "is to improve and understand errors of judgment and choice, in others and eventually in ourselves."[13]

My favorite chapter in the book came early. In Chapter 3, "The Lazy Controller," Kahneman reminds us that cognitive effort is mental work. And as with all work, many of us have a tendency to get lazy when the task gets harder. We simply run out of gas. Several psychological studies show that people who are simultaneously challenged by demanding cognitive tasks and temptation are more likely to yield to temptation. If you are continually forced to do something over and over that is challenging, there is a tendency to exert less self-control when the next challenge arrives. Kahneman tells us that activities that put demands on System 2 thinking require self-control, and continuous exertion of self-control can be unpleasant.

Kahneman is surprised by the ease with which intelligent people appear satisfied enough with their initial answer that they stop thinking. He is reluctant to use the word "lazy" to describe the lack of System 2 monitoring, but lazy is what it seems to be. Kahneman notes that we often say of people who give up on thinking, "He didn't bother to check whether what he said made sense" or "Unfortunately, she tends to say the first thing that comes into her mind." What we should be thinking, he says, is "Does he usually have a lazy System 2 or was he unusually tired?" Or, for the second example, "She probably has trouble delaying gratification—a weak System 2."

According to Kahneman, "Those who avoid the sin of intellectual sloth could be called 'engaged.' They are more alert, more intellectually active, less willing to be satisfied with superficially attractive answers, more skeptical about their intuitions."[14] What does it mean to be engaged? Quite simply, it means your System 2 thinking is strong, vibrant, and less prone to fatigue. So distinct is System 2 thinking from System 1 thinking that Keith Stanovich has termed the two as having "separate minds."

But a "separate mind" is only separate if it is distinguishable. If your System 2 thinking is not adequately armed with the required understanding of the major mental models collected from the study of several different disciplines, then its function will be weak—or, says Kahneman, lazy.

Having been schooled in modern portfolio theory and the efficient market hypothesis, will you quickly and automatically default to this physics-based model of how markets operate, or will you slow down your thinking and also consider the possibility that the market's biological function could be altering the outcome? Even if the market looks hopelessly efficient, will you also consider that the wisdom of the crowds is only temporary—until the next diversity breakdown?

When you analyze your portfolio, will you resist the almost uncontrollable urge to sell a losing position, knowing full well the angst you feel is an irrational bias—the pain of loss being twice as discomforting as the pleasure of an equal unit of gain? Will you stop yourself from looking at your price positions day in and day out, knowing that the frequency with which you do is working against your better judgment? Or will you bow down to your first instinct and sell first and ask questions later?

When thinking about companies, markets, and economies, will you rest with your first description of events? Knowing that more than one description is possible and the dominant description is most often determined by the extent of media coverage, will you dig deeper to uncover additional, perhaps more appropriate, descriptions? Yes, it takes mental energy to do this. Yes, it will take more time to reach a decision. Yes, this is more difficult than defaulting to your first intuition.

Lastly, with all that you have to read to get through the requirements of your job, will you read a new book that will increase your understanding? As Charlie Munger has said so many times, it is only by reading that you are able to continuously learn.

All this and more are the mental exercises that help to close the mindware gap and strengthen your System 2 thinking. It serves to keep you engaged. It works to fully develop your separate mind.

My hope with this book is that it will inspire you to begin thinking about investing in a different way, as something more than a kaleidoscope of shifting numbers. But thinking about investing differently means thinking creatively. It requires a new and innovative approach to absorbing information and building mental models. You will recall from Chapter 1 that to construct a new latticework of mental models, we must first learn to think in multidisciplinary terms and to collect (or teach ourselves) fundamental ideas from several disciplines, and then we must be able to use metaphors to link what we have learned back to the investing world. Metaphor is the device for moving from areas we know and understand to new areas we don't know much about. To build good mental models, we need a general awareness of the fundamentals of various disciplines, plus the ability to think metaphorically.

The art of model building depends on our skill at constructing building blocks.[15] Think of the classic children's toy, Lincoln Logs. To build a model of a cabin, children construct, using various logs, a replica of what they think a log cabin looks like. Now, the set comes with many different logs. Some are short and some are long; some are used for connecting the roof, others are used to frame the doors and windows. To build a good log cabin, the builder has to combine the logs together in such a way as to create a good model.

Constructing an effective model for investing is very similar to building a log cabin. We have, throughout this book, provided a number of different building blocks. Good model building is very much about combining the building blocks in a skillful, artful way. Properly combined, these building blocks will give you a reasonable model of how markets work and, I hope, add some insight that will help you become a better investor. Of course, what we can quickly appreciate is that if you have only a couple of building blocks, it will be very difficult to construct an exact model of a log cabin. This is also true of investing. If you possess only a few building blocks, how will you ever be able to construct a useful model?

The first rule in building an effective model, then, is to start with enough building blocks. To build our all-encompassing model of the market—a meta-model, if you will—we will use as building blocks the various mental models described in this book, the key ideas taken from individual disciplines. After we have collected enough building blocks, we can start to assemble them into a working model.

One critical difference between building a model of a log cabin and building a model of market behavior is that our investing model must be dynamic. It must have the ability to change as the circumstances change. As we have already discovered, the building blocks of fifty years ago are no longer relevant because the market, like a biological organism, has evolved.

A model that changes shape as its environment changes may be difficult to envision. To get a sense of how that could work, imagine a flight simulator. The great advantage of a simulator is that it allows pilots to train and perfect their skills under different scenarios without the risk of actually crashing the plane. Pilots learn to fly at night, in bad weather, or when the plane is experiencing mechanical difficulties. Each time they perform a simulation, they must construct a different flight model that will allow them to fly and land safely. Each one of those models may contain similar building blocks but assembled in a different sequence; the pilot is learning which building blocks to emphasize for each of the scenarios.

The pilot is also learning to recognize patterns and extrapolate information from them to make decisions. When a certain set of conditions presents itself, the pilot must be able to recognize an underlying pattern and to pull from it a useful idea. The pilot's mental process goes something like this: I haven't seen this exact situation before, but I saw something like it, and I know what worked in the earlier case, so I'll start there and modify it as I go along.

Building an effective model for investing is very similar to operating a flight simulator. Because we know the environment is going to change continually, we must be in a position to shift the building blocks to construct different models. Pragmatically speaking, we are searching for the right combination of building blocks that best describes the current environment. Ultimately, when you have discovered the right building blocks for each scenario, you have built up experiences that in turn enable you to recognize patterns and make the correct decisions.

One thing to remember is that effective decision making is very much about weighting the right building blocks, putting them into some hierarchical structure. Of course, we may never fully know what all the optimal building blocks are, but we can put into place a process of improving what we already have. If we have a sufficient number of building blocks, then model building becomes very much about reweighting and recombining them in different situations.

One thing we know from recent research by John Holland and other scientists (see Chapter 1) is that people are more likely to change the weighting of their existing building blocks than to spend any time discovering new ones. And that is a mistake. We must, argues Holland, find a way to use productively what we already know and at the same time actively search for new knowledge—or, as Holland adroitly phrases it, we must strike a balance between exploitation and exploration. When our model reveals readily available profits, of course we should intensely exploit the market's inefficiency. But we should *never* stop exploring for new building blocks.

Although the greatest number of ants in a colony will follow the most intense pheromone trail to a food source, there are always some ants that are randomly seeking the next food source. When Native Americans were sent out to hunt, most of those in the party would return to the proven hunting grounds. However, a few hunters, directed by a medicine man rolling spirit bones, were sent in different directions to find new herds. The same was true of Norwegian fishermen. Each day most of the ships in the fleet returned to the same spot where the previous day's catch had yielded the greatest bounty, but a few vessels were also sent in random directions to locate the next school of fish. As investors, we too must strike a balance between exploiting what is most obvious while allocating some mental energy to exploring new possibilities.

By recombining our existing building blocks, we are in fact learning and adapting to a changing environment. Think back for a moment to the description of neural networks and the theory of connectionism in Chapter 1. It will be immediately obvious to you that by choosing and then recombining building blocks, what we are doing is creating our own neural network, our connectionist model.

The process is similar to genetic crossover that occurs in biological evolution. Indeed, biologists agree that genetic crossover is chiefly responsible for evolution. Similarly, the constant recombination of our existing mental building blocks will, over time, be responsible for the greatest amount of investment progress. However, there are occasions when a new and rare discovery opens up new opportunities for investors. In much the same way that a mutation can accelerate the evolutionary process, so too can newfound ideas speed us along in our understanding of how markets work. If you are able to discover a new building block, you have the potential to add another level to your model of understanding.

It's important to understand that you have the opportunity to discover many new things and add new building blocks to your mental models *without ever taking undue risk.* You can throw a lot of theories and ideas into your thinking mix, assemble them into a model, and, like a pilot in a flight simulator, try them out in the marketplace. If the new building blocks prove useful, then keep them and give them the appropriate weight. But if they appear to add no value, you simply store them away and draw them up again some day in the future.

But remember, none of this will happen if you conclude that you already know enough. Never stop discovering new building blocks. When a corporation cuts its research and development budget to focus on the here and now, that may produce greater profits in the short term, but more likely it places the company in competitive jeopardy at some point in the future. Likewise, if we stop exploring for new ideas, we may still be able to navigate the stock market for a while, but most likely we are putting our-selves at a disadvantage for tomorrow's changing environment.

At the center of the University of Pennsylvania campus, where Locust Walk crosses the Thirty-Seventh Street walkway, a life-size bronze statue depicts Benjamin Franklin sitting on a park bench. He wears a ruffled shirt and knickers, a long coat and vest, and square-buckled shoes. A pair of round bifocals sits on the very tip of his nose, and he is reading a copy of the *Pennsylvania Gazette*. Of the forty-one statues of Benjamin Franklin in Philadel-phia, this one, designed by George W. Lundeen, is by far my favorite. The bench, underneath a beautiful shade tree, is a comfortable spot for a person to sit and reflect about a latticework of mental models, next to the man who so passionately advocated the value of a liberal arts education.

The Thirty-Seventh Street walkway is a major thoroughfare on the Penn campus. Each morning when class is in session, students spill out of the dormitory building called The Quadrangle and head uphill on Thirty-Seventh. When they reach the intersection with Locust Walk, they splinter off into separate groups, each group heading in a different direction to-ward the classes in their chosen discipline.

The physics and math majors turn right and head over to the David Rittenhouse Laboratory on Thirty-Third Street. Biology majors turn left and walk to the Leidy Laboratories on University Avenue. Sociology majors turn left for the Sociology Building located on Locust Walk. Psy-chology majors continue straight on Thirty-Seventh to the Psychology Building on Walnut Street. Philosophy majors turn right onto Locust and walk down to Logan Hall. The English majors walk a few more steps to Fisher Bennett Hall.

The finance students at Penn, who study at the famous Wharton School of Business, have the shortest distance to travel. As Benjamin Frank-lin watches silently, they turn right at the intersection and walk just a few steps to Steinberg Hall, Diedrich Hall, and Huntsman Hall. There they will spend the next four years taking courses on economics, management, finance, accounting, marketing, business, and public policy. At the end of the four years, with college degree in hand, most will seek a job in the fi-nancial services industry. A few will attend graduate school and earn an MBA degree for intensely studying for two more years what they have al-ready learned in the previous four.

Sitting next to Benjamin Franklin one spring afternoon, I wondered to myself what opportunities these hard-charging finance students will have when they graduate, and what additional advantages they would receive if they had spent more of their college experience studying other disciplines. With just one course in physics, they would have learned about Newton's principles, thermodynamics, relativity, and quantum mechanics. They might have been exposed to wave motion, turbulence, and nonlinearity. They might have realized that the same laws that describe the flow of lava at the earth's center or demonstrate how small-scale shifts in plate tectonics cause large earthquakes also govern the forces in financial markets.

Biology majors at Penn spend four years studying molecular biology and evolution, microbiology and genetics, neurobiology, and the biology of invertebrates and vertebrates as well as botany and plant development. But a finance major who took but one course, The Molecular Biology of Life, would have learned about the genetics of animals, bacteria, and viruses, with particular attention to the ways in which modern cell and biological molecular genetic methods contribute to our understanding of evolutionary processes. From that one course, in one semester, a perceptive student might have recognized that the patterns that exist in biology look very similar to the patterns that occur in companies and markets.

Students at the Wharton School will have spent a great deal of time studying the theory and structure of financial markets, but what additional insights could they have learned by taking Social Problems and Public Policy, Technology and Society, Sociology at Work, or Social Stratification? To be a successful investor, you need not spend four years studying sociology, but even a few courses in this discipline would increase the awareness of how various systems organize, operate, thrive, fail, and then reorganize.

Today there is little debate over the fact that psychology affects investing. How much value-added benefit to their education would finance students derive from some basic courses in psychology? Consider, perhaps, a class on Physiology of Motivated Behaviors, where students seek to learn the links between brain structure and behavioral function. Or Cognitive Psychology, which investigates the mental processes in humans, including how people use pattern recognition to determine action. Surely no finance student would pass up the opportunity to take Behavioral Economics and Psychology, which applies psychological research to economic theory to examine what happens when agents with limited cognitive capacities make strategic decisions.

To work in finance, which is a job about making decisions, how could finance majors pass up courses in modern philosophy, logic, and critical thinking? What mental tools might they acquire by studying the theories of knowledge, mind, and reality expressed by Descartes, Kant, Hegel, James, and Wittgenstein? Think of the competitive advantages they could gain from a course on critical thinking, which would give them techniques for analyzing arguments in both natural and statistical language.

Yes, I know there is a lot to read in college, but why not use one of your three unrestricted electives and take Nineteenth Century American Literature, where you will read the outstanding literary treatments of American culture from the early Federalist period to the beginnings of the First World War? Better yet, take the Creative Nonfiction Writing class, a workshop course in writing expository prose; you will learn to write formal essays on topics such as autobiography, review, interview, analysis of advertising, and popular culture.

Of course, in being a finance major you will have a great deal of math to contend with in your accounting and economics courses, but what about adding Mathematics in the Age of Information? You would learn about mathematical reasoning and the media. Often there are mathematical assumptions embedded in stories printed in the media, and this course will teach you how to recognize and question the different mathematical postulates.

Watching the students pass one by one on their way to classes in their chosen major, I can't help but wonder where they will all be in twenty-five years. Will their college education have adequately prepared them to compete at the highest level? Once they reach retirement age, will they be able to look back and measure their life's work as a success or will they see it as something less than that?

These are the same questions Charlie Munger asked his classmates at the fiftieth reunion of the Harvard Law School class of 1948.[16] "Was our education sufficiently multidisciplinary?" he asked. "In the last fifty years, how far has elite academia progressed toward attainable best-form multidisciplinarity?"

To make his point about single-focus thinking, Charlie often employs the proverb "To a man with only a hammer, every problem looks pretty much like a nail." Now, said Charlie, "One partial cure for man-with-hammer tendency is obvious: if a man has a vast set of skills over multidisciplines, he, by definition, carries multiple tools and therefore will limit bad cognitive effects from the 'man with a hammer' tendency. If 'A' is a narrow professional doctrine and 'B' consists of the big, extra-useful concepts from other disciplines, then, clearly, the professional possessing 'A' plus 'B' will usually be better off than the poor possessor of 'A' alone. How could it be otherwise?"

Charlie believes that the broadscale problems we as a society face can be solved only by placing them on a latticework that spreads across many disciplines. Therefore, he argues, educational institutions should raise the fluency of a multidisciplinary education. Admittedly, Charlie is quick to add, "We don't have to raise everyone's skill in celestial mechanics to that of Laplace and also ask everyone to achieve a similar level in all other knowledge." Remember, he said, "it turns out that the truly big ideas in each discipline, learned only in essence, carry most of the freight." Furthermore, he continued, to attain broad multidisciplinary skills does not require us to lengthen the already expensive commitment to a college education. "We all know individuals, modern Benjamin Franklins, who have achieved a massive multidisciplinary synthesis with less time in formal education than is now available to our numerous brilliant young and thus become better performers in their own disciplines, not worse, despite diversion of learning time to matters outside the normal coverage of their own disciplines." It is Charlie's belief that society would be better off if more college courses across a broader spectrum were made mandatory rather than elective.

So as we near the end of this book, we find we have come back full circle to its beginning. The challenge we face as investors and very much as individuals has less to do with the knowledge that is available than with how we choose to put the pieces together. Similarly, the main problem in education revolves around assembling the pieces of curriculum. "The ongoing fragmentation of knowledge and resulting chaos are not reflections of the real world but artifacts of scholarship," explains Edward O. Wilson in *Consilience: The Unity of Knowledge.*[17] Consilience, which Wilson describes as the "jumping together" of knowledge from various disciplines, is the only way to create a common framework of explanation.

One of the principal goals of this book is to give you a broader explanation of how markets behave and in the process help you make better investment decisions. One thing we have learned thus far is that our failures to explain are caused by our failures to describe. If we cannot accurately describe a phenomenon, it is fairly certain we will not be able to accurately explain it. The lesson we are taking away from this book is that the descriptions based solely on finance theories are not enough to explain the behavior of markets.

The art of achieving what Charlie Munger calls "worldly wisdom" is a pursuit that appears to have more in common with the ancient and medieval periods than with contemporary studies, which mostly emphasize gaining specific knowledge in one particular field. No one would disagree that over the years we have increased our baskets of knowledge, but what is surely missing today is wisdom. Our institutions of higher learning may separate knowledge into categories, but wisdom is what unites them.

Those who make an effort to acquire worldly wisdom are beneficiaries of a special gift. Scientists at the Santa Fe Institute call it emergence. Charlie Munger calls it the lollapalooza effect: the extra turbocharge that comes when basic concepts combine and move in the same direction, reinforcing each other's fundamental truths. But whatever you decide to call it, this broad-based understanding is the foundation of worldly wisdom.

The Roman poet Lucretius writes:

> Nothing is more sweet that full possession
> Of those calm heights, well built, well fortified
> By wise men's teaching, to look down from here
> At others, wandering below, men lost,
> Confused, in hectic search for the right road.

For many, many people, the financial markets are confusing, and investing has become a hectic search for the right road. But traveling more quickly down well-worn roads is not the answer. Rather, looking down from the calm heights of knowledge gained from wise men's teaching is. Those who constantly scan in all directions for what can help them make good decisions will be the successful investors of the future.

Seated on the campus park bench, Benjamin Franklin and I watch as the last of the finance students, now late for class, rush past us. I can't help but wonder if he too is thinking about their education and their future. Does he wonder if they have read broadly enough to develop "the connected idea of human affairs" he so eloquently advocated in his 1749 pamphlet? If they have begun to cultivate the habits of mind that will permit them to make connections and link ideas? If they are set on a course of lifelong learning?

He must be thinking about those things, for I think I can hear him quietly read aloud the headline on the *Gazette* he is holding: "The good education of youth has been esteemed by wise men in all ages as the sweet foundation of happiness." It is a simple formula for personal and societal success, as valid today as it was 250 years ago. It is also a timeless road map for achieving worldly wisdom.

READING LIST OF
ST. JOHN'S COLLEGE

Freshman Year

Homer: Iliad, Odyssey
Asechylus: Agamemnon, Libation Bearers, Eumenides, Prometheus Bound
Sophocles: Oedipus Rex, Oedipus at Colonus, Antigone, Philoctetes
Thucydides: History of the Peloponnesian War
Euripides: Hippolytus, Bacchae
Herodotus: Histories
Aristophanes: Clouds
Plato: Meno, Gorgias, Republic, Apology, Crito, Phaedo, Symposium, Parmenides,
    Theaetetus, Sophists, Timaeus, Phaedrus
Aristotle: Poetics, Physics, Metaphysics, Nicomachean, Ethics, On Generation and
    Corruption, Politics, Parts of Animals, Generation of Animals
Euclid: Elements
Lucretius: On the Nature of Things
Plutarch: "Lycurgus," "Solon"
Nicomachus: Arithmetic
Lavoisier: Elements of Chemistry
Harvey: Motion of the Heart and Blood
Essays by: Archimedes, Fahrenheit, Avogadro, Dalton, Cannizzaro, Virchow, Mariotte,
    Driesch, Gay-Lussac, Spemann, Stears, J. J. Thomson, Mendeleyev, Berthollet, J. L.
    Proust

Sophomore Year

The Bible
Aristotle: De Anima, On Interpretation, Prior Analytics, Categories
Apollonius: Conics
Virgil: Aeneid
Plutarch: "Caesar," "Cato the Younger"
Epictetus: Discourses, Manual
Tacitus: Annals
Ptolemy: Almagest
Plotinus: The Enneads
Augustine: Confessions
St. Anselm: Proslogium
Aquinas: Summa Theologica, Summa Contra Gentiles
Dante: Divine Comedy
Chaucer: Canterbury Tales
Des Prez: Mass
Machiavelli: The Prince, Discourses
Copernicus: On the Revolution of the Spheres
Luther: The Freedom of a Christian
Rabelais: Gargantua and Pantagruel
Palestrina: Missa Papae Marcelli
Montaigne: Essays
Viete: "Introduction on the Analytical Art"
Bacon: Novum Organum
Shakespeare: Richard II, Henry IV, Henry V, The Tempest, As You Like It, Hamlet,
    Othello, Macbeth, King Lear, Coriolanus, Sonnets
Poems by: Marvell, Donne, and other sixteenth- and seventeenth-century poets
Descartes: Geometry, Discourse on Method
Pascal: Generation of Conic Sections
Bach: St. Matthew Passion, Inventions
Haydn: Quartets
Mozart: Operas
Beethoven: Sonatas
Schubert: Songs
Stravinsky: Symphony of Psalms

Junior Year

Cervantes: *Don Quixote*
Galileo: Two New Sciences
Hobbes: Leviathan
Descartes: Meditations, Rules for the Direction of the Mind

Milton: Paradise Lost
La Rochefoucauld: Maxims
La Fontaine: Fables
Pascal: Pensées
Huygens: Treatise on Light, On the Movement of Bodies by Impact
Eliot: Middlemarch
Spinoza: Theological-Political Treatise
Locke: Second Treatise on Government
Racine: Phaedra
Newton: Principia Mathematica
Kepler: Epitome IV
Leibniz: Monadology, Discourse on Metaphysics, Essay on Dynamics, Philosophical
   Essays, Principles of Nature and Grace
Swift: Gulliver's Travels
Hume: Treatise on Human Nature
Rousseau: The Social Contract, On the Origin of Inequality
Molière: The Misanthrope
Adam Smith: Wealth of Nations
Kant: Critique of Pure Reason, Foundations of the Metaphysics of Morals
Mozart: Don Giovanni
Jane Austen: Pride and Prejudice
Dedekind: Essays on the Theory of Numbers
Essays by: Young, Maxwell, Taylor, Euler, D. Bernoulli

Senior Year

Articles of Confederation
Declaration of Independence
Constitution of the United States
Supreme Court Opinions
Hamilton, Jay, and Madison: *The Federalist Papers*
Darwin: *Origin of Species*
Hegel: *Phenomenology of Mind*, "*Logic*" (from the *Encyclopedia*)
Lobachevsky: *Theory of Parallels*
De Tocqueville: *Democracy in America*
Kierkegaard: *Philosophical Fragments, Fear and Trembling*
Wagner: *Tristan and Isolde*
Marx: *Capital, Political and Economic Manuscripts of 1844, The German Ideology*
Dostoyevsky: *Brothers Karamazov*
Tolstoy: *War and Peace*
Melville: *Benito Cereno*
Twain: *Adventures of Huckleberry Finn*
O'Connor: Selected Stories

William James: *Psychology: Briefer Course*
Nietzsche: *Birth of Tragedy, Thus Spake Zarathustra, Beyond Good and Evil*
Freud: *General Introduction to Psychoanalysis*
Valery: Poems
Booker T. Washington: Selected Writings
Du Bois: *The Souls of Black Folk*
Heidegger: *What Is Philosophy?*
Heisenberg: *The Physical Principles of the Quantum Theory*
Einstein: Selected Papers
Millikan: *The Electron*
Conrad: *Heart of Darkness*
Faulkner: *The Bear*
Poems by: Yeats, T. S. Eliot, Wallace Stevens, Baudelaire, Rimbaud
Essays by: Faraday, J. J. Thomson, Mendel, Minkowski, Rutherford, Davisson, Schrodinger, Bohr, Maxwell, de Broglie, Dreisch, Ørsted, Ampère, Boveri, Sutton, Morgan, Beadle and Tatum, Sussman, Watson and Crick, Jacob and Monod, Hardy

NOTES

1. A Latticework of Mental Models

1. Charles Munger's complete presentation to Dr. Babcock's class, in lightly edited form, appears in the May 5, 1995, edition of *Outstanding Investor Digest* (*OID*), from which the passages quoted here are taken.

2. Benjamin Franklin, "Proposals Relating to the Education of the Youth in Pensilvania," 1749. All quotes from Franklin in this section of the chapter are taken from this pamphlet, with his original spelling intact.

3. Professor Richard Beeman, interviewed by author, December 23, 1999.

4. George Lakoff and Mark Johnson, *Metaphors We Live By* (Chicago: University of Chicago Press, 1980), 3.

5. Munger's remarks to the Stanford class and his answers to questions from students appear in two issues of *Outstanding Investor Digest*, December 29, 1997, and March 13, 1998. Readers are encouraged to read the lecture, which *OID* editor Henri Emerson aptly describes as "Worldly Wisdom Revisited," in its entirety.

2. Physics

1. Sir Isaac Newton's first law of motion states that a moving object will continue to move in a straight line at a constant speed, and a stationary object will remain at rest unless acted on by an unbalanced force; this is the law of inertia. The second law

states that the acceleration produced on a body by a force is proportional to the magnitude of the force and inversely proportional to the mass of the object. The third law states that for every action there is an equal and opposite reaction.

2. Alfred Marshall takes another turn on our stage in Chapter 3.

3. Alfred Marshall, *Principles of Economics*, 8th ed. (Philadelphia: Porcupine Press, 1920), 276.

4. Ibid., 269.

5. Ibid., 287.

6. Ibid., 288.

7. Paul Samuelson, quoted in Peter L. Bernstein, *Capital Ideas: The Improbable Origins of Modern Wall Street* (New York: The Free Press, 1992), 113.

8. Ibid., 37.

9. Louis Bachelier, quoted in Bernstein, *Capital Ideas*, 21.

10. Paul Samuelson, "Proof That Properly Anticipated Prices Fluctuate Randomly," *Industrial management review* 6 (Spring 1965).

11. William F. Sharpe, "Capital Asset Prices: A Theory of Market Equilibrium under Conditions of Risk," *Journal of finance* 19, no. 3 (Summer 1964), 4336.

12. Brian Arthur et al., "Asset Pricing under Endogenous Expectations in an Artificial Stock Market" (working paper 96-12-093, Santa Fe Institute Economics Research Program, 1996).

3. Biology

1. Erasmus Darwin, a prominent and highly successful doctor, was also a poet. It was in his poetry, principally "Zoonomia," that he chose to express his speculations about evolution, in which he was decidedly ahead of his time. His contemporary, Samuel Taylor Coleridge, took to calling his friend's theories "darwinizing." Although in later years Charles Darwin would claim he was not particularly influenced by his grandfather's theories, it seems impossible that he was unaware of them.

2. Francis Darwin, ed., *The Autobiography of Charles Darwin* (New York: Dover Publications, 1958).

3. For all that Charles Darwin was able to accomplish, he was not able to explain how variations in species occurred. That question was settled by Gregor Johann Mendel, an Austrian botanist and plant experimenter, who was the first to present a mathematical foundation of the science of genetics. Today, biologists understand that variations within a species are caused by the variations of the genes of its individual members.

4. Richard Dawkins, "International Books of the Year and the Millennium," *Times literary supplement* (December 3, 1999).

5. American economists were paying attention, too. Most notable among them at the time was Thorstein Veblen at the University of Chicago. Today his reputation rests on his primary work, *The Theory of the Leisure Class,* in which he described his notion of conspicuous consumption. In his own time, his scholarly reputation was

somewhat overshadowed by his eccentric personal behavior and by his sardonic, satiric style of writing. Many contemporaries simply missed the satire. He frequently called for an evolutionary, post-Darwinian approach to the study of economics; unfortunately, he was light on specific details. Nonetheless, some of today's scholars credit him as a pioneer in this approach. British economist Geoffrey Hodgson, for example, claims "Veblen's writings constitute the first case of an evolutionary economics along Darwinian lines." (G. M. Hodgson, "On the Evolution of Thorstein Veblen's Evolutionary Economics," *Cambridge journal of economics* 22 [1998]: 415–431.)

6. The poignancy is that, despite years of work, he never completed volume 2.

7. *The Theory of Economic Development* was of course written in Schumpeter's native German. The common translation of the title is somewhat misleading. The German word *entwicklung*, usually translated as "development," also means "evolution." In fact, Schumpeter himself wrote to a colleague, while the book was in press, that the title was *The Theory of Economic Evolution*. (Esben Andersen, "Schumpeter's General Theory of Social Evolution" [paper presented at the Conference on Neo-schumpeterian Economics, Trest, Czech Republic, June 2006].)

8. Christopher Freeman, in *Techno-economic Paradigms: Essays in Honor of Carlota Perez* (London, UK: Anthem Press, 2009), 126.

9. Sylvia Nasar, *Grand Pursuit: The Story of Economic Genius* (New York: Simon & Schuster, 2011).

10. Ibid.

11. Alfred Marshall, *Principles of Economics* (Philadelphia: Porcupine Press, 1994).

12. Thomas S. Kuhn, *The Structure of Scientific Revolutions* (Chicago: University of Chicago Press, [1962] 1970), 90.

13. In an intriguing bit of serendipity, the conference, many months in the planning, was held in 1987, the same year as the stock market debacle that caused many people to question the concept of absolute equilibrium in the market.

14. J. Doyne Farmer, "Market Force, Ecology, and Evolution" (working paper, version 4.1, Santa Fe Institute, February 14, 2000).

15. Ibid., 1, 34.

16. J. Doyne Farmer and Andrew W. Lo, "Frontiers of Finance: Evolution and Efficient Markets" (working paper 99–06–039, Santa Fe Institute April 11, 1999).

17. Ibid.

18. Jane Jacobs, *The Nature of Economies* (New York: Modern Library, 2000), 137.

4. Sociology

1. *Church of England quarterly review* (1850), 142.

2. Norman Johnson, S. Ramsussed, and M. Kantor, "The Symbiotic Intelligence Project: Self-Organizing Knowledge on Distributed Networks Driven by Human Interaction," Los Alamos National Laboratory, LA-UR-98–1150, 1998.

3. Marco Dorigo, Gianni Di Caro, and Luca M. Gambardella, "An Algorithm for Discrete Optimization," *Artificial life* 5, no. 3 (1999): 137–172.

4. We have observed anecdotal evidence of emergent behavior, perhaps without realizing what we were seeing. The bestseller *Blind Man's Bluff: The Untold Story of American Submarine Espionage*, by Sherry Sontag and Christopher Drew, presents a very compelling example of emergence. Early in the book, the authors relate a story of the 1966 crash of a B-52 carrying four atomic bombs. Three of the four bombs were soon recovered, but a fourth remained missing, with the Soviets quickly closing in. A naval engineer named John Craven was given the task of locating the missing bomb. He constructed several different scenarios of what possibly could have happened to the fourth bomb and asked members of his salvage team to wager a bet on where they thought the bomb could be. He then ran each possible location through a computer formula and—without ever going to sea— was able to pinpoint the exact location of the bomb based on a collective solution.

5. James Surowiecki, *The Wisdom of Crowds: Why the Many Are Smarter Than the Few and How Collective Wisdom Shapes Businesses, Economics, Societies, and Nations* (New York: Doubleday, 2004), xvi.

6. Ibid., xvi.

7. Ibid., xv.

8. Ibid., 41.

9. Scott E. Page, *The Difference: How the Power of Diversity Creates Better Groups, Firms, Schools, and Societies* (Princeton, NJ: Princeton University Press, 2007).

10. Ibid., 13.

11. Ibid., 13.

12. Michael J. Mauboussin, *Think Twice: Harnessing the Power of Counterintuition* (Boston: Harvard Business Press, 2009, 50.

13. Ibid., 55.

14. Per Bak, M. Paczuski, and M. Shubik, "Price Variations in a Stock Market with Many Agents" (working paper 96–09–078, Santa Fe Institute Economics Research Program, 1996).

15. Diana Richards, B. McKay, and W. Richards, "Collective Choice and Mutual Knowledge Structures," *Advances in complex systems* 1 (1998): 221–236.

5. Psychology

1. Michael Lewis, "The King of Human Error," *Vanity fair* (December 2011): 154.

2. Richard Thaler and Shlomo Benartzi, "Myopic Loss Aversion and the Equity Risk Premium Puzzle," *Quarterly journal of economics* 110, no. 1 (February 1995): 80.

3. Buffett paraphrases Benjamin Graham's famous quote, "Investment is most intelligent when it is business-like." Benjamin Graham, *The Intelligent Investor* (New York: Harper & Row, [1949] 1973), 286.

4. The frequency with which stocks and portfolios outperform the market on a frequency basis is rarely 100 percent. I have spent a good deal of time looking at holding periods of both individual stocks and portfolios and have found that the ones that

do outperform over long periods of time seem to do so about 40–60 percent of the periods. (See Robert G. Hagstrom, *The Warren Buffett Portolio: Mastering the Power of the Focus Investment Strategy* [New York: John Wiley & Sons, 1999].) Still, there is much work to be done in this research area.

5. Charles Ellis, "A Conversation with Benjamin Graham," *Financial analysts journal* (September/October 1976): 20.

6. Graham, *Intelligent Investor,* 107.

7. Terrance Odean, "Do Investors Trade Too Much?" *American economic review* (December 1999).

8. Terrance Odean and Brad Barber, "Trading Is Hazardous to Your Wealth: The Common Stock Investment Performance of Individual Investors," *Journal of finance* 55, no. 2 (April 2000).

9. Terrance Odean and Brad Barber, "The Internet and the Investor," *Journal of economic perspectives* 15, no. 1 (Winter 2001).

10. Hagstrom, *Warren Buffett Portfolio,* 155.

11. Ibid.

12. Ibid.

13. Michael Lupfer and Mark Jones, "Risk Taking as a Function of Skill and Chance Orientations," *Psychological reports* 28 (1971): 27–32.

14. In this respect, the phrase "mental models" as used here is more specific than Charlie Munger's use of the same phrase; his meaning is closer to "key principle, core idea" than to a sense of dimensional representation.

15. Kenneth Craik, *The Nature of Explanation* (London: Cambridge University Press, 1952).

16. Michael Shermer, *How We Believe* (New York: W. H. Freeman, 2000), 36.

17. Fischer Black, quoted in Peter L. Bernstein, *Capital Ideas: The Improbable Origins of Modern Wall Street* (New York: The Free Press, 1992), 124.

18. Claude Shannon, "A Mathematical Theory of Communication," *The Bell Systems technical journal* (July 1948).

19. Charles T. Munger, *Outstanding investor digest* (May 5, 1995): 51.

6. Philosophy

1. Lee McIntyre, "Complexity: A Philosopher's Reflections," *Complexity* 3, no. 6 (1998): 26.

2. Ibid., 27.

3. Ibid., 28.

4. Benoit Mandelbrot, "Introduction," *The Fractal Geometry of Nature* (New York: W. H. Freeman, 1982).

5. Brian McGuinness, *Wittgenstein: A Life—Young Ludwig 1889–1921* (Berkeley, CA: University of California Press, 1988), 118.

6. Ludwig Wittgenstein, *Philosophical Investigations* (Englewood Cliffs, NJ: Prentice-Hall, 1958), v.

7. Douglas Lackey, "What Are the Modern Classics? The Baruch Poll of Great Philosophy in the Twentieth Century," *Philosophical forum* 30, no. 4 (December 1999): 329–345.

8. Wittgenstein, *Philosophical Investigations*, 200.

9. Amazon.com has been owned in my portfolios at Legg Mason Capital Management since 2003. It continues to be a top holding for the fund as well as our firm's institutional separate accounts.

10. Susan Crawford, "The New Digital Divide," *New York times, Sunday review* (December 4, 2011): 1.

11. Rita Charon, MD, PhD, "Narrative Medicine," *JAMA* 286, no. 15 (October 17, 2001).

12. C. P. Snow, *The Two Cultures* (The Rede Lecture, Cambridge, UK, May 7, 1959), in *The Two Cultures and the Scientific Revolution* (1963).

13. John Allen Paulos, *Once Upon a Number: The Hidden Mathematical Logic of Stories* (New York: Basic Books, 1998), 12.

14. John Allen Paulos, "Stories vs. Statistics," *New York times* (October 24, 2010), http://www.NYTimes.com.

15. Ibid.

16. James Boswell, quoted in John Allen Paulos, *A Mathematician Reads the Newspaper* (New York: Basic Books, 1995), 6.

17. Charles S. Peirce, "How to Make Our Ideas Clear," *Popular science monthly* (January 1878). Also in *Pragmatism: A Reader*, ed. Louis Menand (New York: Random House, 1997), 26.

18. William James, "Pragmatism: Conception of Truth," lecture 6 in *Pragmatism* (New York: Dover Publications, [1907] 1995), 30.

19. Ibid., 22.

20. Ibid., 23.

21. Ibid., 24.

22. Ibid., 26.

23. Ibid., 31.

24. Correct use of the dividend discount model requires us to make difficult calculations. What will be the future growth rate of the company over its lifetime? How much cash will the company generate? What is the appropriate discount rate for projecting the growth of cash flows? Answers to these tough questions are necessary input variables. Adding to the difficulty is the fear that the uncertainty of long-range forecasts makes using the model suspect. A further difficulty is that determining value is highly sensitive to its initial condition; even a slight change in growth rate or discount factor can have a large effect on value. For this reason, investors often use shortcuts (second-order models) to determine value.

25. James, *Pragmatism*, 321–324.

26. I am grateful to my friend and colleague Bill Miller for his insights on the philosophy of pragmatism and how it relates to the philosophy of investing.

7. Literature

1. A number of other institutions of higher learning have special liberal arts programs grounded in the works of history's greatest thinkers. Some are part of the university's honors programs while others are short-term intensive-study programs. St. John's is the only university I am aware of that is dedicated to teaching the "great books," and its list of curriculum materials is continuously reviewed and updated.

2. Indeed, St. John's dates back to 1696, five years before Yale was founded, fifty years before Princeton, and fifty-three years before Franklin's famous education manifesto.

3. Don Bell and Lee Munson were interviewed by the author June 7, 2000; Greg Curtis was interviewed November 10, 2011; Steve Bohlin was interviewed December 15, 2011.

4. Mortimer Adler served as editor of the fifty-four-volume *Great Books of the Western World* and as chairman of *Encyclopedia Britannica's* board of editors for twenty years. Until his death on June 28, 2011, he remained active writing and speaking on his lifelong passion: the value of a broad general education based in the humanities.

5. Few reference works in any discipline have the staying power of *How to Read a Book*. The copy I own is from the thirty-sixth printing of the revised edition.

6. Mortimer Adler and Charles Van Doren, *How to Read a Book*, rev. ed. (New York: Simon & Schuster, [1940] 1972), 46–47.

7. Ibid., 291.

8. Ibid., 301.

9. Ibid., 205.

10. Benjamin Doty was interviewed by the author on November 27, 2011.

11. Rolf Potts, "Cannon Fodder," *The New Yorker* (May 2, 2011): 22–23.

12. Robert G. Hagstrom, *The Detective and the Investor* (New York: John Wiley & Sons, 2002).

13. Alan Jacobs, *The Pleasure of Reading in an Age of Distraction* (Oxford: Oxford University Press, 2011).

14. Charlie Munger (address at Stanford Law School, Stanford, CA, 1996), reprinted in *Outstanding investor digest* (March 13, 1998): 58.

15. Ibid., 61, 63.

8. Mathematics

1. Warren Buffett, *Berkshire Hathaway 2000 Annual Report*, 13.

2. Robert G. Hagstrom, *The Warren Buffett Way: Investment Strategies of the World's Greatest Investor* (New York: John Wiley & Sons, 1994).

3. Peter L. Bernstein, *Against the Gods: The Remarkable Story of Risk* (New York: John Wiley & Sons, 1996), 3.

4. Ibid.

5. Ibid.

6. Sharon Bertsch McGrayne, *The Theory That Would Not Die* (New Haven: Yale University Press, 2011), 8.

7. Charles T. Munger, *Outstanding investor digest* (May 5, 1995): 49.

8. Robert L. Winkler, *An Introduction to Bayesian Inference and Decision* (New York: Holt, Rinehart and Winston, 1972), 17.

9. J. L. Kelly's most celebrated moment occurred in 1962 when he programmed an IBM 704 computer to synthesize speech. Kelly had built a "vocoder" (voice recorder synthesizer) and recreated the song "Daisy Bell" with musical accompaniment from Max Mathews. Coincidentally, Arthur C. Clarke was visiting the Bell Labs at the same time. Science fiction buffs already get the connection. In *2001: A Space Odyssey*, the computer HAL 9000 sings "Daisy Bell" as he is being put to sleep by astronaut Dave Bowman.

10. J. L. Kelly Jr., "A New Interpretation of Information Rate," *The Bell Systems technical journal* 35, no. 3 (July 1956).

11. Ed Thorp, interviewed by the author, November 25, 1998.

12. The following section is based on a 1985 article in *Discover* titled, "The Median Isn't the Message" and on Stephen Jay Gould, "Case One: A Personal Story," chap. 4 in *Full House: The Spread of Excellence from Darwin to Plato* (New York: Three Rivers Press, 1996).

13. Sam L. Savage, *The Flaw of Averages: Why We Underestimate Risk in the Face of Uncertainty* (New York: John Wiley & Sons, 2009), 11.

14. Robert G. Hagstrom, "Who's Afraid of a Sideways Market?" *Legg Mason perspectives* (January 2010).

15. Gould, *Full House*, 41.

16. Bernstein, *Against the Gods,* 162.

17. Sir Francis Galton, quoted in Bernstein, *Against the Gods,* 167. It is referenced in the biography by D. W. Forest, *Francis Galton: The Life and Work of a Victorian Genius* (New York: Taplinger, 1974).

18. Gottfried Leibniz, quoted in Bernstein, *Against the Gods,* 329.

19. Nassim Nicholas Taleb, *The Black Swan: The Impact of the Highly Improbable* (New York: Random House, 2007), xvii.

20. William Safire, "On Language: Fat Tail," *New York Times* (2009), http://www.nytimes.com/2009/02/08/magazine/08wwwln-safire-y.html.

21. Kenneth Arrow, quoted in Bernstein, *Against the Gods,* 7.

22. Bernstein, *Against the Gods,* 207.

23. Gilbert Keith Chesterton, "The Paradoxes of Christianity," chap. 6 in *Orthodoxy* (Charleston, SC: BiblioBazaar, [1908] 2007).

9. Decision Making

1. These three puzzles can be found in Shane Frederick, "Cognitive Reflection and Decision Making," *Journal of economic perspectives* 19, no. 4 (Fall 2005): 25–42. The ball costs $.05. It takes 5 minutes for 100 machines to make 100 widgets. It will take 47 days for the lily pad to cover half the lake.

2. Daniel Kahneman, *Thinking Fast and Slow* (New York: Farrar, Straus, and Giroux, 2001), 241.

3. Daniel Kahneman and Shane Frederick, "Representativeness Revisited: Attribute Substitution in Intuitive Judgment," in *Heuristics and Biases: The Psychology of Misjudgment,* ed. Thomas Gilovich, Dale Griffin, Daniel Kahneman (Cambridge: Cambridge University Press, 2002), 54.

4. Philip E. Tetlock, *Expert Political Judgment: How Good Is It? How Can We Know?* (Princeton: Princeton University Press, 2005).

5. Philip Tetlock, "Why Foxes Are Better Forecasters Than Hedgehogs," Seminars About Long-Term Thinking, hosted by Stewart Brand, January 26, 2007.

6. Jahanbegolo Ramin, *Conversations with Isaiah Berlin* (London: Halban Publishers, 2007), 188.

7. Philip Tetlock, "Coming to Existential Terms with Unpredictability" (presentation to the Legg Mason Capital Management Thought Leader Forum, Baltimore, MD, October 6–7, 2011).

8. Keith Stanovich, *What Intelligence Tests Miss: The Psychology of Rational Thought* (New Haven: Yale University Press, 2009). Also see Keith Stanovich, "Rationality versus Intelligence," Project Syndicate (2009–04–06), http://www.project-syndicate.org.

9. Keith Stanovich, "Rational and Irrational Thought: The Thinking That IQ Tests Miss," *Scientific American mind* (November/December 2009): 35.

10. D. N. Perkins, "Mindware and Metacurriculum," *Creating the Future: Perspectives on Educational Change,* comp. and ed. Dee Dickinson (Baltimore: Johns Hopkins University School of Education, 2002).

11. Ibid.

12. Ibid.

13. Kahneman, *Thinking Fast and Slow,* 4.

14. Ibid., 46.

15. I am indebted to John Holland, professor of psychology and engineering and computer science at the University of Michigan, for his graceful presentation on the concepts of building blocks, the need for models that are dynamic, and the flight simulator analogy.

16. Charles T. Munger, "The Need for More Multidisciplinary Skill," (presentation, Fiftieth Reunion of the Harvard Law School Class Graduated in 1948, Cambridge, MA, May 1998). The full text of the speech appears in Appendix B of Janet Lowe's book, *Damn Right: Behind the Scenes with Berkshire Hathaway Billionaire Charlie Munger* (New York: Vintage Books, 1999), 8.

17. Edward O. Wilson, *Consilience: The Unity of Knowledge* (New York: Vintage Books, 1999), 8.

BIBLIOGRAPHY

Chapter 1—A Latticework of Mental Models

Bell, Daniel. *The Reforming of General Education*. New York: Columbia University Press, 1996.

Bevelin, Peter. *Seeing Wisdom: From Darwin to Munger*. Malmo, Sweden: Post Scriptum AB, 2003.

Birkhoff, Garrett. *Lattice Theory*. Providence, RI: American Mathematical Society, 1979.

Black, Max. *Models and Metaphors: Studies in Language and Philosophy*, rev. ed. Ithaca, NY: Cornell University Press, 1966.

Burke, James. *Connections*. Boston: Little Brown, 1978.

Farmer, J. Doyne. "A Rosetta Stone for Connectionism." *Physica D*, vol. 42 (1990).

Franklin, Benjamin. *Autobiography*. Numerous editions of Franklin's fascinating work are available today.

Holland, John H. *Emergence: From Chaos to Emergence*. Reading, MA: Helix Books, a division of Addison-Wesley, 1995.

———. *Hidden Order: How Adaptation Builds Complexity*. Reading, MA: Addison-Wesley, 1995.

Lakoff, George and Mark Johnson. *Metaphors We Live By*. Chicago: University of Chicago Press, 1980.

Locke, John. *Some Thoughts Concerning Education*. 1693.

Lucas, Christopher. *Crisis in the Academy: Rethinking American Higher Education in America*. New York: St. Martin's, 1998.

Milton, John. "Of Education." 1644.

Munger, Charles T. *Poor Charlie's Almanack*. Virginia Beach, VA: Dunning Company, 2005.

Van Doren, Carl. *Benjamin Franklin*. This Pulitzer Prize–winning biography of Franklin, originally written in 1934, has been produced in numerous editions by several publishers.

Wilson, Edward O. *Consilience: The Unity of Knowledge*. New York: Alfred A. Knopf, 1998.

Chapter 2—Physics

Anderson, Philip W., Kenneth J. Arrow, and David Pines, eds. *The Economy as an Evolving Complex System*. Reading, MA: Perseus Books, 1988.

Arthur, Brian W., Steve N. Durlauf, and David A. Lane, eds. *The Economy as an Evolving Complex System II*. Reading, MA: Addison-Wesley, 1997.

Arthur, Brian, et al. "Asset Pricing under Endogenous Expectations in an Artificial Stock Market." Working paper for SFI Economics Research Program, 96–09–075, 1996.

Bak, Per, M. Paczuski, and M. Subik. "Price Variation in a Stock Market with Many Agents." Working paper for SFI Economics Research Program, 96–09–075, 1996.

Bernstein, Peter L. *Capital Ideas: The Improbable Origins of Modern Wall Street*. New York: The Free Press, 1992.

Bronowski, Jacob. *The Ascent of Man*. Boston: Little Brown, 1973.

Dolnick, Edward. *The Clockwork Universe: Isaac Newton, the Royal Society and the Birth of the Modern World*. New York: Harper Collins, 2011.

Fama, Eugene. "Efficient Capital Markets: A Review of Theory and Empirical Work." *Journal of Finance* vol. 25, no. 2 (May 1970).

Farmer, J. Doyne. "Physicists Attempt to Scale the Ivory Towers of Finance." Working paper for SFI Economics Research Program, 99–10–073, 1999.

Farmer, J. Doyne and Andrew Lo. "Frontier of Finance: Evolution and Efficient Markets." Working paper for SFI Economics Research Program, 99–06–039, 1999.

Gell-Mann, Murray. *The Quark and the Jaguar: Adventures in the Simple and the Complex*. New York: W. H. Freeman, 1994.

Gleick, James. *Chaos: Making a New Science*. New York: Penguin Books, 1987.

———. *Isaac Newton*. New York: Pantheon Books, 2003.

Johnson, George. *Fire in the Mind: Science, Faith, and the Search for Order*. New York: Vintage Books, 1996.

Lo, Andrew W. and Craig A. MacKinlay. *A Non-Random Walk down Wall Street*. Princeton, NJ: Princeton University Press, 1999.

Mantegna, Rosario and Eugene H. Stanley. *An Introduction to Econophysics: Correlations and Complexity in Finance*. Cambridge: Cambridge University Press, 2000.

Marshall, Alfred. *Principles of Economics*. 8th ed. Philadelphia: Porcupine Press, 1920.

Newton, Issac. *The Principia: Mathematical Principles of Natural Philosophy*. Los Angeles: University of California Press, 1999.

Nicolis, Gregoire and Illya Prigogine. *Exploring Complexity: An Introduction*. New York: W. H. Freeman, 1989.

Samuelson, Paul A. "Proof That Properly Anticipated Prices Fluctuate Randomly." *Industrial Management Review* vol. 6 (Spring, 1965).

Samuelson, Paul A. and William D. Nordhaus. *Economics*. 12th ed. New York: McGraw-Hill, 1985.

Sharpe, William F. "Capital Asset Prices: A Theory of Market Equilibrium under Conditions of Risk." *Journal of Finance* vol. 19, no. 3 (Summer 1964).

Strathern, Paul. *The Big Idea: Newton and Gravity*. New York: Doubleday, 1997.

Trefil, James and Robert M. Hazen. *The Sciences: An Integrated Approach*. New York: John Wiley & Sons, 2000.

Westfall, Richard S. *The Life of Isaac Newton*. New York: Cambridge University Press, 1994.

Chapter 3—Biology

Christensen, Clayton. *The Innovator's Dilemma*. Boston: Harvard Business School Press, 1997.

Christensen, Clayton and Michael E. Raynor. *The Innovator's Solution*. Boston: Harvard University Press, 2003.

Colinvaux, Paul. *Why Big Fierce Animals Are Rare*. Princeton, NJ: Princeton University Press, 1978.

Darwin, Charles. *The Origin of Species*. Reprint, New York: Gramercy Books, 1979.

———. *Voyage of the Beagle*. Reprint, London: Penguin Books, 1989.

Darwin, Francis, ed. *The Autobiography of Charles Darwin*. Reprint, New York: Dover Publications, 1958. Originally published in 1893 as *Charles Darwin, His Life Told in an Autobiographical Chapter and in a Selected Series of His Letters, edited by his son*.

Dawkins, Richard. *The Selfish Gene*. New York: Oxford University Press, 1976.

———. *The Blind Watchmaker*. New York: W. W. Norton, 1996.

Dennett, Daniel C. *Darwin's Dangerous Ideas*. New York: Simon & Schuster, 1995.

Foster, Richard and Sarah Kaplan. *Creative Destruction*. New York: Doubleday, 2001.

Frank, Robert H. *The Darwin Economy*. Princeton, NJ: Princeton University Press, 2011.

Gould, Stephen Jay. *Dinosaur in a Haystack*. New York: Crown, 1995.

Haeckel, Stephan. *Adaptive Enterprise*. Boston: Harvard University Press, 1999.

Jacobs, Jane. *The Nature of Economies*. New York: Modern Library, 2000.

Jones, Steve. *Almost Like a Whale*. London: Doubleday, 1999.

Kuhn, Thomas S. *The Structure of Scientific Revolutions*. Chicago: University of Chicago Press, (1962) 1970.

Marshall, Alfred. *Principles of Economics*. Philadelphia: Porcupine Press, 1994.

Martel, Leon. *Mastering Change.* New York: Simon & Schuster, 1986.

Mayr, Ernst. *The Growth of Biological Thought.* Cambridge: Harvard University Press, 1982.

McCraw, Thomas K. *Prophet of Innovation: Joseph Schumpeter and Creative Destruction.* Cambridge: Harvard University Press, 2007.

Nasar, Sylvia. *Grand Pursuit: The Story of Economic Genius.* New York: Simon & Schuster, 2011.

Ormerod, Paul. *Butterfly Economics.* New York: Pantheon Books, 1998.

Ridley, Mark. *Evolution.* Cambridge, MA: Blackwell Science, 1996.

Rothschild, Michael. *Bionomics: Economy as Ecosystem.* New York: Henry Holt, 1990.

Schumpeter, Joseph A. *Capitalism, Socialism and Democracy.* New York: Harper & Row, 1950.

Weibull, Jorgen. *Evolutionary Game Theory.* Cambridge: The MIT Press, 1995.

Chapter 4—Sociology

Axelrod, Robert. *The Complexity of Cooperation.* Princeton, NJ: Princeton University Press, 1997.

Axelrod, Robert and Michael D. Cohen. *Harnessing Complexity.* New York: The Free Press, 1999.

Bak, Per. *How Nature Works.* New York: Copernicus, Springer-Verlag, 1996.

Barabasi, Albert-Laszlo. *Linked: The New Science of Networks.* Cambridge, MA: Perseus Publishing, 2002.

de la Vega, Joseph. *Confusion de Confusiones* (Confusion of Confusions). New York: John Wiley & Sons, (1688) 1996.

Fydman, Roman and Michael D. Goldberg. *Beyond Mechanical Markets.* Princeton, NJ: Princeton University Press, 2011.

Grodon, Deborah. *Ants at Work: How an Insect Society Is Organized.* New York: The Free Press, 1999.

Holland, John H. *Emergence: From Chaos to Order.* Reading, MA: Addison-Wesley Publishing, 1998.

Holldobler, Bert and Edward O. Wilson. *Journey to the Ants.* Cambridge: Harvard University Press, 1994.

Johnson, Steve. *Emergence: The Connected Lives of Ants, Brains, Cities, and Software.* New York: Scribner, 2001.

Kindleberger, Charles P. *Manias, Panics, and Crashes.* New York: John Wiley & Sons, 1978.

Krugman, Paul. *The Self-Organizing Economy.* Malden, MA: Blackwell, 1996.

Le Bon, Gustave. *The Crowd: A Study of the Popular Mind.* New York: Penguin Books, 1970.

Mackay, Charles. *Extraordinary Popular Delusions and the Madness of Crowds.* Published together with De La Vega, Joseph. *Confusion de Confusiones* (Confusion of Confusions). New York: John Wiley & Sons—Investment Classics, 1996.

Mauboussin, Michael J. *More Than You Know: Finding Financial Wisdom in Unconventional Places*. New York: Columbia University Press, 2006.

———. *Think Twice: Harnessing the Power of Counterintuition*. Boston: Harvard Business School Press, 2009.

Miller, John H. and Scott E. Page. *Complex Adaptive Systems*. Princeton, NJ: Princeton University Press, 2007.

Page, Scott E. *The Difference: How the Power of Diversity Creates Better Groups, Firms, Schools, and Societies*. Princeton, NJ: Princeton University Press, 2007.

———. *Diversity and Complexity*. Princeton, NJ: Princeton University Press, 2011.

Schweitzer, Frank, ed. *Self-Organization of Complex Structures: From Individuals to Collective Dynamics*. Amsterdam: Gordon and Breach Science Publishers, 1997.

Smith, Adam. *An Inquiry into the Nature and Causes of the Wealth of Nations*. Reprint, New York: Modern Library, 1937.

Sontag, Sherry and Christopher Drew. *Blind Man's Bluff: The Story of American Submarine Espionage*. New York: Public Affairs, 1998.

Sumner, William Graham. *Social Darwinism: Selected Essays*. Englewood Cliffs, NJ: Prentice-Hall, 1963.

Surowiecki, James. *The Wisdom of the Crowds: Why the Many Are Smarter than the Few and How Collective Wisdom Shapes Businesses, Economics, Societies, and Nations*. New York: Doubleday, 2004.

Wilson, Edward O. *In Search of Nature*. Washington, DC: Island Press, 1996.

Chapter 5—Psychology

Belsky, Gary and Thomas Gilovich. *Why Smart People Make Big Money Mistakes*. New York: Simon & Schuster, 1999.

Bernstein, Peter L. *Capital Ideas: The Improbable Origins of Modern Wall Street*. New York: The Free Press, 1992.

Chancellor, Edward. *Devil Take the Hindmost*. New York: Farrar, Straus & Giroux, 1999.

Cialdini, Robert B. *Influence: The Psychology of Persuasion*. New York: William Morrow, 1993.

Craik, Kenneth. *The Nature of Explanation*. London: Cambridge University Press, (1943) 1952.

de la Vega, Joseph. *Confusion de Confusiones* (Confusion of Confusions). New York: John Wiley & Sons, 1996.

Fox, Justin. *The Myth of the Rational Market*. New York: Harper Business, 2009.

Gilovich, Thomas. *How We Know What Isn't So*. New York: The Free Press, 1991.

Gilovich, Thomas, Dale Griffin, and Daniel Kahneman. *Heuristics and Biases: The Psychology of Intuitive Judgment*. Cambridge: Cambridge University Press, 2002.

Graham, Benjamin. *The Intelligent Investor*. New York: Harper & Row, (1949) 1973.

Graham, Benjamin and David Dodd. *Security Analysis*. New York: McGraw-Hill, (1934) 1951.

Hagstrom, Robert G. *The Warren Buffett Portfolio: Mastering the Power of the Focus Investment Strategy.* New York: John Wiley & Sons, 1999.

Johnson-Laird, Philip N. *Mental Models.* Cambridge: Harvard University Press, 1983.

Kahneman, Daniel, Paul Slovic, and Amos Tversky. *Judgment under Uncertainty: Heuristics and Biases.* Cambridge: Cambridge University Press, 1982.

Kindleberger, Charles P. *Manias, Panics, and Crashes.* New York: John Wiley & Sons, 1996.

Le Bon, Gustave. *The Crowd.* New York: Penguin Books, (1895) reprint 1977.

Mackay, Charles. *Extraordinary Popular Delusions and the Madness of Crowds.* New York: John Wiley & Sons, (1841) reprint 1996.

McCloskey, Donald N. *If You're So Smart: The Narrative of Economic Expertise.* Chicago: University of Chicago Press, 1990.

Russo, Edward J. and Paul J. H. Schoemaker. *Winning Decisions: Getting It Right the First Time.* New York: Doubleday, 2002.

Shefrin, Hersh. *Beyond Fear and Greed.* Boston: Harvard University Press, 2000.

Sherden, William A. *The Fortune Sellers.* New York: John Wiley & Sons, 1998.

Shermer, Michael. *Why People Believe Weird Things.* New York: W. H. Freeman, 1997.

———. *How We Believe.* New York: W. H. Freeman, 2000.

———. *The Believing Brain: From Ghosts and Gods to Politics and Conspiracies—How We Construct Beliefs and Reinforce Them as Truths.* New York: Times Books, 2011.

Shiller, Robert J. *Market Volatility.* Cambridge: The MIT Press, 1997.

———. *Irrational Exuberance.* Princeton, NJ: Princeton University Press, 2000.

Shleifer, Andrew. *Inefficient Market: An Introduction to Behavioral Finance.* Oxford: Oxford University Press, 2000.

Thaler, Richard H. *The Winner's Curse: Paradoxes and Anomalies of Economic Life.* Princeton, NJ: Princeton University Press, 1992.

Tucket, David. *Minding the Markets: An Emotional Finance View of Financial Stability.* New York: Palgrave Macmillan, 2011.

Tvede, Lars. *The Psychology of Finance.* New York: John Wiley & Sons, 1999.

Von Neumann, John and Oskar Morgenstern. *Theory of Games and Economic Behavior.* Princeton, NJ: 1944.

Chapter 6—Philosophy

Audi, Robert. *The Cambridge Dictionary of Philosophy.* Cambridge: Cambridge University Press, 1995.

Baker, Gordon, ed. *The Voices of Wittgenstein: The Vienna Circle.* New York: Routledge, 2003.

Carroll, Noel. *The Poetics, Aesthetics, and Philosophy of Narrative.* Chichester, UK: Blackwell Publishing, 2009.

De Botton, Alain. *The Consolations of Philosophy.* New York: Pantheon Books, 2000.

Dickstein, Morris. *The Revival of Pragmatism: New Essays on Thought, Law, and Culture.* Durham, NC, and London: Duke University Press, 1998.

Hans, Sluga, and David G. Stern, eds., *The Cambridge Companion to Wittgenstein*. Cambridge: Cambridge University Press, 1996.

Honderich, Ted, ed. *The Oxford Companion to Philosophy*. Oxford: Oxford University Press, 1995.

James, William. *Pragmatism*. New York: Dover Publications, (1907) 1995.

James, William and Henry James. *Letters of William James*. Boston: Atlantic Monthly Press, 1920.

Klagge, James C. *Wittgenstein: Biography and Philosophy*. Cambridge: Cambridge University Press, 2001.

Lakoff, George and Mark Johnson. *Metaphors We Live By*. Chicago: University of Chicago Press, 1980.

McCloskey, Donald N. *If You're So Smart: The Narrative of Economic Expertise*. Chicago: University of Chicago Press, 1990.

Menand, Louis, ed. *Pragmatism: A Reader*. New York: Random House, 1997.

———. *The Metaphysical Club: The Story of Ideas in America*. New York: Farrar, Straus and Giroux, 2001.

Paulos, John Allen. *A Mathematician Reads the Newspaper*. New York: Basic Books, 1995.

———. *Once Upon a Number: The Hidden Mathematical Logic of Stories*. New York: Basic Books, 1998.

Richardson, Robert D. *William James: In the Maelstrom of American Modernism*. Boston: Houghton Mifflin, 2005.

Satz, Debra. *Why Some Things Should Not Be For Sale*. Oxford: Oxford University Press, 2010.

Simon, Linda. *Genuine Reality: A Life of William James*. New York: Harcourt, Brace, 1998.

White, Morton. *Pragmatism and the American Mind*. New York: Oxford University Press, 1973.

Wittgenstein, Ludwig. *Philosophical Investigations*. 3rd ed. Englewood Cliffs, NJ: Prentice Hall, 1958.

Chapter 7—Literature

Adler, Mortimer J. *How to Speak, How to Listen*. New York: Simon & Schuster, 1983.

Adler, Mortimer J. and Charles Van Doren. *How to Read a Book*, rev. ed. New York: Simon & Schuster, 1972.

Bloom, Harold. *The Western Canon: The Books and Schools for the Ages*. New York: Riverhead Books, 1994.

———. *How to Read and Why*. New York: Scribner, 2000.

———. *Where Shall Wisdom Be Found?* New York: Riverhead Books, 2004.

Denby, David. *Great Books*. New York: Simon & Schuster, 1996.

Dreiser, Theodore. *The Financier*. Lexington, KY: Seven Treasures Publication, 2008.

Eco, Umberto. *On Literature*. London: Harcourt, 2002.

Fischer, Steven Roger. *A History of Reading*. London: Reaktion Books, 2003.

Hagstrom, Robert G. *The Detective and the Investor*. John Wiley & Sons, 2002.

Jacobs, Alan. *The Pleasures of Reading in an Age of Distraction*. Oxford: Oxford University Press, 2011.

Kirsch, Adam. *Why Trilling Matters*. New Haven, CT: Yale University Press, 2011.

Krystal, Arthur. *A Company of Readers*. New York: The Free Press, 2001.

Lyons, Martyn. *Books: A Living History*. Los Angeles: Getty Publications, 2011.

Manguel, Alberto. *A History of Reading*. New York: Penguin Books, 1996.

———. *The Library at Night*. New Haven, CT: Yale University Press, 2006.

Samet, Elizabeth D. *Soldier's Heart: Reading Literature Through Peace and War at West Point*. New York: Farrar, Straus and Giroux, 2007.

Shiller, Robert J. *The Subprime Solution*. Princeton, NJ: Princeton University Press, 2008.

Woolf, Virginia. *The Common Reader: The First Series*. Edited and introduced by Andrew McNeillie. New York: Harcourt Brace Jovanovich, (1925) 1984.

Chapter 8—Mathematics

Bernstein, Peter L. *Against the Gods: The Remarkable Story of Risk*. New York: John Wiley & Sons, 1996.

Brown, Aaron. *Red-Blooded Risk*. Hoboken, NJ: John Wiley & Sons, 2012.

Byers, William. *How Mathematicians Think*. Princeton, NJ: Princeton University Press, 2007.

Connor, James A. *Pascal's Wager: The Man Who Played Dice with God*. San Francisco: Harper Collins, 2006.

Devlin, Keith. *The Man of Numbers: Fibonacci's Arithmetic Revolution*. New York: Walker & Company, 2011.

Epstein, Richard. *The Theory of Gambling and Statistical Logic*. New York: Academic Press, 1977.

Fingar, Thomas. *Reducing Uncertainty: Intelligence Analysis and National Security*. Stanford, CA: Stanford University Press, 2011.

Fitzgerald, Michael and Loan James. *The Mind of the Mathematician*. Baltimore: Johns Hopkins University Press, 2007.

Gould, Stephen Jay. *The Full House: The Spread of Excellence from Plato to Darwin*. New York: Three Rivers Press, 1996.

Hagstrom, Robert G. *The Warren Buffett Way: Investment Strategies of the World's Greatest Investor*. New York: John Wiley & Sons, 1994.

———. *The Warren Buffett Portfolio: Mastering the Power of the Focus Investment Strategy*. New York: John Wiley & Sons, 1999.

Hersh, Reuben. *What Is Mathematics Really?* Oxford: Oxford University Press, 1997.

Keynes, John Maynard. *The General Theory of Employment, Interest, and Money*. New York: First Harvest, Harcourt Brace, 1964.

Knight, Frank H. *Risk, Uncertainty, and Profit*. Washington DC: Beard Books, 2002.

McGrayne, Sharon Bertsch. *The Theory That Would Not Die*. New Haven, CT: Yale University Press, 2011.

Paulos, John Allen. *Innumeracy: Mathematical Illiteracy and Its Consequences*. New York: Hill and Wang, 1988.

———. *A Mathematician Plays the Stock Market*. New York: Basic Books, 2003.

Poundstone, William. *Fortune's Formula*. New York: Hill and Wang, 2005.

Rappaport, Alfred. *Creating Shareholder Value*. New York: The Free Press, 1986.

Rappaport, Alfred and Michael J. Mauboussin. *Expectations Investing*. Boston: Harvard Business School, 2001.

Savage, Sam L. *The Flaw of Averages: Why We Underestimate Risk in the Face of Uncertainty*. New York: John Wiley & Sons, 2009.

Stanovich, Keith E. *What Intelligence Tests Miss: The Psychology of Rational Thought*. New Haven, CT: Yale University Press, 2007.

Taleb, Nassim Nicholas. *Fooled by Randomness: The Hidden Role of Chance in Life and in the Markets*. New York: Texere/Thomson Corporation, 2004.

———. *The Black Swan: The Impact of the Highly Improbable*. New York: Random House, 2007.

Thorp, Edward O. *Beat the Dealer*. New York: Vintage Books, 1966.

Thorp, Edward O. and Sheen T. Kassouf. *Beat the Market*. New York: Random House, 1967.

Weisstein, Eric W. *CRC Concise Encyclopedia of Mathematics*. London: Chapman & Hall/CRC, 1999.

Wilson, Edward O. *Consilience: The Unity of Knowledge*. New York: Vintage Books, 1999.

Chapter 9—Decision Making

Arum, Richard and Josipa Roksa. *Academically Adrift: Limited Learning on College Campuses*. Chicago: University of Chicago Press, 2011.

Biggs, Barton. *Hedge Hogging*. New York: John Wiley & Sons, 2006.

Carr, Nicholas. *The Shallows: What the Internet Is Doing to Our Brains*. New York: W. W. Norton & Company, 2010.

Derman, Emanuel. *Models Behaving Badly*. New York: The Free Press, 2011.

Gardner, Dan. *Future Babble: Why Expert Predictions Fail—and Why We Believe Them Anyway*. Toronto: McClelland & Stewart, 2010.

Gawande, Atul. *The Checklist Manifesto: How to Get Things Right*. New York: Henry Holt, 2009.

Gould, Stephen Jay. *The Hedgehog, the Fox, and Magister's Pox: Mending the Gap Between Science and the Humanities*. Cambridge: Harvard University Press, 2003.

Kahneman, Daniel. *Thinking Fast and Slow*. New York: Farrar, Straus, and Giroux, 2011.

Kronman, Anthony T. *Education's End: Why Our Colleges and Universities Have Given Up on the Meaning of Life*. New Haven, CT: Yale University Press, 2007.

Mauboussin, Michael J. *More Than You Know: Finding Financial Wisdom in Unconventional Places*. New York: Columbia University Press, 2006.

———. *Think Twice: Harnessing the Power of Counterintuition*. Boston: Harvard Business Press, 2009.

Meehl, Paul E. *Clinical Versus Statistical Prediction: A Theoretical Analysis and a Review of the Evidence.* Northvale, NJ: Jason Aronson, 1996.

Pariser, Eli. *The Filter Bubble: What the Internet Is Hiding from You.* New York: Penguin Press, 2011.

Russo, J. Edward and Paul J. H. Schoemaker. *Decision Traps: The Ten Barriers to Brilliant Decision-Making & How to Overcome Them.* New York: Doubleday, 1989.

Sapolsky, Robert M. *Why Zebras Don't Get Ulcers.* New York: Henry Holt, 2004.

Tetlock, Philip E. *Expert Political Judgment: How Good Is It? How Can We Know?* Princeton, NJ: Princeton University Press, 2005.

Watts, Duncan J. *Everything Is Obvious: Once You Know the Answer.* New York: Crown Business, 2011.

ACKNOWLEDGMENTS

To begin at the beginning, I wish to acknowledge, with appreciation and gratitude, Charlie Munger and his wonderful concept of the latticework of mental models. That idea inspired this book, and it continues to inspire me in the conduct of my professional life every single day.

Then, for the actual writing of the book, I must start by expressing my deepest appreciation to my writing partner, Maggie Stuckey. This is the eighth book we have written together over the past eighteen years, and quite honestly I don't think I could have written one book without her. Maggie works and lives in Portland, Oregon. I live in Pennsylvania and work on the East Coast. A collaboration that is separated by a continent might pose a problem for many, but Maggie's hard work, dedication, and her special gift of connecting immediately to the work has always made me feel she lives next door. As I mentioned in the Preface, this was a particularly difficult book to write, but Maggie's talent for immediately connecting to the material has made the challenge much easier. She always was able to come up with an additional tidbit that enlivened the story. You the reader and I the author are very fortunate that Maggie has willingly shared her natural gifts with us.

I am fortunate to have many friends, colleagues, and professors who were willing to share their valuable time with me, each patiently explaining the nuances of their particular area of expertise and how what they learned might also benefit people struggling to make sense of the investment world.

A special thanks goes to Bill Miller, who introduced me to the Santa Fe Institute and the world of complex adaptive systems. Bill is a walking library who has allowed me to "check out," for free, countless books and ideas.

Michael Mauboussin, investment strategist, professor, and talented writer is equally curious about the world of investing. His generosity in sharing ideas and willingness to walk me through the most difficult parts were incredibly helpful. Thanks, Michael.

I would like to thank Richard Beeman, Paul Sniegowski, Larry Gladney, and William Wunner at the University of Pennsylvania. At Villanova University, my alma mater, both Maria Toyoda and Markus Kruezer are passionate about a liberal arts interpretation of the world. Their academic passion was an important and timely spark motivating me to dig just a little deeper.

At St. John's College, a special thanks is extended to President Christopher Nelson. Chris was an eager supporter of the project and introduced me to several people who helped me better understand the benefits of a Great Books education. Thanks to Walter Sterling, tutor; Greg Curtis, honorary alumnus; and to Don Bell, Lee Munson, and Steve Bohlin. Go Johnnies!

I especially enjoyed my conversation with Benjamin Doty, senior investment director at Koss Olinger and adjunct professor at the University of Michigan. Ben is a professional investor who took his valuable time to teach a course on the benefits of reading literature and how doing so makes for being a better investor. His reading list is a thoughtful and welcome distraction from the stacks of information that dominate our reading hours.

I am greatly indebted to Laurie Harper at Sebastian Literary Agency. Laurie is the perfect agent who navigates the world of publishing with great integrity. She is smart and loyal. Her professionalism, forthright honesty, and great sense of humor have always been appreciated. She is, in a word, special.

I also wish to thank, wholeheartedly, Myles Thompson at Columbia University Press. When Myles asked if I might consider revisiting *Investing: The Last Liberal Art*, I immediately jumped at the opportunity. Not only is Myles a talented publisher, he is also my friend. Thank you for your continued support.

Writing is a time-consuming endeavor. The time you spend writing a book requires your family to be patient and understanding. For their unwavering support I owe more than I can say to my wife Maggie and to John, Rob, Kim, and Jaques.

For all that is good and right about this book, you may thank the people I have mentioned here. For any errors and omissions, I alone am responsible.

INDEX